GUARINO GUARINI AND HIS ARCHITECTURE

GUARINO GUARINI

AND HIS ARCHITECTURE

H. A. MEEK

YALE UNIVERSITY PRESS · NEW HAVEN AND LONDON

Copyright © 1988 by Yale University
Second Printing 1989

Designed by Faith Brabenec Hart
Typeset in Linotron Bembo by Best-set Typesetter Ltd, Hong Kong
Printed in Hong Kong by South Sea International Press Ltd

I. (*frontispiece*) Turin, S. Lorenzo. The dome octagon.

The vignette on the title-page was used in Guarini's
Coelestis mathematica (1683). It appears to represent
a Guarinian 'nine spot' plan (compare p. 139).

Library of Congress Cataloging-in-Publication Data

Meek, H.A. (Harold Alán), 1922–
  Guarino Guarini and his architecture/H.A. Meek.
    p.   cm.
  Bibliography: p.
  Includes index.
  ISBN 0-300-03989-1
  ISBN 0-300-04748-7 (pbk)
  1. Guarini, Guarino, 1624–1683—Criticism and interpretation.
2. Architecture, Baroque—Italy. I. Title
NA1123.G8M44 1988
720′.92′4–dc19   87-24636
                                                CIP

In memory of Irene

אֵשֶׁת נְעוּרִים

ACKNOWLEDGEMENTS

Cordial thanks for their advice and help are due to Professor W. J. Kidd and Emeritus Professor J. A. Potter, of Queen's University, Belfast; to Dr J. Quentin Hughes, of Liverpool University; the late Professor Nino Carboneri; Dr Vittorio Viale and his successors at the Accademia delle Scienze di Torino; Professor Mario Abrate, Turin; and to Dr Vladimír Novotný, Státní Ústav Památkové Peče, Prague.

I am also grateful to the staff of the Archivio di Stato di Torino and of the Biblioteca dell'Istituto di Archeologia e Storia dell'Arte, Rome. I am glad of the opportunity to acknowledge the kindness of the University libraries of Cambridge, Berlin and Bonn in making rare publications available, and to Sarah O'Brien, of the Science Library, Queen's University, Belfast, for procuring the texts for me.

Credit has been given in the Photographic Acknowledgements to artists, photographers and holders of copyright for permission to reproduce pictures and diagrams, but especial gratitude is due to Dr Chiara Passanti, Turin, for consenting to the use of drawings commissioned by her late father, Professor Mario Passanti; to Professor G. Torretta, of the Politecnico di Torino, for the use of his drawings and for other kindnesses; and to Professor Daria de Bernardi Ferrero, also of the Politecnico di Torino.

Finally, I should like to thank Faith Hart and John Nicoll, of Yale University Press.

PHOTOGRAPHIC
ACKNOWLEDGEMENTS

Guarino Guarini, *Dissegni d'architettura civile et ecclesiastica* (Turin 1686) 145, 149
Guarino Guarini, *Architettura civile* (Turin 1737) 1, 5, 6, 7, 9, 17, 18, 19, 20, 25, 26, 27, 32, 46, 48, 70, 80, 81, 98, 111, 118, 119, 120, 121, 123, 133, 134, 135, 136, 137, 138, 139, 144, 146, 150, 151, 164.
Jean Marot, *L'Architecture françoise* ('Le grand Marot') (Paris n.d. [c.1670]) 30
B.A. Vittone, *Istruzioni diverse concernenti l'officio dell'architetto civile* (Lugano 1766) 154, 155, 159, 160

P. Abercrombie (*Town and Country Planning*. Oxford University Press 1945) 31
A. Blunt (*Art and Architecture in France, 1500–1700*. © Anthony Blunt 1973, p. 328). Reproduced by permission of Penguin Books Ltd 29
A.E. Brinckmann 33
P. Buscalioni 125
Institut Prof Cento, by kind permission of Dr M. Anderegg, Zürich 113, 114
L. Denina and A. Protto 47
Hans Eckstein 176, 177
Professor Daria de Bernardi Ferrero 127, 130, 132, 140
Professor H.G. Franz 168, 169, 170, 174
Walter Hege 162, 163
E. Hempel (*Baroque Art and Architecture in Central Europe*. © Eberhard Hempel 1965). Reproduced by permission of Penguin Books Ltd 167, 171
Brian Knox. Reprinted by permission of Faber and Faber Ltd from *The Architecture of Prague and Bohemia* 172
G.L. Marini 106, 110
Professor H.A. Millon 96, 141
Professor W. Oechslin 108
Professor M. Passanti, by courtesy of Dr Chiara Passanti 14, 15, 23, 24, 28, 37, 40, 49, 53, 54, 56, 59, 60, 78, 84, 87, 88, 92, 105, 112
Erika Schmauss 161
Professor G.C. Sciolla 148
Professor G. Torretta 38, 41, 42
J. Vanderperren and J. Kennes, by courtesy of *A*[+], Brussels 34

Karlsruhe: Staatliche Kunsthalle 67, 71, 74, 75
London: Courtauld Institute of Art 21
Messina: Museo Regionale 8, 13
Munich: Germanisches Nationalmuseum 175
Paris: Musée des Arts Décoratifs 157
Schwerin: Staatliches Museum 35
Turin: Archivio di Stato 45, 62, 63, 64, 65, 66, 68, 69, 77, 82, 83, 85, 86, 126, 131
Turin: Biblioteca Nazionale 50, 124
Turin: Biblioteca Reale 51
Turin: Istituto Bancario S. Paolo di Torino 79
Turin: Museo d'Arte Antica 2, 3, 4, 156, 158
Turin: Museo Civico 152, 153
Turin: Palazzo Reale 73
Turin: Soprintendenza per i beni ambientali e architettonici 127
Vatican: Biblioteca Apostolica Vaticana 142, 143
Vienna: Graphische Sammlung Albertina 122, 165
Wiesbaden: Archiv Groenesteyn 173

Alinari (Florence) 44(b)
Arxiu Mas (Barcelona) 10, 44(a)
Riccardo Moncalvo (Turin) 36, 39, 43, 52, 55, 57, 58, 89, 90, 91, 93, 94, 95, 99, 100, 102, 103, 104, 107, 116, 117, 128, 129, I, II, III, IV, V, VI, VII, VIII, IX, X, XI

CONTENTS

1   INTRODUCTION

FEW DISCIPLINES can be as replete with paradox as the history of artistic taste. The eighteenth-century visitor to the Uffizi – perhaps Goethe himself, though he is not specific – would hasten past the Botticellis and Fra Angelicos without a second glance, and make straight for the works of the sublime Salvator Rosa . . .

In the field of architecture, no body of work has been the subject of such wildly divergent critical opinion as that of Guarino Guarini.[1] It was well thought of by the architect's contemporaries. In 1690, seven years after Guarini's death, Maximilien Misson, author of the *Théâtre sacré*, wrote to the Marquis Arthur de la Motte Chatelard: 'The Abbé Guarini has built a master-piece, a marvel, a portent . . . Rome itself, even in the brilliance of its thousand monuments, has nothing to equal it.'[2] He was referring to the church of S. Lorenzo in Turin.

Less than eighty years later, the spread of the neoclassical taste had led to a revulsion against what were perceived as late Baroque extravagances. F. Milizia in his celebrated *Memorie dei più celebri architetti* (Rome 1768) used the space of his article on Guarini to mount an attack on his architecture of unparalleled sarcasm and detestation, ending with the words 'whoever likes Guarini's architecture, much good may it do him, but he would be a nitwit'.[3] Stefano Ticozzi in his *Dizionario degli architetti scultori, pittori & c* (Milan 1830) was yet more vicious, ending his piece on Guarini with the words 'He died, to the advantage of art, in 1683.'

Towards the end of the nineteenth century, it was Cornelius Gurlitt who reinstated the taste for late Baroque in nearly all countries, starting with his *Geschichte des Barokstils in Italien* (Stuttgart 1887).[4] The English-speaking world, however, perhaps because of the influence of Ruskin (who referred to the Baroque as the Grotesque Renaissance), took much longer to change its mind. Martin S. Briggs, in his later years honorary secretary of the R.I.B.A. (where I met him in 1952), observed in his *Baroque Architecture* (London 1913), 'the chapel of S. Sindone . . . and the church of S. Lorenzo are profusely and vulgarly decorated, but their chief interest lies in the extraordinary complicated and absurd way in which they are domed. For sheer lunacy of design they would be hard to parallel.'

A reprint house in New York[5] deemed it opportune to reissue Briggs's 'antiquated' book (the expression is Wittkower's) in 1967. It was the very next year that saw the apotheosis of Guarinian revaluation: a six-day congress under the banner of *Guarino Guarini e l'internazionalità del barocco* was held in one of Guarini's own buildings in Turin – the Collegio dei Nobili, now occupied by the Academy of Sciences – where a brilliant assembly of scholars from Europe and America delivered a series of papers on every aspect of the life, work, thought and influence of Guarini; the 'internationality' of the conference title referred to the circumstance of Guarini's 'radical elimination of the historical component'[6] from architectural style, which promoted the spread of Baroque architecture in Europe, by the same process as Guarini himself describes in connection with Gothic architecture, which was 'born without a master'.[7] And as Baroque architecture reaches Germany and beyond, it is not hard to trace Guarini's influence on it. Art historians, in fact, have been doing so for the last seventy years. In 1915 Paul Frankl addressed the Kunstwissenschaftliche Gesellschaft in Munich on the Guarinian antecedents of Banz and Vierzehnheiligen. His reception was somewhat acrimonious.[8] A. E. Brinckmann had better luck seventeen years later when he read his paper 'Von Guarino Guarini bis Balthasar Neumann' to the Deutscher Verein für Kunstwissenschaft in Berlin,[9] while at the 1968 Turin conference a whole section of the proceedings was devoted to the topic.[10]

But if we know where Guarini led to, so to speak, it is much more difficult to say where he came from. He was a Theatine novice in Rome when Cortona, Bernini and Borromini were in practice there. S. Carlo alle Quattro Fontane had just been finished, S. Ivo was still going up. 'Stimuli for him, but not training', was how Brinckmann put it.[11] He was surely right. The works of these great masters of the Baroque afford no key to the phenomenon of Guarini. If we look at an architect more contemporary with him, Carlo Fontana, we find that he is easily explicable in the terms of his Roman experience: he was simply a man of his times. But Guarini's architectural language is so fantastic, original and strange, that it defies any attempt to classify it. Guarini, in a word, is not the product of an ambience: he is the creator of one.

On the basis of a stone and brick technology which was exploited with a daring that outstripped the masters of the Gothic, he pushed architectural creativity and inventiveness beyond the familiar Baroque world of emotional manipulation and *trompe-l'oeil* illusionism. He was free to do it because he had broken loose from the constraints of classic precedent. The Romans, he suggests in his treatise *Architettura civile*, did not always follow Vitruvius, nor the moderns the ancients. Architecture changes as custom changes.[12] And hence 'the symmetries of architecture can be varied between themselves without discord'.[13] So classical architecture is no longer taken as the universal model, while Gothic is justified because it conforms to the taste and mode of its time. Guarini did not disguise his appreciation of the fashionable French architecture of his day; and he employed Islamic forms for his openwork domes. The freedom he enjoyed in using non-traditional solutions, however, did not result in the emergence of a type of eclectic imitation. Instead, there was a process of thematic assimilation, which has been likened to the harmonic development we find in music, where what is important is not so much the melodic theme, but the development it receives via the quasi-mathematical rules of counterpoint, until a rich harmonic texture is achieved.[14] Thus, the interlacements of the SS. Sindone dome, and the stellate embroidery of the facade of the Palazzo Carignano show that, for Guarini, architecture was not the closed, formal system of a tradition-based style, but a rich and profound interweave or texture.

How near can we get to Guarini as a person? The record is amazingly uneven. The Archivio di Stato in Turin preserves a note of the 10 soldi that were spent one rainy day in September 1679 to send the architect home in a sedan chair from the site of the Palazzo Carignano.[15] And yet nothing is known for certain of his whereabouts between 1657 and 1660. Some writers candidly accept these limitations. 'We do not know', writes Umberto Chierici, 'with what mind and with what hopes Guarini arrived in Turin from Paris.'[16] Others, however, exert their imagination to fill the lacuna. Andreina Griseri tries to picture the architect on site in Turin: 'Thin, gaunt, electric, tireless, Guarini must have appeared like an obsessive phantom; a black habit in restless movement amongst the stones, the mortar and the close-packed scaffolding.'[17]

There are more dramatic fragments than this, from real life. Turin Civic Library preserves a respectful but exasperated letter from Guarini to the Archbishop of Turin, dated 19 April 1677, complaining of the six bad years he has had at the hands of Fr Virle, the local Theatine *preposito*, and asking permission to leave Turin for the remaining two years of Virle's term of office, as Guarini despaired of changing his attitude to anything more amicable 'or at least of reducing it to a reasonable indifference'.[18] Three days later, as a flurry of frantic letters in the Archivio di Stato show, Guarini could stand it no longer and went over the wall.[19] But as a Theatine cleric put it later that week, writing to the Marchese di San Tomaso: 'Her Royal Highness told me several times in reply that she had more need of Fr Guarino than of Fr Virle.'

Such glimpses are tantalizing. For the most part we must make do with the impressions that may be derived from Guarini's own books and buildings. He appears to us, across three centuries, as learned, courteous and quietly ironical.[20] He was an artist, scholar and priest, interested in theology, architecture, astronomy, mathematics and philosophy, but he could still find the time and inclination to write a play for Sicilian schoolboys to perform.

It will be the object of this book to explore some aspects of our heritage from this complex and profound man, who was born in Modena in 1624 and entered the Theatine Order of monks at an early age. Documentary sources and stylistic evidence will be scanned for clues about his early travels, in particular to Spain and Portugal. We shall trace his career in Sicily, in France and finally in Piedmont, where most of his surviving works are to be found, in and around the city of Turin.

Guarini's architecture exploits openwork stone domes in a manner never before practised, while concealing the true statical bases of the structure. This work will be analyzed in detail and set into its art-historical context, with particular reference to Islamic and Gothic sources and to the views expressed by the architect in his posthumously published *Architettura civile*.

Buildings by Guarini that either were not completed or have been destroyed will be studied from the engravings in his book; every scheme illustrated in it is, in fact, reproduced and analyzed here. We shall look at the architect's relationship to the Piedmontese court, and examine his various scientific and philosophical treatises. In conclusion, the influence of Guarini's work will be traced on the Baroque architecture of Austria, Bohemia and southern Germany.

P. D. Guarinus Guarinus Cleric: Regul:ᵃ Sciētiarum Sane'
oīum ornamenta exacta morum innocentia, modestia Regu=
lari disciplina pulchrius exornauit, ex hac uita
discessit Pridie' nonas Martÿ anno 1683
etatis   sue. 59.

2 EARLY DAYS

WHEN GIROLAMO TIRABOSCHI was compiling his *Biblioteca Modenese*, 'or notices of the life and works of the writers born in the States of the most serene Signor the Duke of Modena', published in 1783, he was able to list Guarini's buildings and comment briefly on all his publications, but he could find practically nothing to say of his life. He does not even give the date of his birth, only when he made his profession in Rome.

A hundred years later, Fr Tommaso Sandonnini, after prolonged research in the Archivio dell'Opera Pia in Modena, was able to cast a great deal more light on the matter, particularly about Guarini's early days in Modena.[1] Sandonnini established that the Guarini family was a branch of the Guarinis of Verona.[2] A distinguished forerunner had been the mathematician Antonio Guarini, who was born in Ferrara, but had lived in Modena from 1545 and was superintendent of works there.[3]

Guarino Guarini was born in the parish of S. Margherita, Modena, on 17 January 1624, the son of Rinaldo Guarini and his wife Eugenia Marescotti. Modena in those days was experiencing the full effects of a century's religious campaigning by the spiritual shock troops of the embattled Church of Rome. After the initial onslaughts of Lutheranism, a vigorous counter-movement had been initiated. New Orders and Sodalities were founded with the object of consolidating the faith of those who still remained true to the traditional doctrines, while endeavouring to recover the ground that had been lost to Protestantism.

The medieval term 'clerics regular' (*chierici regolari*)[4] was revived and applied to the members of these new Orders. The first to be founded, a hundred years before Guarini's birth, was the Theatine Order, which took its name from Chieti, in Latin Teate,[5] a town in the Abruzzi of which one of the four founders (afterwards Pope Paul IV) was then bishop. The Barnabites followed in 1530, the Somaschi in 1532 and the Jesuits in 1534.[6]

The Theatines made rapid progress. Abroad, their missions reached as far afield as Prague, Paris and Lisbon, while in Italy there was hardly a city or small town where they did not make their presence felt. They established themselves in Modena in 1604, moving to the old parish church of S. Vincenzo in 1614. They proceeded to build themselves a new house beside that of the Guarini family,[7] and in 1617 started to reconstruct S. Vincenzo, at first to the designs of Paolo Reggiani.[8]

The chronicler Spaccini remarks that the Theatines in Modena put people's backs up at first 'because of their jealousy of other Orders and their instability',[9] but they made up for this in 1631 by their selfless devotion when the plague broke out, as the many bequests and donations recorded in their

1. Portrait of Guarino Guarini.

5

archives testify. This must have made an impression on the seven-year-old Guarini, as would the sound, and the even more sensational sight, of Alfonso III, Duke of Modena, turned Capuchin monk and preaching repentance from the pulpit of Modena Cathedral, two years later.

The ubiquity of the Theatines in general, and their proximity to the Guarini household in particular, render it probable that Guarino Guarini and his five brothers received their schooling from them. There has been some speculation on what he might have learned:

> he probably dedicated the greater part of his youthful studies to philosophy, theology, astronomy and mathematics, getting to architecture through the latter, an abstract procedure, not supported, at least at first, by the daily practice of a craft, nor ever sustained by professional activity in the proper sense of the term.[10]

These words have a resonance. We may recall what has been said of an older contemporary of Guarini:

> Inigo Jones comes into the architectural history of his time in an oblique and slightly mysterious way: neither by rising from a craft, nor by early introduction to the Works.[11]

At the end of September 1639 the fifteen-year-old Guarini applied to join the Theatine Order.[12] His brother Eugenio was already a member; his three other brothers and his cousin eventually followed him. 'Strange fate of a family', says Portoghesi, 'which decided its end in this way.'[13] The young Guarini was presented as a novice in the next month, was accepted, and left for Rome on 22 October 1639.

The years of Guarini's novitiate – six in all – were spent at the Theatine monastery of S. Silvestro, on the Quirinal. The Theatines, like the other militant Orders founded in the previous century to combat the inroads of the Reformation, were active church builders. They were also, it seems, keen exploiters of all those strange theatrical devices which they, and most notoriously the Jesuits, used 'to catch men's affections and to ravish their understanding'.[14] When the Theatines were invited to Paris by Cardinal Mazarin, they introduced the astonished French to this kind of spectacle. The churches were transformed into opera houses.[15] The Jansenists were shocked, but the Queen, Anne of Austria (who had installed the Theatines in a house on the present Quai Voltaire), turned up in person at Ste Anne-la-Royale to see the 'représentations . . . en forme de théâtre', with a perspective at the end of which the Holy Sacrament was exposed on the altar. On one side stood the Emperor Augustus with his court, while on the other were the mathematicians who described the world, in accordance with the Evangelist: 'there went out a decree from Caesar Augustus that all the world should be described' (Luke 2:1).[16] In the end, the Archbishop of Paris had enough of it all and forbade these spectacles.

In Rome, the Theatine church was S. Andrea della Valle, begun in 1591 to the design of Giacomo della Porta. It was taken over in 1608 by Carlo Maderno, who completed it, except for the facade, in 1623.[17]

Although the Theatines were not averse to the employment of lay architects, especially in the case of prestige buildings such as their church in Rome, their common practice was to employ clerics of their own Order who had trained as architects. The most noted of these was Fr Francesco Grimaldi, who is believed to have had a hand in the design of S. Andrea.[18] His finest work is to be found in Naples.[19] We know, too, of Fr Pietro Carraciolo, who

6

built the church of S. Vincenzo in Piacenza,[20] and Fr Bernardo Castagnini, who did the design for the remodelling of the Theatine house in Modena, and was involved in the extensions and improvements to S. Bartolomeo in Bologna.[21]

The more able of the Theatine architects were sent round the country working wherever their services were needed, though there was a certain tendency to re-use successful designs. S. Andrea della Valle, for example, is re-echoed in S. Vincenzo at Modena, and shows up again at the Annunziata in Messina,[22] while Fr Caracciolo's plan for S. Vincenzo in Piacenza saw service once more for S. Cristina in Parma.[23]

It is in the context of this tradition that Guarini discovered his bent for architecture and was encouraged to develop it. We do not know the details of his training. We know, in fact, virtually nothing of his *Lehrjahre* in Rome, save that on 11 April 1641 he appeared before the Vice-Regent of Rome (who was acting in his capacity of *tutore dei minori*) and made formal profession of his desire to leave the world and retire into religion.[24]

Nevertheless, Guarini's novitiate in Rome coincided with the *floruit* of Borromini, Bernini and Cortona. Here indeed was a school for any Baroque architect. The eighteenth-century neoclassical denigrators of Guarini regarded him as the *reductio ad absurdum* of Borromini. Milizia, for example, opens his article on Guarini with the words: 'If there has ever been an architect who carried to excess the extravagances of Borromini, it is certainly Father Guarino Guarini.'[25] By the time of Sandonnini, a hundred years later, this has become 'this famous exaggerator of the architectural vices of his time'.[26] But a few pages later the same writer paradoxically observes:

> It cannot be believed that he [Guarini] was a follower or bad pupil of Borromini. The few years spent in the great metropolis, the ancient monuments, the renaissance palaces, the grandiose buildings erected by Bernini, Borromini, Fontana and so many other great architects of the seventeenth century will have certainly left a profound impression on his mind, but this and no other was the influence they exercised on him.[27]

Hans Sedlmayr was the first historian to descend from generalities and attempt a detailed comparison of the two architects. He devotes the fourth chapter of his book *Die Architektur Borrominis* to an analysis of the two styles, and finds, feature by feature, a difference of approach and a different spirit informing the way that space is treated and structure handled, though, he says, Guarini's forms will not be seen to differ from Borromini's 'as long as we are looking at qualities that are simply typical of the "high Baroque style"'.[28]

No work of Borromini is mentioned in Guarini's own *Architettura civile*,[29] nor is Borromini himself alluded to, though there may be an oblique and critical reference to him in Guarini's remark that 'the architect does not construct walls, roofs, machines, statues, doors, locks or bricks ...' (*AC* I.i) when contrasted with the account given by Fra Juan de S. Bonaventura of Borromini (who started life as a mason, not a priest) at work on S. Carlino: 'Sr Francesco himself guides the bricklayer's trowel, adjusts the stuccatore's tool, the joiner's saw, the stone-dresser's chisel, etc., etc.'[30]

There is an unambiguous and critical reference in Guarini's Treatise to Bernini's work, namely the way that his Cathedra Petri in St Peter's interferes with the view through the same architect's Baldacchino.[31] This remark of Guarini's – he says the Baldacchino looked better before the Cathedra Petri was installed – reveals that whatever he learned from the great masters of the

Roman high Baroque during his novitiate, represents the start of a familiarity, not the end of it. What this familiarity amounted to in human terms is hard to say. The suggestion has been made that the 'particular accents' of Ste Anne-la-Royale, Guarini's Theatine church in Paris, owe something to a Borrominian design for the facade of S. Carlino, not then executed in its entirety.[32] How did Guarini get to see these unpublished and unexecuted designs, it is asked, 'except by supposing there was a notable friendship between Guarini and Borromini'. Paolo Portoghesi in his little monograph on Guarini goes even further and boldly states that it was Borromini who put Guarini up to studying architecture in the first place, but he offers no sources for this assertion.[33]

Since no buildings of Guarini have yet been described or analyzed in this work, it may be best at this stage simply to make the point that while Guarini may exhibit certain superficially Borrominian features, more especially in his earlier works, he has a much wider spread of sources than the 'ordinary' late Baroque architect. These include Islamic and Gothic impulses, but everything employed is utterly transformed in a type of design which, in Guarini's vertical structures (as contrasted with his longitudinal ones), makes use of a succession of 'autonomous' zones, where one zone gives no indication as to what may be expected in the next.

Guarini returned from Rome in 1647 and was ordained priest in Modena on 17 January 1648.[34] On 9 March of that year the Theatine papers in the Archivio di Stato of Modena show that he was made auditor of the monastery. In this office, no doubt, was acquired that respect for economy so sharply expressed thirty years later in the posthumously published *Architettura civile*:

> The architect must proceed discreetly. Since he has to look to the convenience of the building owner, if he puts him to such expense that he either cannot finish the scheme, or by doing so will have to reduce himself to poverty and become a beggar, this will not produce convenience but rather grave inconvenience for the person who ought to be enjoying it.[35]

A later observation in the same chapter reinforces the message:

> Everything should be done with the least expense possible, so materials should not be used which, not being of the country, can only be obtained at great expense.[36]

To the post of auditor (*revisore dei conti*), conferred on Guarini in March 1648, the duties of superintendent of works at the Theatine church of S. Vincenzo were added eighteen months later.[37] The reconstruction of this old church had been started by the Theatines in Modena as far back as 1617, under the patronage of the Infanta Principessa Isabella and Cardinal d'Este.[38] Various architects had had a hand in the work, starting with Paolo Reggiani,[39] who was followed by Bartolomeo Avanzini, the architect of the Ducal Palace in Modena. It was, however, the Theatines' own man, Fr Bernardo Castagnini, who had given the most systematic attention to the long drawn out scheme, helped latterly by the young Guarini after his return from Rome. It was Castagnini whom Guarini ultimately succeeded as superintendent of works in October 1649.[40] The meeting at which he was appointed was actually called to approve the design by Bartolomeo Avanzini for the dome of S. Vincenzo. The work was begun but difficulties arose, and in a memorandum to the Duke of Modena dated 1651,[41] the master builder Ascanio Passeri and his colleagues, the Della Pergola brothers, reported that

II. Turin, S. Lorenzo. Nave. 'The one serliana that gives on to deep real space.'

8

2. Modena, S. Vincenzo. Pilaster capital.

3. Modena, S. Vincenzo. *Coretto.*

4. Modena, S. Vincenzo. Presbytery: side window.

(after thirty years' work on the church) serious doubts had arisen about its structural soundness, and various measures had been devised by Passeri to cope with this situation, measures which had been approved by the monks and endorsed by Avanzini and Guarini. These were put in hand, but disagreements had emerged about rates of pay for the work, and building had ceased. If the Duke wanted 'real information about these works', he should ask the Provost and Fr Guarini.

Two years later they were still struggling with the dome. The Duke of Modena convened a meeting of architects, engineers and clerics,[42] where they discussed a new design for the dome, of timber covered with lead, devised by Guarini, who exhibited a cardboard model of his scheme. This was supposed to be a prodigy of lightness, weighing much less than the structure that was currently roofing the church. It was duly approved in its turn, but for lack of funds or some other reason it was never built. No drawing or engraving of the design survives.

It is a matter of speculation as to what Guarinian details, if any, may be detected in S. Vincenzo today.[43] Perhaps the offbeat column capitals in the nave (Fig. 2) may be an early example of Guarini's fantasy, though they do not figure exactly in the collection of idiosyncratic capitals illustrated in the plates of *Architettura civile*. The surrounds of the *coretti* (Fig. 3) may also be Guarini's forerunners perhaps of the squat and diagrammatic *coretti* in the chapel of the SS. Sindone.[44] Finally, the side windows of the presbytery (Fig. 4) beneath the *coretti* display certain decorative features (a tablet on the keystone of the arch, the flower-like brackets supporting the imposts of the arch itself) which anticipate later Guarinian devices.

Some scholars have suggested that Guarini was the designer of the high altar tabernacle in the church. Carboneri points to the 'singular development upwards, not to mention the over-abundant multiplicity of motifs which swarm in every order . . . unredeemed by a profound tension'.[45] The authorship of Tommaso Loraghi, however, is well attested, with ample details of his payment for the tabernacle by the Theatines,[46] whereas no documentary evidence exists to connect it with Guarini.

When the Theatine fathers, with the help of Bernardo Vittone, brought out the text of Guarini's *Architettura civile*, they prefaced it with a dedication to his 'Sacred Royal Majesty'[47] in which they refer to four buildings by name as testifying to the architect's 'Somma perizia': the chapel of SS. Sindone, 'our famous church of S. Lorenzo in Turin' (Col. Pl. II), Ste Anne in Paris and S. Vincenzo in Modena. It is curious that S. Vincenzo should have been selected for mention in that illustrious company, where Guarini's only documented contribution, the dome, was never actually realized. Presumably the fathers found some reference to the church in the papers of Guarini, then fifty years dead, and interpreted his interventions as authorship of the design.

The records of the Theatine Order in Modena, now transferred to the Archivio di Stato of that city, enable us to trace Guarini's progress through the *cursus honorum* of his house. We have seen him made auditor in 1648 and superintendent of works in 1649. The next year brought the appointment of *cassiere* or treasurer, and with it, trouble. The Provost, in the chapter held on 19 April 1650,[48] told the assembled fathers that a discrepancy was evident in the accounts. He implied that Guarino's elder brother Eugenio Guarini was the cause of that discrepancy, and the treasurer himself clearly in debt. The matter was referred all the way along the line to the Father General of the Order, who quashed the charge on 20 November 1650.[49]

While bad feeling may have been aroused between the Provost and the

Guarini brothers by these incidents, they do not seem to have interrupted the progress of their careers. Guarino was appointed lecturer in philosophy in 1650, while Eugenio was elected *procuratore* in 1653. In the following year Eugenio was transferred to Ferrara to teach philosophy, and on 30 May Guarino was appointed *procuratore* in his place.[50] There was only one higher position in the Theatine house, that of provost, and Guarini was elected to it in the next year, at the age of thirty-one.[51]

At this point disaster struck. The appointment was made without consultation with the civil authorities, and did not find favour with Prince Alfonso, the son of Duke Francesco I, who was acting as viceroy in the absence of his father. The reasons for this are uncertain. A note in the List of Provosts in the Theatine Archive at Modena reveals the Prince as 'having been annoyed that the fathers had not appointed Fr Castagnini as Provost'.

The Theatines, who like the Jesuits sedulously cultivated kings and princes, hastened to withdraw the appointment. The evidence for this is a letter dated 25 February 1655 from the Father General of the Order to the Duke of Modena informing him that Guarini had renounced the post.[52] A document dated 7 January 1656, however, in the Archivio di Stato at Parma refers to a request received for the services of a certain preacher from 'il R.do D. Guarino Guerini Preposito di Modena',[53] so it is evident that Guarini remained in post throughout 1655, though the List of Provosts notes in connection with this contretemps that 'the house remained for a year without a provost'. In 1656, however, the Theatines of Modena elected the man the Prince wanted: the architect Fr Bernardo Castagnini. He was to die in office two years later, on 14 September 1658.[54]

The pressure of ducal disfavour now obliged Guarini to leave his native city and begin those travels that made him 'the Mercury of our age'.[55] The capitular registers of the Theatine house in Parma show that the 'R.do D. Guarino Guarini Preposito di Modena' was unanimously accepted as a member on 9 September 1656. Three months later he was at Guastalla, a small town between Parma and Mantua, whence on 3 December 1656 he wrote a letter to the Duke of Modena assuring him of his devotion and unshakeable obedience.[57] The Duke was unmoved, and continued to remain so; fourteen years later, when the Duke of Savoy intervened on Guarini's behalf, Laura, Duchess of Modena, politely but firmly rejected his request, writing 'it is just as necessary that Father Guarini should not return to his monastery here for the present as was the original resolution proper, that for various reasons he should leave it'.[58]

That Guarini was briefly back in Modena in 1657 is attested by references in the Theatine papers.[59] After that, however, there is a gap in our certain knowledge of his whereabouts. It is not until 1660 that his reappearance is attested at Messina, in Sicily. These *Wanderjahre* will now engage our attention.

3   SPAIN AND PORTUGAL

OF THE NAMED DESIGNS illustrated in the plates of *Architettura civile*, all but three are of buildings in Italy. The three named buildings abroad are Ste Anne-la-Royale in Paris, S. Maria della Divina Providenza in Lisbon and S. Maria Ettinga in Prague.

We know in detail the dates of Guarini's stay in Paris, but about a possible stay in Prague or Lisbon there is no documentary evidence. This has led some scholars to assert that no such visits took place, and one even goes so far as to see it as a mark of Guarini's 'open mindedness' that he was prepared, as he puts it, to design buildings for cities he did not know, and whose erection he could not direct, in contrast, say, to Bernini, who experienced 'paralysis of his creative genius' in the alien urban space of Paris.[1] R. Wittkower, however, who elsewhere has shown himself sceptical about a possible Guarinian visit to Spain,[2] maintains that each of Guarini's buildings (like each of his books) was an architectural *summa*, on which construction would founder without the architect's personal supervision.[3] There is, for example, a letter in the Archivio di Stato, Modena, written by Madama Reale in Turin to the Duke of Modena (when Guarini, at the end of his life, was once more working briefly in his native city), which asks the Duke in tones of barely suppressed panic to send Guarini back to Turin, as a matter of urgency, so that he might resume his supervision of the work on the Sindone chapel.[4] We know, too, that it was the Theatines' practice to employ monks of their own Order as architects, and to send the more successful of them from place to place, to work wherever their services were required.

Bearing all this in mind, one may, in the absence of documentary evidence, be tempted to look instead for circumstantial evidence in support of the hypothesis that Guarini visited Prague and Lisbon in the blank years – blank to us, that is – between 1657 and 1660. For Prague there is little to show, for Lisbon a great deal. The circumstantial evidence of a visit by Guarini to the Iberian peninsula is of two main kinds: what Guarini brought back from Islamic Spain to put into his own architecture in France and Italy, and what he actually proposed for his Lisbon church.

The Spanish–Islamic heritage of Guarini will be discussed in detail later in this work, in particular when considering the design of S. Lorenzo, Turin. At this point, when no buildings have as yet been described or analyzed, we may summarize the position in this way: one of the most striking of all Guarini's architectural devices is the openwork dome, made up of interlaced parabolic arches that sweep over the centre of the space they roof leaving an octagonal opening in the middle, above which (in the case of the nave at S. Lorenzo) further structures are superimposed. The closest parallel to this type of

12

construction is to be seen in two of the domes at the Great Mosque of Cordoba (see Fig. 44), completed before AD 976, where the superficial similarity between the two designs is very striking.

The other Guarinian feature that seems to have Arabo-Spanish and Mudejar origins is the 'telescopic' disposition of vertical space; that is, the development of the section as a series of independent regions of decreasing horizontal dimension as the building rises (see for example the section through the church of the Padri Somaschi, Fig. 18). This type of volumetric design is characteristic of Mudejar architecture, as exemplified in La Seo (the cathedral of Saragossa), begun in the twelfth century, and the cathedrals of Tarazona and Teruel. Although none of these Spanish buildings is referred to in the *Architettura civile*, Guarini does allude to 'the great church of Seville in Andalusia and the cathedral of Salamanca in Castille'.[5]

Both the interlaced arches and the 'telescopic' vertical development are already present in Guarini's Padri Somaschi church in Messina, designed between 1660 and 1662. The implication is accordingly that they are the outcome of a recent architectural experience, gained while travelling; the introduction to Guarini's play *La pietà trionfante* published in Messina in 1660 refers to him as the 'Mercury of our age' – a metaphor for a traveller.

It may also be relevant in this connection to note that Guarini's next book, *Placita philosophica*, which was published in Paris in 1665, bears a dedication to the Portuguese nobleman Francesco de Mello, which Guidoni suggests 'does not seem to be dictated by chance interest, but from a long and friendly familiarity'.[6] Always ready to push speculation to the limits of the possible, Guidoni even hazards the thought that de Mello, when serving as Portuguese ambassador to England, might have taken Guarini with him, 'which many indications make one consider necessary for his scientific and philosophical training'.

———

All discussions of a possible visit by Guarini to the Iberian peninsula presuppose that it would have been in connection with building a church for the Theatine Order in Lisbon. Permission to erect a church there was given to the Theatines in the year 1650 by King João IV.[7] The moving spirit here was the Theatine father Antonio Ardizone, and it is to him that Guarini dedicated the two plates, a plan and a long section, of his design for the church of S. Maria della Divina Providenza in the *Dissegni d'architettura civile et ecclesiastica*, published posthumously without accompanying text in Turin in 1686. When Guarini's plates were reissued in 1737, however, to accompany a text conflated by Bernardo Vittone from two of the author's manuscripts in the possession of the Theatine house in Turin, the dedication to Fr Ardizone was blanked out.

Lisbon's first Theatines were accommodated temporarily in some houses within the convent of S. Catalina. A site was made available to them in the Rua dos Fies de Deus, in the district known as the Bairro Alto.[8] It was here that a kind of scratch church was run up in three months[9], between July and September 1653, perhaps in wood, as when its replacement was commenced in 1698, Fray Agostinho de Santa Maria makes the specific point that it was 'a new and magnificent one *in stone* [my italics]'.[10]

The 1653 church cannot possibly be the one designed by Guarini, as suggested, for example, by R. C. Smith Jnr.[11] Guarini's Divina Providenza must

13

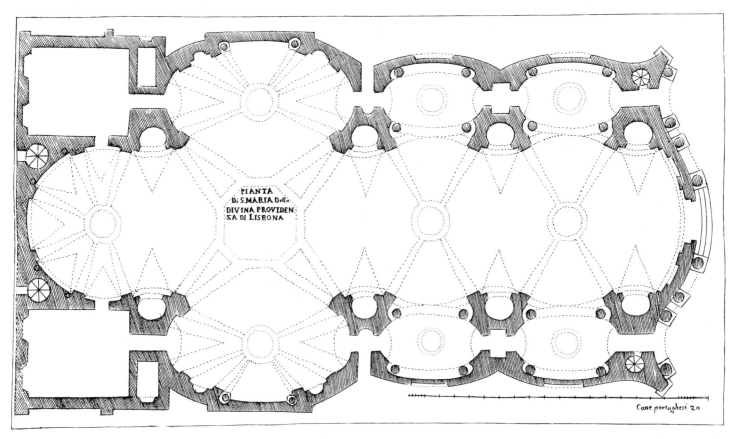

5. Lisbon, S. Maria della Divina Providenza. Plan.

6. Lisbon, S. Maria della Divina Providenza. Long section.

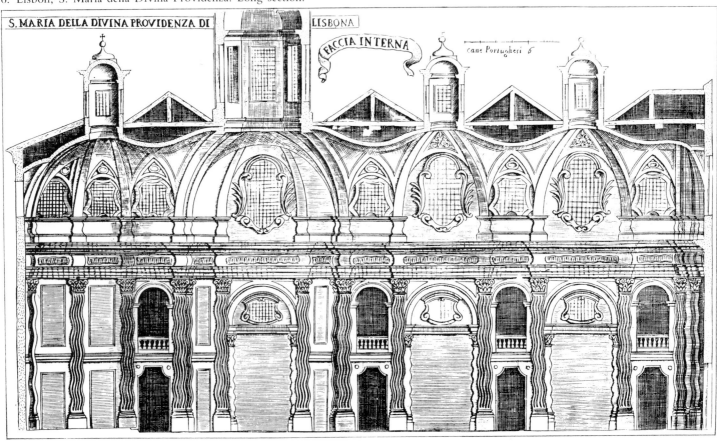

have been its intended replacement; hence the dedication to Fr Ardizone. What the omission of this dedication in the 1737 edition of the Treatise betokens, we can only guess.

Permission to build a new and permanent church was granted by King Pedro II in 1681, two years before Guarini died, and the first stone of this was only laid in 1698.[12] This new church in its turn has disappeared, destroyed in the earthquake of 1775. 'It does not seem probable', writes J. A. Ramírez, 'that it followed the plan, drawn by Guarino Guarini some forty years before the commencement of construction works; after such a long period of time the plan would have been considered old-fashioned, however prestigious its author.'[13] But Lisbon in the late seventeenth century was scarcely a hotbed of architectural progress. When, for instance, the royal architect João Antunes was called upon in 1682 to produce a monumental building, the outcome was the church of S. Engracia, which has been called 'thoroughly *retardataire . . .* a monument to the unsettled times and the inefficient architects of the period'.[14] The fact is that we cannot at this distance in time know whether Guarini's church was ever actually built, or with what possible modifications.[15]

———————

All we know for certain of Guarini's design for S. Maria della Divina Providenza in Lisbon[16] is contained in the two plates (Figs. 5 and 6) printed in the *Dissegni* and subsequently (minus dedication) in the *Architettura civile*. A first glance at these plates – a plan and a long section – shows a condensed Latin cross plan deriving ultimately from north Italian models. Closer inspection reveals that the whole church has been set into undulating motion, in both plan and section. Like Borromini's S. Carlo alle Quattro Fontane, with which Daria de Bernardi Ferrero compares it,[17] it hardly contains a single straight line.[18] The nave consists of two intersecting circular bays, each capped by a ribbed quadripartite dome surmounted by a lantern. The presbytery is likewise covered by a circular dome, which is, however, somewhat smaller. The huge dome at the crossing intersects both the presbytery dome and the second dome of the nave. Two longitudinally elliptical chapels serve as transepts. The plan shows the side walls undulating continuously from the cylindrical surface of the entrance end until they meet in the circular rear wall of the presbytery. The major convexities of the trabeation over the side chapels, sunk and compressed between the piers, are linked by what Passanti aptly calls 'the rapid repetition of this motif between their two heads'.[19]

Further study of the sectional elevation shows that the undulatory movement is transmitted to all the chief members which articulate the composition: the shafts of the major Order of pilasters wriggle from side to side, all the way from the plinth to the capital, while the minor Order, framing the side chapels, is twisted. The architraves and friezes undulate, too. Nor is this all: where the individual bays interpenetrate at vaulting level, the lines of intersection are not clear-cut, but take the form of soft curves; edges are rounded off, and the ceiling, in long section, is a mathematically indefinable wavy line, dipping over a series of windows, set in the lunettes between the domes. The way that all the spatial cells of the church melt into each other at their intersections was first noted by Sedlmayr, who coined the expression 'spatial fusion' to describe the effect.[20]

The search for an explanation of this extraordinary motif has produced

7. 'The Supreme Corinthian Order, which I make undulating.'

some answers that are hardly less baffling. Professor Portoghesi, in one of those abstruse pronouncements that so exasperated the late Anthony Blunt,[21] observed:

> It might be said that at Lisbon the application of the undulatory order contained an iconic allusion, albeit prophetic, to a jerky seismic motion, but the procedure of extending to the design of the order the process of undulation, not controlled in its spatial outcome, appears to be a distortion motivated by extradisciplinary reasons and not controlled in the specificity of the architectural meaning.[22]

Marcello Fagiolo invokes the aid of cosmology to explain the scheme.[23] He refers to Guarini's book *Placita philosophica* where the author claims that the stars move through the heavens on an undulating, sinusoidal and spiral course, deriving from the combination of diverse movements of rotation and revolution, and the conciliation of opposites. When this notion is transferred from astronomy to architecture, it serves (Fagiolo says) to elucidate the design of S. Maria della Divina Providenza:

16

The reasoning behind this construction is so logical, so captious, that it could seem natural to see men roaming about in this labyrinth as satellites immersed in a system which towers above them, conditions them, binds them in its spirals.[24]

The real clue to the design is contained in *Architettura civile*, where Guarini refers to a 'Supreme Corinthian Order which I make undulating'.[25] This Order is extrapolated from a twisted Corinthian column, which is provided with an undulating cornice and all the requisite trimmings, so that, as Guarini says, 'they might constitute an individual and entire Order'. The details are shown in a plate in the Treatise (Fig. 7).

The impetus to design a complete undulating Order derived from the curious belief, widely entertained during the Renaissance, that Solomon's Temple in Jerusalem featured twisted columns, and that these columns were preserved in Old St Peter's in Rome.[26] Though the Temple itself was lost, it should thus be possible by applying the rules of module and proportion to reconstruct an entire twisted or undulating Order from the columns. This was in fact done by a Spanish Benedictine monk, Juan Andres Ricci or Rizi (1600–1681), the son of Antonio Ricci, a Bolognese artist who had settled in Spain. In his treatise *Tratado de la pintura sabia*[27] Fray Juan Ricci sets out the details of a complete Salomonic Order, where, with a kind of maniacal logic, the twisted shaft of the column serves as a kind of *primum mobile* for inducing undulation into bases, pedestals, capitals, entablatures, friezes and pediments, producing what Ricci calls *un Orden Salomónico totalmente entero*. Like a tell-tale speck of dust or a hair in forensic medicine, the *entero* in the Spaniard's title finds a revelatory echo in the Italian's *Ordine proprio e intiero*.[28] Ricci's treatise was not published till this century: together with six others on theology, geometry and anatomy, it lay in archives in Madrid (the F. Boix Collection) and Montecassino. The significant adjective recurs in the Benedictine's *Brebe tratado de arquitectura acerca del Orden Salomónico entero*, written in 1663 and dedicated to Pope Alexander VII and Queen Christina of Sweden. This treatise, too, languished at Montecassino until published by Lafuente Ferrari in 1930.

Fr Celestino Gusi, in the life of Ricci contributed to Lafuente Ferrari's edition of Ricci's treatise, suggests that it was written between 1659 and 1662; Ramírez argues, however, that his 'ideas concerning the Salomonic Order could have been developed and partially disseminated prior to the writing of the manuscript'.[29] This is the nub of the matter: in the absence of contemporary publication, 'dissemination' must in any case have taken place orally, and Guarini's familiarity not simply with twisted columns, but with the idea of *a complete undulating Order*, as early as his stay in Sicily (1660–2)[30] where, on his own evidence, he employed it 'in practice in a chapel in Messina, albeit in stucco',[31] reinforces the impression that he had been in contact with Ricci or his immediate circle in Spain. Other undulatory details characterize Guarini's early designs, most notably at Ste Anne-la-Royale in Paris (1662–6), which features an undulating cornice, but the Divina Providenza in Lisbon is the only known case where he employed the Supreme Corinthian Order, with its undulating shafts, architraves and friezes. Guarini's use of this Order, however, for precisely this site, his subsequent Islamic borrowings and the other circumstances mentioned above may well be deemed persuasive evidence that the winged sandals that bore the Mercury of our Age to Sicily in 1660 had indeed passed over the Iberian peninsula.

Messina. Chiesa Annunziata
prima del 28-12-1908

4   SICILY

IN THE YEAR 1660 a *tragicommedia morale* entitled *La pietà trion-fante* was published in the Sicilian city of Messina, intended for performance by the youths of the local Theatine seminary. The play was dedicated to His Most Serene Highness Alfonso, Duke of Modena, and its author was the regular cleric Guarino Guarini, lecturer in mathematics at the Theatine school. The dateline of this book is really the only firm chronological evidence for Guarini's stay in Sicily. We know when he left, but there is no saying exactly when he arrived: it might have been 1659 or 1660. Three centuries of earthquakes, wars and invasions have destroyed any archival evidence that might have pinpointed Guarini's movements. We learn from the publisher's preface to *La pietà trionfante* that the play was composed in Modena, but due to its author's forced departure from his native city the manuscript 'was carried from town to town following the voyages of its author, the Mercury of our age'.

The gloss put on this observation by Sandonnini was that in his *Wander-jahre* Guarini's name had become famous 'for the numerous voyages he undertook and the works he executed, and it is probable that for just this reason he was called to Messina by the Theatines, who were desirous of erecting a house and a temple of great size'.[1] The Messina where Guarini found himself was in the grip of a building boom, and had the wealth to pay for it. Its riches derived from intensive silkworm breeding and silk weaving.[2] Messina silk products were in wide demand; they were exported in great quantities and Messina itself enjoyed the privilege of being a free port, its harbour thronged with Genoese, Flemish and Dutch ships.

An ample proportion of the wealth thus generated was consumed in an unparalleled building boom, in an exuberant late Mannerist style of architecture: 'Year by year a new church, a fountain, a portal, a palazzo.'[3] The whole Messina littoral resembled a building site, from the Royal Palace, which was undergoing restoration, to the famous street known as the Palazzata, where twelve uniform palaces were going up. This *bâtissomanie* affected the religious Orders, too: Jesuits, Theatines, Augustinians and other pious squadrons of the Counter-Reformation – fathers of the Minori Osservanti, for example. They are said to have torn down the church of Portosalvo in a single night to clear the site for rebuilding.

The Theatines themselves had settled in Messina at the beginning of the seventeenth century and begun their church of S. Maria Annunziata in the second decade of the century, on the lines of their Roman basilica, S. Andrea della Valle. They were supported in their efforts by the Archbishop of Messina and the Contessa Cibo.[4] By the time Guarini made his appearance,

8. Messina, S. Maria Annunziata. Elevation (pre-1908 photograph).

9. Messina, S. Maria Annunziata. Elevation and strip plan.

10. Valencia, S. Miguel de los Reyes. Elevation.

the body of the church was virtually completed.[5] Guarini was invited to design the facade. This scheme is illustrated as a plate in *Architettura civile*, but the building itself no longer exists. It was damaged in the earthquakes of 1783 and 1894, and demolished after that of 1908. Several old photographs survive, showing the front elevation before (Fig. 8) and after (Fig. 13) the 1908 catastrophe, and a number of fragments are preserved in the grounds of the Museo Nazionale in Messina.

The facade was placed diagonally to the nave (Fig. 9), thus masking the tower that was set forward to one side of it, and conforming to the building line of the street. A comparison of the plate in *Architettura civile* with the pre-1908 photograph shows that the engraver has misunderstood Guarini's intentions, displaying full columns on both ground and upper levels where pilasters were intended. The way that Guarini has disposed them in the built version provokes Hager to say:

> The powerful columns and pilasters of the plinth level do not remain ... generically arranged by groups so that loadbearing units are recognized in them, they are rather lined upon both sides in a continuous succession, apparently without regard to where the individual member comes to rest in the structure.[6]

Viewed overall, the facade may be read as a flat version of the characteristic Guarinian telescopic development of three-dimensional space, as we shall see shortly, for example, at the Padri Somaschi church in Messina. The facade is dished inwards, like Borromini's front to the Oratory of S. Filippo Neri in Rome, with a counter-movement in the convex central feature at plinth level, analogous to that on the S. Filippo Neri facade. There are Borrominian borrowings in the decorative details, too, such as the winged cherub heads on the plinth level niche windows and the stuck-on foliage of the upper central light, the latter, incidentally, already missing in the photograph.

The build-up of the Annunziata facade was to be repeated in broad lines some years later in an altar Guarini designed for the church of S. Nicolò, Verona. In a study of the S. Nicolò altar, a similarity has been noted to Spanish and South American *retablos*, 'which become complicated symbolic machines of mystical suggestion'.[7] But in Spanish art the term *retablo* is also applied by analogy to a type of church facade development where the elevation is built up in the same way, 'towering portals like extruded retables', as G. Kubler explains them.[8] Martin de Olinda's facade at the church of S. Miguel de los Reyes near Valencia (Fig. 10) is a characteristic example. It was completed in 1644, and either it or one like it may have been seen by Guarini during his time in Spain. Certainly the general composition of the Annunziata facade with its three main storeys (of which the topmost unit, or superstructure, is again divided into three storeys) is something radically different from the broad Roman gable. Whether what we have here is a flat harbinger of the Guarinian 'telescoped' development of volume, or a reminiscence of a Spanish *retablo* front, the general effect is that of a synthesis of heterogeneous elements which produces an unresolved tension – basically a Mannerist usage.

A common practice of the Italian religious Orders in the seventeenth century was to abut their house or college onto their church. A typical example in Messina is the Jesuit College by the local architect Natale Masuccio (Fig. 11), annexed to their church of S. Giovanni Battista, by the same architect. The Theatines adopted a similar layout for their establishment, illustrated most readily in an engraving by Francesco Sicuro (Fig. 12).[9] This reveals the

20

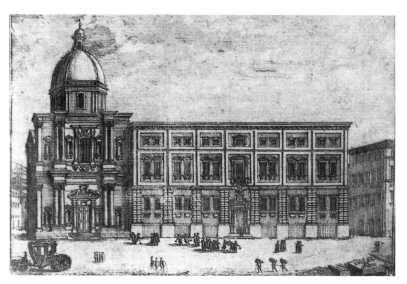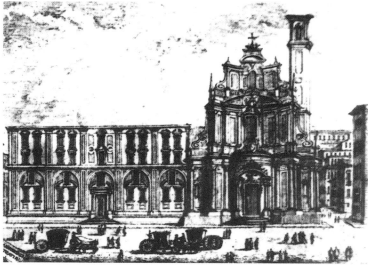

11. Messina, Jesuit College and church of S. Giovanni Battista (from Sicuro, *Vedute*).

12. Messina, Theatine College and church of S. Maria Annunziata (from Sicuro, *Vedute*).

house of the Order to be articulated in a similar manner to the Jesuit College, though with five bays of paired windows as against the Jesuits' seven. Both have ornate entrances in the centre bay. A long tradition, which can be traced back through successive generations of topographical writers and compilers of guidebooks, attributes the Theatine house to Guarini as well. A recollection of the Ducal Palace at Modena has been seen in the coupled windows,[10] but a more local model is offered by Masuccio's design for the Jesuits (built about 1630).[11] The fenestration at ground floor level is in groups of three per bay, with a central window sitting astride the lower two; but a photograph of the house, next to the church, taken after the 1908 earthquake (Fig. 13), shows that Sicuro's engraving is inexact in its details, since the centre window as built intersects a semicircular arch, of which the surviving lunette fragments on each side are likewise open; while the half-open pediments of the lower windows cut into its frame. Hager suggests that the triangular disposition of the windows 'has obviously been chosen to harmonize with the church facade'[12] 'Obviously' is not the adverb that leaps at once to the mind; 'possibly' might be more appropriate.

In his 'observation' on the Supreme Corinthian Order – the undulating Order – in the *Architettura civile*, Guarini remarks that it turned out well when he used it in practice 'in a chapel, albeit in stucco, in Messina'.[13] It is not possible to identify this chapel with certainty. An anonymous guidebook to Messina published in 1902 refers to the altar of St Anthony of Padua in the church of the Annunziata as being 'first on the right, decorated with heavy stucco and serpentine columns, designed by the same Guarini'.[14] The suggestion has been made that the location may actually have been at the base of the octagonal bell tower, included in the strip plan annexed to the facade in Guarini's book.[15] This would have been, strictly speaking, 'the first on the right' as you went in (if somewhat tucked away), but there is no means of knowing now.

Sandonnini, writing before the earthquake of 1908, refers to the church of S. Filippo in Messina as part of those works which 'attest to the uncommon worth of this architect'.[16] This was a church, on basilican lines, and an oratory, started in 1618. Guarini's connection with it is another tradition of Messina, but both the church and any documentation that might have existed in connection with it have vanished.

A question of a slightly different nature hangs over Guarini's last scheme for Messina, the church he designed for the Somasian Fathers, or the Padri Somaschi, first illustrated in plates 29 and 30 of the *Dissegni* and subsequently reproduced in *Architettura civile*. This question is whether the design was ever built? Portoghesi thinks that it was never finished 'and perhaps never even started'.[17] It was not among the buildings destroyed in 1908, earlier guidebooks do not refer to it, [18] and it is not illustrated in Francesco Sicuro's 1768 set of *Vedute e prospetti della citta di Messina*. Portoghesi, furthermore, assigns the scheme to a latter stage in the architect's career,[19] in which he is followed by Hager[20] and Millon,[21] but as Wittkower remarks,[22] there is no stringent reason to follow them in this, and it is logical to regard the church of the Padri Somaschi as the first statement of a number of themes that preoccupied Guarini: centrality, telescoped space and the idiosyncratic treatment of vaulting, which were destined to pass through a series of variations in his subsequent career.

The plan of the church is completely centralized (Fig. 14). It consists at ground floor level of a hexagonal inner area, bounded at the angles by six

13. Messina, S. Maria Annunziata. Detail of facade.

triangular piers, each articulated at the three arrises with attached columns. Beyond this central area there runs an ambulatory bounded by the outer walls on one side, and by major arches on the other, between the column triads giving on to the central hexagon. The ambulatory comprises six long groin-vaulted spaces, interspersed by six much smaller ones. These smaller units, which act as 'articulations' between the larger vaulted ones, are capped by circular lanterns (Figs. 17 and 18). The plan shape of the smaller units is, at least by implication, a triangle with inward curving sides. The curved base of this triangle is constituted by the rear wall of an elevational niche: the other two sides are reflected by the two minor arches that close off the short ends of the adjoining vaulted spaces; and these two arches turn not in vertical planes, but in cylindrical surfaces normal to the inner sides of each pair of columns.

So much for the hexagonal plan of the ground floor zone. The transition to the next zone up is achieved internally by pendentives, above which is a circular cornice. This does not run, however, round the interior of a cylindrical drum, but around a hexagon with six large windows. Between the windows a series of parabolic ribs spring from hidden bases located at the angles of the hexagon, and hence independent of the balustraded ring. They are arranged in such a way as to form a six-pointed star, with a regular hexagon in the centre. (Fig. 15). But this is not all. The interweaving of the ribs creates the effect of a diaphanous or basket-work dome which crowns the hexagonal space below: thus we have for the (vertically) intermediate zone a hybrid feature that is at the same time drum and dome, which, as Wittkower remarks, is no less surprising than the use of pendentives for the transition of the ground floor hexagon into the round, only to return to the hexagon again.[23]

We shall encounter this device of interwoven ribs to form an openwork dome once again in the church of S. Lorenzo in Turin, but this time elevated to a greater degree of complexity. A discussion of its possible sources will be postponed till then.

The six ribs or binding arches cross and intersect in such a way as to create a regular open hexagon in the centre, rotated in relation to the hexagon at the base, so that its angles coincide with the centre points of the lower hexagon's sides.[24] Precariously based on this open hexagon is a proper small drum and dome, the two of them together exactly as high as the pseudo-dome. The method employed to locate this heavy mass of masonry on the intersections of the binding ribs was to be refined and perfected in Guarini's later church of S. Lorenzo, Turin.

Here, in one of the first buildings designed by Guarini, we are at once confronted by the peculiarity which above all characterizes his style: 'the superimposition along a vertical axis of several autonomous volumetric entities'.[25] In ascending through the section of this church, and of other Guarinian buildings, it is not possible to foretell from the conformation of a lower zone how, on the basis of normal compositional procedure, the next zone is going to develop. In this respect Guarini differs from Borromini, whose influence is traceable in other respects. Borromini's structures are admittedly complex, but in true Baroque fashion he aimed to create a homogeneous structure that could be 'read' along the main lines of the walls.[26] Guarini's anti-homogeneous tendencies look back in this respect to the Mannerist tradition. But both Guarini and Borromini were indisputably indebted to that 'indefatigable, almost maniacal draftsman'[27] Giovanni Batista Montano (d. 1621), whose posthumously published fantasies, in particular the *Scielta di varij tempietti antichi* (Rome 1624), include studies of

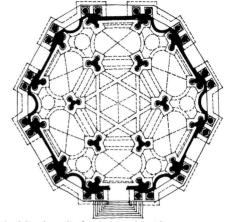

14. Messina, Padri Somaschi. Plan.

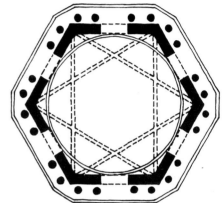

15. Messina, Padri Somaschi. Plan at level of drum.

16. G.B. Montano: Tempietto on the Via Appia (from *Scielta di varij tempietti antichi*).

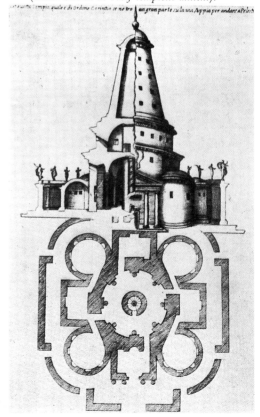

23

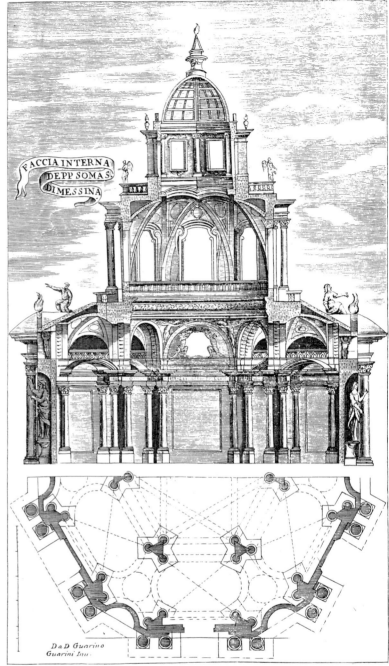

17. Messina, Padri Somaschi. Elevation.

18. Messina, Padri Somaschi. Section and part plan.

possible hierarchical aggregations, on both horizontal and vertical planes, of autonomous volumetric units (Fig. 16).[28]

It was from Montano's studies that Guarini may have derived the impetus that led him to design the church of the Padri Somaschi on a centralized plan, though the line of descent for such layouts can of course be traced through Alberti back to such late Roman circular churches with an ambulatory as S. Costanza (c.320).[29] One effect that Guarini's design would have achieved was the differentiation in levels of internal illumination, so beloved of the Baroque.[30] There would have been a dramatic contrast between the great flood of light pouring into the central area from the large windows of the intermediate zone and (through the lattice-work of the parabolic arches) from the large lantern above, with the half-light prevailing in the ambulatory

24

chambers at ground floor level, where illumination is derived from the six little apertures of the groin-vaulted chambers, and the minor lanterns crowning the six intermediate 'joint' areas.

The superimposition of three apparently autonomous volumes internally is duly reflected in the elevation, where the common Baroque device of progressive upward simplification cannot alone account for the virtual lack of relationship between the tiers – a feature that Wittkower considers to be more reminiscent of a late mannerist tabernacle than of a church.[31]

Guarini's centralized plan produces six identical elevations. At the level of the lowest zone these appear as a chain of sumptuous portals in full relief, interconnected by the sinuous line produced by the alternation of curvilinear pediments and acroteria. These create a continuously undulating movement that runs right round the building, and the usual Roman Baroque tendency is hence absent that sees the facade as an outward expression of the spatial movement and direction within.

A parallel to the Baroque complexity of the Padri Somaschi can be found in the plot structure of the play published by Guarini in Messina in 1660, *La pietà trionfante*.[32] Indeed, Enrico Guidoni, in a remarkable paper read to the Guarini Congress in 1968, attempted to use the text of the play to demonstrate the link between Guarini's architecture and the Renaissance Art of Memory: 'the secret technique of rhetoric, of the combinatorial art, of memory understood as a valid instrument in a universal sense'.[33] We shall not attempt to cut a path through this metaphysical forest.

Guarini's play, 'a tragicomedy', had been composed in Modena, but the contretemps with Prince Alfonso and the Theatine's forced departure from his native city prevented it from being performed there. It was staged instead at Messina,[34] where the boys of the Archiepiscopal Seminary, at which Guarini taught mathematics, provided the thirty-seven speaking parts the cast list demands.

Clodoald, King of Denmark, is discovered lamenting the loss of his son Enchirion,[35] stolen from him by a wolf, and his daughter Hildegard, seized by pirates. The son, in fact, has been saved by a shepherd, while the daughter, sold into slavery in Saxony, has (thanks to her beauty) been made chief of the Vestal Virgins. Clodoald, expelled from his kingdom by Hyrcanus, seeks refuge in Saxony, then in rebellion against the Emperor Charlemagne. Here, through violating a wood dedicated to Mars, he loses his sight. To recover it, he swears to sacrifice to the god the first person he encounters. For this foolhardy resolve, he meets of course with the same retribution as befell Jephtha and Idomeneus: the first comer is another of his sons, Hyacinth (Giacinto), who, prompted by filial piety, at once offers to sacrifice himself to placate the cruel god:

> Tu pur dell'occhi tuoi lume, e pupille
> più fiate mi giurasti:
> ma se a gli orrori tuoi lume non porge
> d'inutile pupilla,
> di tenebrosa luce io godo i vanti.

In Guarini's reference here to *tenebrosa luce*, a prophetic interest has been seen in the manipulation of light that finds its apotheosis in the Chapel of the Holy Shroud (SS. Sindone) in Turin.[36]

Giacinto's kind gesture is accepted with alacrity, if regret, and the unfortunate youth is abandoned to the savage beasts of the forest, whence he is rescued in the nick of time by Enchirion and his companion Faustino, who providentially find themselves in the neighbourhood. Enchirion and Giacinto are cast into prison, where they are shortly joined by the fair Hildegard, who, moved by sisterly pity, has been trying to free them.

The prospects of the young Danes are now markedly gloomy, when, with an unexpectedness of incident comparable to that of a Guarinian section, Charlemagne arrives with his whole army. He captures the city, defeats Hyrcanus and restores the *Königskinder* to their father, who, converted to Christianity, recovers his vision at the moment of baptism, and thereafter his kingdom. With true Christian piety Clodoald pardons his adversary Hyrcanus, and the play ends amid general gratification. Guarini notes in his preface that 'the story is true and is related by good authors', but he adds that he has filled it out a little 'to make it more suitable for the stage'.

As an architectural dramatist, Guarini can hardly be placed in the same league as his younger contemporary Sir John Vanbrugh (who was nineteen when Guarini died). *La pietà trionfante* is certainly not lacking in imagination and learning, but the complicated plot, the involved language and the prolixity of the dialogue, including lengthy comments on the action by allegorical characters, make it an unlikely candidate for revival, even by the Architectural Association's Dramatic Society. It is pertinent to add, however, that in Guarini's scientific and architectural books, where he did not feel compelled to aim at a lofty and poetic style, the writing is simple, clear and strictly to the point.

———

From the beginning of 1662, the health of Guarini's mother began to fail,[37] and Guarini obtained permission from his superiors to leave Messina and to take up residence in the Theatine house in Modena,[38] whence he was able to attend his mother's death bed.

Guarini did not prolong his stay in his native city. He was *persona non grata* with the court, and even eight years later, when the Duke of Savoy solicited permission for the architect to be allowed to settle permanently in Modena, the request was refused.[39] His presence on this occasion was merely tolerated on humanitarian grounds. The last reference to Guarini in the papers of the Theatine house in Modena is dated 3 July 1662, when he is noted as being charged with the task of designing sepulchres in the church of S. Vincenzo. Shortly afterwards Guarini's journey north, started in Messina, was resumed. By September or October of 1662 he was in Paris.[40]

5 PARIS

A THEATINE MISSION, despatched by the General Chapter of the Order, arrived in Paris in August 1644. They were not actually invited by the Italian-born Cardinal Mazarin, but were welcomed by him and promised his protection.[1] Mazarin bought a house for the Theatines on what is now the Quai Voltaire on the south bank of the Seine, opposite the Louvre.[2] The small chapel it contained was dedicated to St Anne, and named Ste Anne-la-Royale at the desire, it is said, of Louis XIV, who as a boy of not quite ten was present at the consecration in 1648. The choice of name was evidently intended to honour the Queen Dowager, Anne of Austria, with whom Mazarin was on close, if not indeed intimate, terms.

Shortly before Mazarin died in 1661 he made over to the Theatine Order the adjoining house, which he had acquired in the meantime, together with some additional property at the back. In his will he left the Parisian Theatines the sum of 100,000 écus.[3]

It was Mazarin's intention that this legacy should be applied to the construction of a new church for the Theatine Order in Paris, to replace the small chapel in their house. Already in his lifetime he had brought over from Italy the engineer Antonio Maurizio Valperga,[4] who had produced a scheme for a church that was oval on plan, with a cross-vault and a cupola, facing the Seine; the actual designs are lost. Five months after the death of Mazarin, the Theatine fathers decided, in the chapters of 15 and 30 August 1661, to accept Valperga's plan and put it into execution. An agreement was drawn up with a contractor to dig the foundation trenches. Between then and the autumn of 1662 there are various notices in capitular registers of building decisions being taken, generally on a consensus of advice from 'skilled architects and masons' or 'skilled architects and craftsmen', which seem to indicate the absence of the author of the scheme. Valperga was in fact occupied at the time in fortifying the town of Brissach on the Rhine near Colmar.[5]

An end was put to all hesitancy and shilly-shallying in the autumn of 1662, when the Father General of the Order sent Guarino Guarini to direct the work, 'a man excellent in architecture', who arrived in Paris some time between the chapters held on 29 August and 26 October 1662.

Guarini did not think highly of Valperga's scheme. He considered that it would turn out 'very inconvenient, dark and narrow, and as if divided into three separate portions'.[6] He proposed accordingly, to draw up a new scheme, using the existing foundations, which would be 'much lighter, more convenient and graceful'. Guarini's scheme was approved by the Commissioner appointed by the executors of Mazarin's estate, and adopted at the chapter of 3 November 1663. The foundation stone was laid on 22 Novem-

27

ber by the Prince de Conti, representing Louis XIV, and building operations began in earnest in the following year.

While the Padri Somaschi was on a completely centralized plan, Ste Anne represents the conventional compromise between centralization and a longitudinal layout (Fig. 19). It takes the form of a Greek cross, with a presbytery annexed to the far side of the east arm. But as the four main piers that define the central area are set on a 45 degree diagonal, and as this obliquity is reflected by the responds in the opposite angles of the arms, the four areas become contiguous to each other, and a powerful 'wraparound' movement is imparted to the arms vis-à-vis the central space. This contiguity is emphasized – two-dimensionally, at least – by the fact that each arm is prolonged by two elliptical minor spaces at each end,[7] which abut each other, though they do not interpenetrate.

A vertical impetus is given to each of the main piers (see section, Fig. 20) by the fact of their being articulated by a pair of pilasters (on separate bases) on each face; and these pilasters, having made their presence felt by the appropriate breaks forward in the entablature they support, carry on upwards, in the shape of pairs of band-like ribs which run over the segments of the cross-vaults that roof the four arms of the cross, to create an elongated open hexagon at the apex, capped in each case by a lantern. Here again is the true Guarinian note: the lattice feature, defining in its uppermost reaches a shape that is broken through to reveal a space beyond. In the present instance it is a harbinger, sounding four times, and in two variations of proportion, a motif that will be taken up and elaborated in a higher zone of the central area. A similiar design feature was to be employed some years later in the little church of S. Maria Ettinga which Guarini designed for his Order in Prague.

So much for the upward projection, in the form of band-like ribs, of the pilasters on the faces of the angled piers, where they are turned out towards the arms. An examination of the plan and section of the church shows that on the side towards the central area these bands serve to frame the major soffit-less arch, where the lunettes of the central square meet the pendentives of the arms.[8] These pendentives support a drum – a cylindrical one this time, not a hexagon as at Messina. At least the interior is cylindrical, with a gallery articulated by a series of serlianas; the exterior is articulated by a number of pairs of attached and quarter-attached columns,[9] which support a deep entablature. This entablature winds its way round the top of the drum in eight concave loops, lending the drum the appearance of an octagon: but the eight points where the concave surfaces should meet have been replaced by re-entrant angles, so that the entablature repeatedly comes out to a point and breaks back. In the middle of each convex stretch of entablature, though set well back, is placed a diminutive cylindrical lantern, through the sides of which light penetrates, to filter through the serlianas of the gallery inside, thus contributing to the complex interplay of illumination.

The drum is surmounted by the Guarinian speciality *par excellence* of the scheme. This consists of a dwarf dome, decorated on the interior by a complex interlace of double band-like ribs. We have already seen what we have referred to as the harbinger of this motif in the treatment of the vaulted roofs over the arms, where the pilasters framing the four angles of the room continue up beyond the entablature as flat ribs. Here, in the dwarf dome, the first ribs can be read as a continuation, in a higher zone, of the coupled columns of the serlianas that frame the gallery of the drum. As may be seen from the sectional elevation, they create their interlace pattern by springing in pairs from their plinths, and vaulting over the next plinth to the one beyond.

28

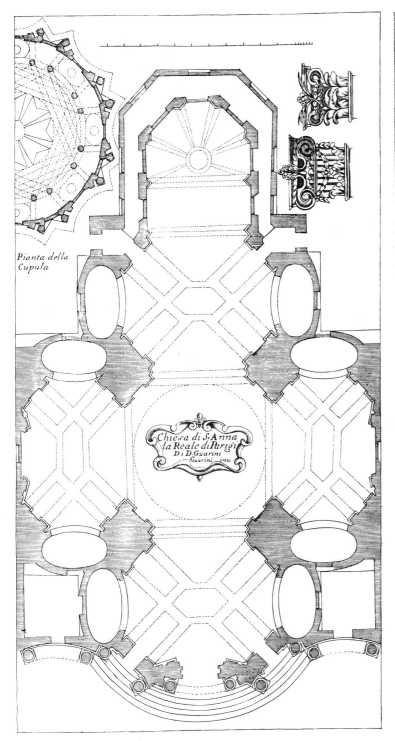

Pianta della Cupula

Chiesa di S. Anna la Reale di Parigi Di D. Guarini. Guarini inu.

PROSPETTO INTERNO DI ANNA REALE DI PARIGI

Trabo 10

Pianta della Cornice

Scala della cornice

Cornice Principale della Chiesa

This basketwork effect may be of Borrominian inspiration, harking back to the treatment of the ceilings in the Oratory of S. Filippo Neri and the church of the Propaganda Fide in Rome (Fig. 21) – which themselves may be inspired by Michelangelo's device at St Peter's of projecting the upward thrust of his giant elevational pilasters into the ribs, which continue that movement over the dome.

In Borromini's earlier building, the Oratory, dating from the 1630s, the lines of the pilasters are continued upwards into rib-like vaults. Twenty years later the same motif was used again in the Re Magi chapel of the Propaganda

19. Paris, Ste Anne-la-Royale. Plan.

20. Paris, Ste Anne-la-Royale. Section and detail of undulating cornice.

29

21. Rome, Collegio di Propaganda Fide (Borromini). Vaulting of the chapel of the Re Magi.

22. Durham, Cathedral Priory. Kitchen vault, 1366 (from R.W. Billings, *Durham Cathedral*, 1843).

Fide, developed into a criss-cross pattern 'that forces one to see the room aerially across the space, instead of around the walls'.[10] But whereas Borromini's use of the device helps to tie in the whole structure, Guarini's recourse to this motif is intended only to articulate the topmost of a series of autonomous units.[11]

In the Parisian building, the architect 'pasted ... Borromini's flat and doubled bands on a closed surface'.[12] The fact of his doing so, Pommer suggests, 'in turn awakened Guarini to those Moorish and medieval Spanish vaults where the cat's cradle of ribs was applied to spherical surfaces in star-like patterns, or ... where the vaults were set in crossing towers that had open drums and stepped exteriors'.[13] The culmination of this development will be seen in Guarini's diaphanous ribbed dome at S. Lorenzo, Turin, where fuller consideration will be given to the question of Islamic antecedents.

A byproduct of the dome interlacement at Ste Anne is represented by the pairs of pointed arches that are brought about directly above the semicircular arches of the serlianas. This type of effect is to be seen in some of the churches in Palermo, Monreale and Cefalù,[14] a legacy of the Fatimid occupation of Sicily which Guarini might have observed during his stay on the island. But pointed arches may also be regarded, perhaps, as a kind of Gothic portent. We shall see that Guarini was an avowed student and a conscious admirer of Gothic architecture.

A still more striking Gothic effect may be discerned in the way Guarini leaves open the wide octagon formed in the centre of his dwarf dome by the interlaced flat ribs. This feature may be compared with the analogous one contrived in the roof of the ocatagon at the crossing of Ely Cathedral (1323), or even more closely, because of the way it follows the overarching rib patterns, with John Lewyn's kitchen vault (Fig. 22) at Durham Cathedral Priory (1366). The latter, in its turn, has also been referred to Islamic prototypes.[15] A closer examination of this particular question follows in the discussion of the sources for S. Lorenzo.

In his Parisian church, Guarini uses the central oculus defined by the rib enlacement to provide a view through to a smaller, truncated dome, which rises above, capped in its turn by a lantern of traditional design. The inspiration for this was much nearer to hand, namely in the Rue St Antoine, Paris, where François Mansart's centralized plan church of Ste Marie-de-la-Visitation (1632–3) has its choir roofed by an oval dome, opened up in the centre to admit a strong influx of light from a tall lantern.[16] Mansart achieved a similar effect at Blois (1635–8), where the central panel of the coved ceiling over the stair-well is left open to give a view at an upper level of a dome on pendentives, ending in a low lantern, a device that creates an illusion of exaggerated loftiness and recession. A cut-off dome was also planned by Mansart for the Val-de-Grâce in 1645,[17] though it was never executed, as Lemercier took over the project in the next year. The whole line of development was raised to a higher plane of monumentality with Le Vau's design of 1663 for the vestibule of the Louvre,[18] which had its vault open to the sky. It is undoubtedly within the context of this climate of architectural thought that Guarini's feature must be considered.

The central area of the ground floor zone of Ste Anne-la-Royale has a feeling of constriction, imparted by the size in plan and elevation of the four great piers that bound it, and by the relative narrowness of the four openings off it towards the arms. This horizontal constriction is counterbalanced, however, by a strong Gothic/Baroque vertical impetus, created in the central area by the fact that the piers are very tall in relation to the radius of the four major arches of the openings to the arms, while in the arms themselves the Guarinian device of continuing the pilasters upwards beyond the entablature, in the form of band-like ribs, draws the eye up to the apex of the vault, where it encounters the breakthrough to the lantern.

In ascending through the section, however, there is an immediate expansion at the level of the drum, where it is the gallery front that aligns with the square below, the main walls of the drum being set back to such an extent that its overall internal diameter is exactly twice the width of the ground floor openings in the arms. Above this zone, however, the interlace-hemisphere, the truncated dome and the lantern create a sequence of ever more restricted spaces, whose reduction is accentuated by their increasing distance from our eyes. And 'after the alternating movement of rise and fall produced in the first two zones by the serlian motifs of the drum and the interlace following it, a pure movement of ascent follows in the last two spaces'.[19]

A parallel to this contraction, expansion and contraction again of internal volume may be discerned in Guarini's treatment of light sources. Meagre at the lowest zone, they penetrate directly only through small apertures in the upper part of the oval altar spaces of the arms. In the zone immediately above, over the entablature, is the maximum invasion of light, pouring through the curious serliana-type windows, almost symmetrical about the horizontal as well as the vertical axis, and augmented by the contribution filtered through the lanterns over the arms. In the next zone up, however, in counterpoint to the expansion of volume, the light diminishes in quantity, percolating through the serlianas of the gallery from much smaller windows in the walls of the drum, and from a ring of tiny lanterns, located on the offset behind the scooped-out octagonal entablature outside. In the zone of the dwarfed dome are curious viol-shaped apertures,[20] smaller again than the windows in the drum, and the diminution continues to the lantern.

The oval, as a plan component, makes its first modest appearance in Guarini's work here at Ste Anne-la-Royale.[21] It is a feature that was later to be exploited with sublime skill in the intersecting ovals of his longitudinal churches, which in their turn proved the inspiration of much late German Baroque architecture. But even here, its use involves consequences that go beyond the immediately obvious.

The conjunction of two ovals behind each of the four major piers has the effect of throwing the latter out of the square (Fig. 23), so that in fact each pier exhibits three different widths of face: narrowest in the north and south side arms, wider in the central square, and widest in the east and west arms. This affects the distance apart of the pilasters that run up them. The discrepancy can be seen at once on plan (Fig. 19) by comparing the distances apart of the coupled ribs shown on the ceiling of the north and south arms with those of the east and west. Furthermore, the width of the opening to the oval chapels is greater in the east and west arms than in the north and south ones,[22] with the result that the east and west chapels are deeper than the other two. The total outcome of these adjustments may have been to produce an illusionistic effect of greater depth, when viewed from certain standpoints. Hence, the fact that the sides of the piers that face towards the central square are narrower than those in the east and west arms, means that the visitor entering the church (Fig. 24) and taking a synoptic view from point A of the four diagonal pier faces presented to him will derive an impression of exaggerated distance from the two farther faces (2, 2), since not only are they foreshortened by perspective, which the visitor knows, but they are also

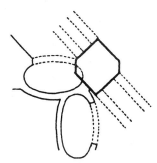

23. Paris, Ste Anne-la-Royale. Different widths of pier faces.

24. Paris, Ste Anne-la-Royale. Effects of synoptic view from point A.

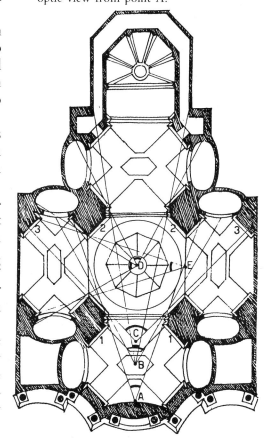

25. Paris, Ste Anne-la-Royale. Elevation.

narrower in actuality, which he does not know; and the extra narrowness is attributed to increased remoteness.[23] A counter-effect is not achieved from point B, in the centre of the west arm, because in looking through to the east end, the furthermost pilasters, which again are actually wider than those in the central square, are partially masked. But the effect of exaggerated perspective is once more achieved from point E, looking towards the side arm. This Baroque illusionism is paralleled to some extent by the effect of exaggerated foreshortening that must have been evident when looking up from the central square, where once again the distant coincides with the small. Guarini's highest development of this technique will be encountered in the dome of the Chapel of the Holy Shroud (SS. Sindone) at Turin, where coloured stone is used to simulate the softening of tone values that occurs at a great distance. But illusionistic devices of this nature cannot really substitute

32

for actual physical depth, since the intensity of impression conveyed is bound to vary with the standpoint.

The tendency already noted of the Guarinian interior to superimpose several autonomous volumetric entities along a vertical axis is once more evident at Ste Anne, where it is also reflected in the elevation (Fig. 27). This presents, in the rather unkind words of one scholar, 'a layer cake arrangement of five superimposed parts'.[24] The arrangement is in fact a further development of the incipient 'telescoping' that we have seen in the Messina facades. Wittkower calls it 'a pagoda-like build-up',[25] and seen in this light it may be said that this tendency is taken to its logical conclusion in the Sanctuary of Oropa, built by Guarini in 1680, where each successive storey of the octagonal structure displays its own piece of roof all round in true pagoda fashion, like a series of petticoats. Precedent for Guarini's general elevational composition at Ste Anne may perhaps be found in such early Baroque buildings in the north of Italy as the hexagonal church of S. Maria del Quartiere, built in Parma in 1604 to the designs of G. B. Aleotti and his pupil G. B. Magnani.[26]

The two lower zones of the elevation have an undulating facade – a convex central portion flanked by concave bays – reminiscent of Borromini's S. Carlo alle Quattro Fontane. The two columns (or four – there is a discrepancy between the engravings of plan and elevation)[27] flanking the central portal have their axes on the segment of the circle that forms the central convexity, while the intermediate and outer columns follow their respective concavities. On top of this comes the drum, the octagonal treatment of which has been discussed above. The drum is surmounted by the dwarfed dome, whose surface inside is covered by the band-like interlacements. Externally it is cased in such a way as to give the appearance of a second drum, its viol-shaped windows flanked by pilasters. A conventional-looking dome with eight exposed ribs caps this, its lower part masked by a circular attic. The whole is surmounted by a lantern, finishing in a helicoidal spire supporting a ball and cross – another Borrominian reminiscence, this time of the finial on top of the university church of S. Ivo della Sapienza in Rome.

Bernini's famous visit to France, made at the invitation of Louis XIV in 1665 in connection with his project for the Louvre,[28] took place during Guarini's residence in Paris. There is no record of their ever having met, though the influence of Bernini's French schemes can be traced in two of Guarini's designs: his Paris Palace and the Palazzo Carignano in Turin. Bernini did, however, visit Ste Anne on 14 June 1665[29] while it was under construction, in the company of his French cicerone, the Sieur de Chantelou, who records that the Master expressed the view that the church would turn out well, at the same time reassuring the Theatine fathers who had misgivings about its proportions.[30]

The same year, 1665, also found Sir Christopher Wren in Paris. In one of his letters Wren speaks of the opportunity he had 'of seeing severall Structures ... while they were in rising, conducted by the best Artists, French and Italian, and having dayly conference with ym and observing ye Engines and Methods'.[31] This is enough for Professor Portoghesi to assert that the reference must be to Guarini ('no other Italian architect was then engaged in Paris on works of any interest'),[32] and he speculates as to whether Wren's astronomical studies were known to the Italian polymath who was later to publish books on the same subject himself.[33] An encounter is possible; it is even probable. But in the letter of Wren's which tells us most about his French visit, Guarini's name does not appear on the list he gives of the architects and artists he had met, a list that includes even such minor figures as Jean Gobert.[34]

If we know that Bernini considered that Ste Anne would 'turn out well', we have little indication as to what Wren thought of it, though the view has been expressed that 'on the whole it seems unlikely that Guarini's imaginative creation would have pleased him, since according to his own testimony, he was suspicious of every excess of architectural "fancy"'.[35] The same scholar suggests elsewhere, however, that the semicircular porticoes that front the transepts of St Paul's might possibly be a reminiscence of the serpentine facade of Ste Anne.[36] Interesting comparisons of the careers of Wren and Guarini have been made by R. Wittkower and M. Tafuri.[37] The latter contrasts Wren's success in integrating his buildings in the London townscape and Guarini's anti-urbanistic tendencies.

If the question is asked, 'What influence did Guarini's work have on French architecture in general?' the answer must be: very little. Guarini's stay in Paris fell within the period of the highest classical brilliance in French architecture. Church design, it is true, had at first lagged behind in the general progress of the art, and even mid-century Parisian churches[38] such as St Sulpice, St Roch, St Nicolas-du-Chardonnet and St Louis-en-l'Ile, despite their classical forms, still have many medieval reminiscences. With the church of the Sorbonne (begun 1635) and the Val-de-Grâce (begun 1645), however, a modified French classical Baroque appeared of great formal perfection and artistic strength. 'There is just as much spatial ingenuity in these plans,' observes N. Pevsner, 'as in those of contemporary Italy, although their detail appears cold and restrained against the Baroque of Rome.'[39] By the 1660s, when Guarini was at work in Paris, a conscious attempt was being made by the state to regulate and control the arts. It was in fact the decade when Colbert was setting up the Academies,[40] which were to codify and propagate the official versions of the arts (although the Academy of Architecture was not established until 1671). This process inevitably had the effect of combating innovation and tended to preserve the status quo. The only building claimed as of 'indisputably Guarinian derivation'[41] in France is the church of St Didier at Asfeld, in the Ardennes, built by Michel Fleury around 1680, which has a dome raised over a pentagonal plan with concave sides.[42] Interesting exchanges on a lesser scale, however, are postulated by Wittkower, who claims that Mansart followed Guarini's type of dome in his design for the Bourbon chapel at St Denis (1665), and that the same kind of dome was used by Jules Hardouin Mansart for his church at Les Invalides (1679 et seq.), though he adjusted the curve of the second vault, which he closed in the centre instead of opening it into a lantern.[43] It is this latest version, Wittkower maintains, that was incorporated by Guarini into his project for S. Gaetano at Vicenza, right at the end of his career. There is undoubtedly an interesting correspondence between the last two schemes, though some uncertainty exists as to whether Mansart's preceded Guarini's in date.

'The architect', Guarini wrote, 'must proceed discreetly. Since he must look to the convenience of whoever builds, if he puts him to such expense that he is either unable to finish the scheme, or must impoverish himself to do so and become a beggar, this will certainly not redound to the convenience, but

34

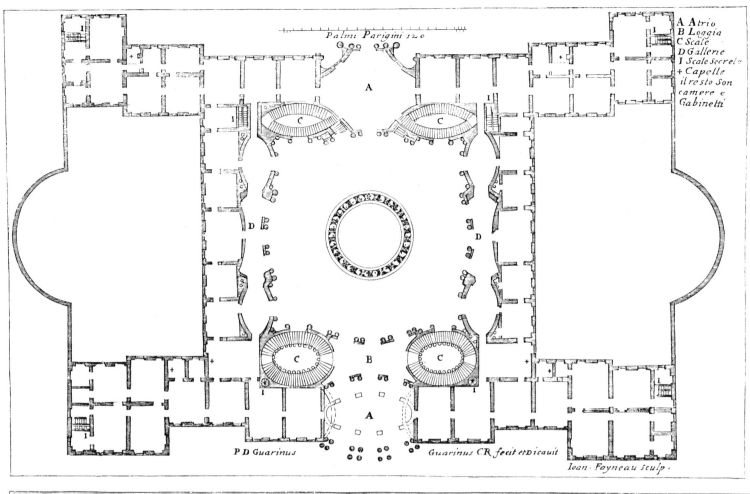

A Atrio
B Loggia
C Scale
D Gallerie
I Scale secrete
+ Capelle
il resto Son
camere e
Gabinetti

Palmi Parigini 120

P D Guarinus

Guarinus CR fecit et Dicauit

Ioan. Fayneau sculp.

D Guarinus
Guarinius in di

FACCIA ESTERIORE

P. d. Parigi 60

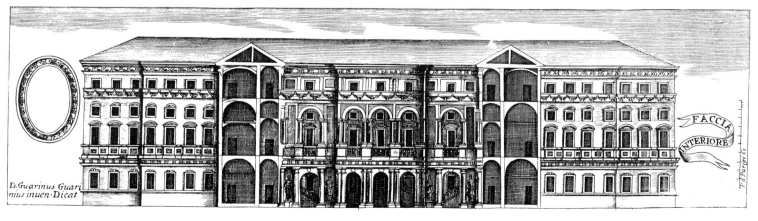

D. Guarinus Guari
nius inuen Dicat

FACCIA INTERIORE

P. d. Parigi 60

rather to the grave inconvenience of him who should enjoy it.'[44] It may well have been Guarini's experience in Paris that prompted these reflections. The Theatines had spent nearly a quarter of Cardinal Mazarin's bequest in acquiring the site for their church.[45] A financial crisis supervened in 1666, and Guarini accused Camillo Sanseverino, head of the Chapter, and superintendent of works, of falsifying the accounts.[46] Sanseverino claimed to have paid out 90,000 écus (270,000 livres) and said that the actual expenses were greater still, while Guarini maintained that it could not have been more than 40,000. Whatever the truth of the matter, it became impossible for Guarini to remain in Paris. He left for Italy in October 1666 with only a third of the church completed,[47] and arrived in Turin on 4 November 1666.[48] In December of that year we find the Duke of Savoy writing to the Father General of the Theatines asking him to allow Guarini to remain in Turin to work for him.[49]

Meanwhile the financial difficulties of the Theatines in Paris increased. Building at Ste Anne-la-Royale ceased early in 1668,[50] and apart from minor works of maintenance, all activity was suspended until 1714, when a lottery was authorized to raise the balance of the funds needed.[51] Building started again to revised designs by Liévain, and the church was eventually dedicated on 21 December 1720. It served the Theatines for seventy-five years, till the Order was suppressed in 1795. From 1800 to 1815 it was used as a dance hall, and then as a café, until it was gradually demolished between 1821 and 1823.[52]

Plates 23 and 24 in the *Architettura civile* (our Figs. 26 and 27) represent a large palace calibrated in 'Parisian palms'.[53] None of the plates illustrating Guarini's designs has any commentary, and these two do not even have a title, but on the basis of the local scale employed, it is generally presumed that they illustrate a scheme intended for erection in Paris.[54] That it was not a mere theoretical exercise, but designed to meet the requirements of an actual client, seems evidenced by various idiosyncratic plan details; the location of the six chapels with which the palace is equipped on the floor shown, the secret stairs provided, and the dimensions of some of the minor rooms, all conspire to suggest a particular brief. The formidable size of the palace – there are 140 rooms in addition to the main reception areas – recalls for a moment the vast town and country houses illustrated in the engraved designs of Antoine Le Pautre,[55] but both the plan and the elevations are a good deal more sober than the French architect's fantastical designs.

Basically the palace is laid out round a hollow square, with the main facades elongated at each end by a set of rooms comprising an *appartement*. Villas built on a hollow square plan, with the main facades extended to give them greater importance, are a well-established architectural type in seventeenth-century Piedmont.[56] The castle of Racconigi,[57] near Turin (*c.* 1650), later to be remodelled by Guarini himself, is a mature example of the genre for which a functional origin is presumably to be found in the need to provide additional accommodation in the more luxurious class of villa, without expanding the central courtyard to unmanageable dimensions. The development can be seen in embryo in the 'ears' projecting from the lateral wings of the Villa Il Verrua near La Crocetta (Fig. 28).

A more immediate link, however, with the Parisian architectural scene is provided in the present instance by Bernini's plans for the Louvre. Bernini's third scheme (Fig. 30), drawn up in 1665 during his stay in Paris and quickly

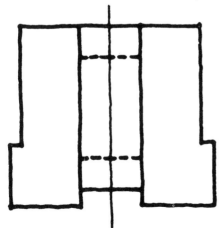

28. La Crocetta, Villa Il Verrua. Block plan.

36

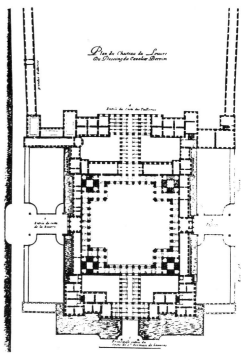

30. Paris. Bernini's third project for the Louvre. Plan.

29. (*above left*) Paris. Bernini's first project for the east front of the Louvre, 1664.

made available in an engraving by Marot, shows a rectangular layout, at the heart of which is a square court with a square staircase at each internal corner. This design feature is paralleled in Guarini's plan, but whereas Bernini's Louvre project is built up entirely of rectilinear elements, this is not the case with Guarini's French Palace. Of the four staircases in the corners of Guarini's courtyard, the two nearest the garden front[58] are oval on plan, whereas the others are almond-shaped. These shapes project into the courtyard and serve as the mainsprings for a swinging sinuous motion that is imparted to the walls of the galleries and atria which surround the courtyard – a movement that penetrates the main body of the building to emerge in curvilinear features at the front and back entrances, enlivening these otherwise staid elevations with an indication of the stir within.

Bernini's first project for the Louvre (Fig. 29), in point of fact, had involved a display of the boldest Baroque plasticity on the east front, with a great oval pavilion bulging out in the centre, flanked by two elliptical wings ending in corner pavilions.[59] Pietro da Cortona was responsible for a comparable scheme, reminiscent of his almost contemporary facade of S. Maria della Pace in Rome.[60] Guarini was to follow their lead at his Palazzo Carignano in Turin, where for the first time the main facade of a palace is set in swaying motion, not on the drawing board alone, but in bricks and mortar. And at the Palazzo Carignano the characteristic sinuosity of the facade is again following the line not of a pavilion, but of a staircase; a staircase, too, that in Guarini's first drafts[61] was placed on an inside wall to project into the central court, as in the French Palace.

A closer examination of the serpentine courtyard walls reveals that their profile is not one of smoothly developing sinuosity, but that each facade is built up of three juxtaposed units, described as 'a dominant concavity set against the forward thrust of the angular convexities flanking them'.[62] This tendency to break up design units into their component parts is very characteristic of Guarini. In this he differs notably from Borromini, whose facades and volumes 'read' without interruptions.[63] We have, in fact, already noticed a parallel usage to this in the plan of Ste Anne-la-Royale, where the undulating entrance wall is also built up of juxtaposed segments of circles, the central convexity being set slightly back from the flanking concavities.

The elevational composition of the French Palace is of a type that Guarini was to use elsewhere on domestic buildings, namely at the villas of Racconigi

37

and Govone: a ground floor forming a kind of plinth for the whole building, surmounted over a heavy entablature by the *piano nobile*, over which there is a mezzanine separated by a cornice from a crowning attic storey. The indications of room usage on the plan engraved in the *Architettura civile* are minimal,[64] but, as has been noted above, the wings that project from the main square constitute *appartements* in the French style, four sets on each floor.

On the main elevation the *appartement* units flanking the central tract are readily identifiable in two separately articulated blocks on each side, progressively narrowing in width and advancing in projection forward from the main building line. The rear elevation differs in treatment from this, but both facades make use of a heightened play of light and shade to lend prominence to the entrance features: on the front elevation by two deep hollows from which the *avant-corps* springs, and on the garden facade by quadrupling the columns on the segmental entrance bay.[65]

During his years in Paris, Guarini lectured on theology.[66] He also completed and prepared for the press his most extensive scientific work, the fruit of the studies and lectures he had undertaken at Modena, Messina and Paris itself. It appeared on 1 May 1665 in the form of a massive folio volume of over 800 pages, published by Dionyse Thierry under the title *Placita philosophica physicis rationibus, experientiis, mathematicisque ostensa*.

Placita philosophica is a work of immense, if occasionally perverse,[67] erudition, presented in an inelegant post-classical Latin. The 'philosophical principles' referred to in the title are meant in the Aristotelian sense: the book in fact attempts to embrace nearly every branch of human knowledge. Its six main divisions comprise: (1) a preparation for logic; (2) preliminary arguments on physics; (3) preliminary arguments against current works on astronomy; (4) against current works on generation and corruption; (5) on separate substances; (6) metaphysics.

Philosophy is divided by Guarini into speculative and practical. Speculative philosophy in its turn is subdivided into physics, mathematics and metaphysics. In the course of his section on physics, the author devotes a complete dissertation to the nature of Art.[68] He distinguishes between divine art – the 'idea' – and human art. The latter species Guarini defines as an action or attitude which brings things together at the same time in accordance with their natural rapport.[69] There are thus three types of art: that which aims at an imitation of nature, such as sculpture; that which aims to produce some natural effect, such as agriculture; and that which aims at convenience. To achieve these ends, every artist must employ the most appropriate means for the purpose. Hence to pursue an art is none other than to apply oneself to the natural rapport (*convenientia*) of the things that pertain to it, and their relevance to the art itself. The first conclusion drawn from this is that all arts in fact depend on either mathematics, philosophy or medicine, these being the sciences which are concerned with the likeness between things, or their proportions or natural rapport.

Guarini's second conclusion is that there are two types of idea: a remote one which represents the mass of different species, and which fertilizes the artist's mind, and a near one, identified with some of the actual species themselves, which the artist chooses, fixes in his mind and proposes to

38

imitate. When the artist wishes to start work, it behoves him to pick the right material, and to know his tools perfectly. In difficult cases, where neither intellect nor imagination suffices, the artist should make little models to prove and perfect the idea.

The third and final conclusion drawn is that art can help the work of nature and perfect it, but cannot exercise any creative action on it.[70] Though fields become more fertile with the help of the art of agriculture, art can only modify works of nature, not create them. The passage ends with an excursus on the 'idea', in the light of Scotist and Thomist controversy about this problem, with a view to determining what type of cause the idea belongs to. In Guarini's view, idea is *extrinsic formal cause*. The idea, in fact, to which a resemblance must be produced, is the effect; hence it is extrinsic form. It is form, in that, through it, the effect is produced *in that manner*; extrinsic, because the idea itself does not pass from the mind of the artist to the work, but the artist at work imitates it. It cannot be *effective cause*, because it has no real influence on the work of art. It cannot be an end, because the artist often does not propose it as an end; as for example the painter, who wishes to express nature as his end, not the idea. It cannot be true form, because it does not show itself. Hence it will only be an extrinsic and improper cause, and a directive condition rather than a cause.

These final remarks show that Guarini was profoundly affected by the philosophical outlook known as occasionalism,[71] a theory propounded by certain followers of Descartes and in particular by Arnold Geulincx and Nicolas Malebranche. Briefly, the occasionalist view maintains that there is really no interaction between body and soul; seeming action of the one at the bidding of the other is due to the direct intervention of God. The sun's rays stimulating the optic nerves is not the *cause* of my sensation of light; but on the *occasion* of the former, God causes in me the latter. My hand does not move because I will it to do so; on the *occasion* of my willing, God causes it to take place.

Some of the mathematical consequences of this outlook were developed by the Oratorian priest Nicolas Malebranche (1638–1715). In his view, the idea of extension or body which we have when we apprehend their mathematical qualities is not the idea of our own mind, since an *idea* cannot belong to the extended world of bodies, nor being an idea of *extension* can it belong to the mind, to which extension is foreign according to Descartes. The idea is the idea of God, in whom we see all things. There is thus an antinomy between matter and mind, extension and thought.[72]

Guarini's *Placita philosophica* appeared in Paris in 1665. This was one year after Malebranche was first introduced to Cartesian philosophy – indeed to philosophy in general – by reading Descartes's *Traité de l'homme* (a work, it is said, that moved him so deeply at the time that he was constantly obliged, by palpitation of the heart, to lay it aside). Whether there was any direct contact between Guarini and Malebranche is a matter for conjecture,[73] but the parallelism of their ideas is striking.

In a philosophical system, such as that of Guarini and Malebranche, where God is considered to be the only creative agent and the only real cause, the problem arises as to how the creative power of the artist is to be explained. It would seem, in part at least, to derive from the stimulus which mathematics, and in particular geometry, can exercise on the intellect, which in Guarini's philosophy is linked inextricably with the imagination, and regulates its functioning. It was in fact Malebranche who had described geometry 'as a kind of universal science which opens the spirit, makes it attentive and provides it with that kind of dexterity which is apt for directing the imagination'.[74]

Guarini's use of geometrical sources as stimuli to the imagination has long been appreciated,[75] and he himself was later to write that 'architecture is a faculty which in all its operations employs measurements, depends on geometry'.[76] And just as in geometry we start off from simple relationships to arrive at more complex theories, so in Guarini's architecture combinations of simple geometric figures develop into forms of extreme complexity.

Both Malebranche and Guarini in their works discuss the problem of human liberty. Man's liberty, according to the occasionalist view, is not damaged by the continuous intervention of God in every human action and by the concept of God as the sole effective cause in the world. The artist, in particular, expresses his freedom in his choice of means and in the manner he applies them in one way rather than another: hence the importance which Guarini assigns, in the passage from *Placita philosophica* cited above, to questions of materials, techniques and mathematical calculations, etc.

We have seen in Guarini's exposition that the artist wants in his work to express nature and not idea. Here 'nature' must be understood as the structure of the universe, created by God, and subject to mathematical and cosmological law. It is this rational nexus of laws regulating nature which the artist imitates. In this light, Guarini's buildings may perhaps be seen as a kind of *a posteriori* proof of the marvellous complex of mathematical laws which underpins the universe; and as G. C. Argan observes: 'What proves more certainly that ideas exist, and find in nature the "occasion" of their miraculous realization?'[77]

6 TURIN

LITTLE DOCUMENTATION has been discovered relevant to Guarini's life in Paris; the circumstances of his leaving have been noted above.[1] In his own Theatine Order his star was rising. His book was admired, and evoked an *enthusiasmus* from his fellow Theatine Olimpio Masotti that concluded with the words:

> In aevum crede, tuis placitis
> Placebis.[2]

Guarini's architectural achievements, too, were becoming well known, and his services were sought for Theatine building projects elsewhere. He had turned down an invitation from his Order in Germany to go to Munich and design a Theatine church there,[3] but the suspension of work on Ste Anne-la-Royale due to exhaustion of funds made him more receptive to a similar approach from the Theatines in Turin.

The city where Guarini took up residence in 1666, and where he was to spend the most fruitful years of his life, was the capital of the Duchy of Savoy-Piedmont; but it had been so for scarcely more than a hundred years. The original dominion of the House of Savoy, which ruled the territory for eight centuries, was the county of Savoy on the west side of the high Alps, incorporated, with its ancient capital of Chambéry, into France since 1860.[4] At an early date territories were acquired on the eastern slopes of the mountains and subsequently in the higher plain of Piedmont, including Turin. But these empty northern plains lay at the hinge between two power systems – those of the kingdom of France, ever seeking to expand its boundaries eastward, and of the ramshackle Holy Roman Empire, periodically galvanized by a ruler with greater ambition or drive than usual. Piedmont was thus for centuries a battlefield over which armies of French, Germans and Spaniards manoeuvered. It had reached a low ebb of ruin and degradation by the mid-sixteenth century, when its recovery and consolidation were set in train by the able Duke Emanuele Filiberto (ruled 1553–80), who in 1563 moved his capital from Chambéry to Turin, 'a decisive step which committed the family to an Italian rather than a French destiny'.[5]

It was also a step that involved the transfer of the Savoyan nobility to Turin, thereby bringing a refined patronage of the arts to the city. Emanuele Filiberto, *auspicium melioris aevi*,[6] encouraged these developments by his personal example. He collected pictures, books and statues, and began introducing poets, philosophers, architects and artists to Turin, including Tasso and Palladio. The latter dedicated the third of his *Quattro libri dell'architettura* to Emanuele Filiberto.

Its history of wars and devastations left a mark on the artistic development of Piedmont. The Renaissance 'breathed on it in a subdued and almost inadvertent fashion'.[7] Throughout the fifteenth and the greater part of the sixteenth centuries, the old medieval traditions in art and architecture persisted in the Duchy,[8] and when the Baroque finally caught up with Piedmont, its early manifestations in Turin (represented mainly by the work of Ascanio Vitozzi and the two Castellamontes) were very sober, reflecting the persistent influence in the north of Palladio and Scamozzi. These inhibitions were now to be dissolved under the unique and idiosyncratic influence of Guarino Guarini's architecture, to such an extent that after the deaths of Bernini and Borromini 'it became more stimulating for an architect to work in Turin than in Rome itself; the latter went on to academic re-elaboration, while the former was renewing a figurative world and defining a European language'.[9] Bernini and Borromini indeed were both still alive in 1666, but the Turin of Carlo Emanuele II was already ripe for original and adventurous works of architecture that would give tangible expression to the self-confidence of the newly consolidated state. Nor was the Church backward in this respect either; in fact an undoubted fillip was given to architecture by the rivalry that existed to some extent between Church and State. The latter ultimately rested on the former, since its legitimacy was based on the claim to rule by the grace of God. In this context the Church sought to maintain and increase its influence by the erection of prestigious buildings.

The battle which had marked the turning point in Piedmont's fortunes was won against the troops of Henri II at St Quentin, in north-eastern France on 10 July 1557 – St Lawrence's day – by Emanuele Filiberto, then a commander in the Imperial army of Charles V. Emanuele Filiberto had vowed to build a church to St Lawrence if a victorious outcome meant that he could recover his Duchy. The Duchy was indeed restored to the House of Savoy, but the poor economic conditions prevailing at the time led the Duke to settle for something less grandiose than a new foundation. Instead, he thought of restoring the little late Lombard church of S. Maria del Presepe, on the Piazza Castello where the Vestibule and Oratorio della Beata Vergine Addolorata now stand,[10] and changing the dedication to St Lawrence. Work was started in 1563, and the building finally consecrated in 1580. It was made the court chapel, and the chapel of the newly merged Orders of S. Lazzaro and S. Maurizio.[11] As such, it soon proved inadequate for the functions it was called on to perform. The building of a newer, larger church was long delayed. When it did come about, however, the body responsible was Guarini's Order, the Theatines.

The first Theatines had arrived in Turin in 1622, at the instance of Carlo Emanuele I.[12] The Duke was on terms of personal friendship with the Apostolic Nuncio to the city,[13] a Theatine by the name of Tolosa Pado, and had heard Theatines preaching on several occasions in the cathedral. Carlo Emanuele had, it seems, a penchant for the Orders, having introduced the Augustinians, Antonians, Barnabites, Capuchins, Camaldolites, Minor Observants and the monks of the SS. Annunziata into Turin,[14] to say nothing of the other cities of his domain. The State, however, was still impoverished, and could not assure the Theatines of a church for their exclusive use. The unfortunate fathers seem to have gravitated from one shabby tabernacle to another, until in 1634 they petitioned Duke Vittorio Amedeo I to cede them the ducal chapel of S. Lorenzo, with the hint that, if they were granted it, they might before long be in a position 'to raise there a new and grandiose church'.

The Theatine petition was allowed, and letters patent were issued on 8 February 1634,[15] which cited, amongst other points, the convenience of having the fathers in close proximity – on the Piazza Castello – so that Madama Reale (the dowager Duchess) and the Duke could hear them say mass and preach.

The Piazza Castello, on to which the new church was to face,[16] had emerged in the Middle Ages as the command zone (*zona di comando*) of Turin. It was located near the Praetorian Gate of the Roman *colonia*,[17] with whose boundaries the medieval town coincided – medieval and indeed Renaissance: for as late as 1563, when Duke Emanuele Filiberto entered Turin, he found it congested and impoverished,[18] still contained within the circuit of its ancient walls and towers, and still laid out on the rectilinear grid of the Roman *castrum*, bisected by its Decumanus.[19] Only an extension beyond this boundary could provide relief for the crowded and insanitary conditions which prevailed, but the economic conditions which existed in the early days of the Restoration prevented this.

When funds were ultimately made available for building purposes, the first call on them was for military rather than civil purposes, and a citadel in the shape of a pentagonal bastion trace was built between 1564 and 1566 immediately beyond the south-west angle of the *castrum* (Fig. 31).

In 1584 Ascanio Vitozzi was commissioned to draw up a scheme for improving and ennobling the appearance of the Piazza Castello, employing a series of frontal arcades to lend uniformity to the layout.[20] Free plots were granted to those who would erect buildings on them in conformity with Vitozzi's master-plan. Work did not begin till 1606,[21] when a patent was issued, and on Guarini's arrival in the city sixty years later, operations were in hand once more for the enlargement of the Piazza. The intention was to increase it to twice its previous size, still to Vitozzi's uniform design, and it was originally proposed to carry the arcades across the front elevation of the church.

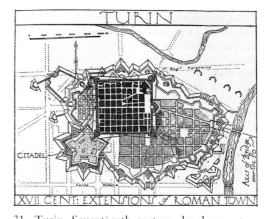

31. Turin. Seventeenth-century developments.

It had long been realized, however, that tearing down old city blocks to widen piazzas and provide more prestigious thoroughfares (not to mention the nascent Baroque desire of the ruling family to symbolize its aspirations to pomp and power) was an inadequate response to the problems posed by the city's population growth.[22] In 1620 work began on a new city quarter, to the immediate south and south-east of the old town. The layout, planned by Ascanio Vitozzi, was a continuation of the *castrum* grid; this, G. C. Argan observes, 'we may call its "humanist" side. But that plan also lent itself to military and civil parades, which display and emphasize the authority of the State, just as religious ceremonies display and emphasize the authority of the Church; this we may call its Baroque side.'[23]

The imposing layout of the new quarter was something novel for Italy, though Henri IV had started his improvements in Paris some years previously. Bernini himself is said to have called it 'the finest sight that could be found in Italy'.[24] At the same time, it has been criticized[25] as an architecture of parade, stage sets for the use of the court, in an 'urban texture extendible at will, without altering its physiognomy'.[26]

Guarini's interventions here, over the decade and a half of his building activities in Turin, were to save the city from becoming 'a planned abstraction'.[27] The undulating facades of buildings such as the Palazzo Carignano were to tear apart the solemn rectangularity of Vitozzi's grid, and a fresh and subtle fluidity was to be lent to the streetscape of Turin by Guarini's innovatory use of brickwork.

7   SAN LORENZO

IN JUNE 1634 the Theatines took possession of the existing ducal chapel of S. Lorenzo, and the first stone of the new S. Lorenzo was laid.[1] Design drawings for this scheme have never been found, though a perspective sketch of it is said to be contained with other souvenirs in a metal cylinder placed inside a cornerstone of the new foundation.[2] The plan was supposedly a large Latin cross,[3] and authorship has been variously ascribed to Ascanio Vitozzi, Carlo Morello and Carlo di Castellamonte.

Once again, however, the Theatines met with disappointment. Lack of funds, domestic crises and foreign wars reduced building operations to a desultory trickle.[4] As late as 1661 payments are recorded as being made to a general contractor and to a stone-cutter,[5] but how much building was actually above ground when Guarini arrived in Turin in 1666 is problematical. What *is* certain is that Guarini did not accept the Latin cross layout he found on the site, but devised instead a centralized plan of a greater geometrical strictness even than Ste Anne-la-Royale.

The centralized plan, revived in Renaissance times by Brunelleschi, Alberti and Bramante,[6] had not made its appearance in Turin until the late sixteenth century,[7] with Ascanio Vitozzi's Capuchin church (1583) and S. Trinità (1590); but neither these nor F. Lanfranchi's much later church of the Visitation (1661) prepared the Torinesi for the extraordinary manifestation of S. Lorenzo.

The plan of S. Lorenzo (Fig. 32) comprises one great centralized congregational space set in a square frame with a smaller presbytery to the east and a retrochoir beyond that. The geometrical basis of the plan has been established by Passanti as being generated by a Greek cross layout with very short arms, which undergoes a series of elastic deformations,[8] though Brinckmann, over fifty years ago, had published a copy of Guarini's plan (Fig. 33) on which he had superimposed a number of circles of equal radius, passing through the major points of articulation, with another one and a half times larger; these, he claimed, underlay the whole geometry of the church.[9]

Brinckmann's scheme was amended a few years ago by the Belgian scholars J. Vanderperren and J. Kennes, in a scheme (Fig. 34) that sees the major circles as key points from which undulatory movements emanate, on the basis of 'wave lengths' located outside the building itself.[10] Something else is needed, however, to explain the dynamic of the building, and in particular to account for its vertical development, which Wittkower could only see as a series of autonomous zones.[11]

If we examine the plan at entrance level, in conjunction with a view of the interior (Fig. 36) – insofar as it is possible to reproduce this in a photograph –

III. Turin, S. Lorenzo. Dome.

32. (*right*) Turin, S. Lorenzo. Plan.

35. (*facing page top*) Rome, S. Maria della Vittoria. Cornaro Chapel (Bernini).

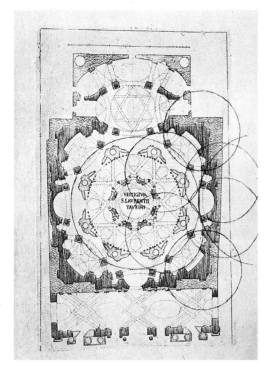

33. Turin, S. Lorenzo. Geometrical bases of the plan, according to Brinckmann.

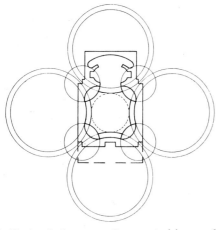

34. Turin, S. Lorenzo. Geometrical bases of the plan, according to Vanderperren and Kennes.

36. (*facing page*) Turin, S. Lorenzo. Nave.

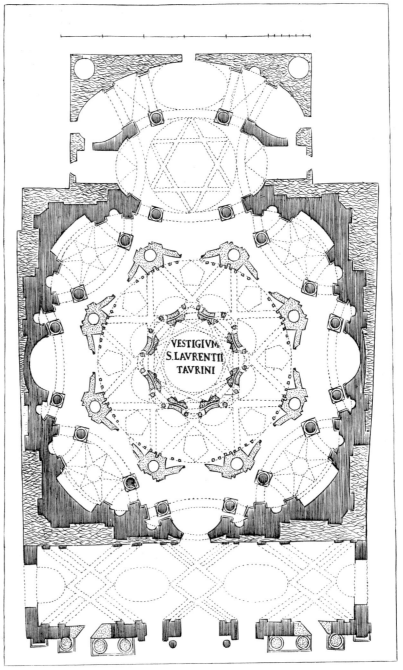

it will be seen that the whole congregational space at this level is surrounded by a succession of convex surfaces that compress it. These eight convexes are, at the cardinal points, smoothly curved, while the diagonal ones are jointed, with a central chamfer flanked by two curved components. These shapes are most readily discernible at cornice level and immediately below, because the walls and entablatures which comprise them are carried in each case on a corresponding serliana, which frames an altar.

A projecting wall unit of this kind is a dynamic feature of great intensity. It was used by Bernini for his St Teresa altar in the Cornaro chapel of the church of S. Maria della Vittoria in Rome (Fig. 35). Here the altar is framed not indeed by a serliana but by heavy coupled columns and pilasters, with a broken pediment placed on a slant, as though some gigantic force had heaved open the curtain of wall and bent it towards us, so that these features come out to meet us and then recede, to focus our attention on the centre of the altar.

The visual pressure exerted in the Cornaro chapel is great, but here the space is confined. In the much broader ambience of S. Lorenzo such an effect would be diluted, but for the circumstance that the entire periphery of the major congregational area is articulated by the eight convexities, which in themselves constitute a rich visual experience. To the spectator passing round the surging periphery, first one convexity acquires predominating importance, then the hollowing out of a pier assumes unexpected depth. The arch of a serliana projects forward sinuously in cantilever for a stretch before combining in a single motif with the great convex arches of the crossing.

A sinuous line runs along the perimeter walls, too (Fig. 37), as a counterpoint to the eight convexities that project into the central area. It is made up by the four convexities at the back of the arms of the Greek cross (that is, on the cardinal points) and the four concavities at the back of the hollowed out piers (that is, the rear walls of the diagonal chapels).

Amidst the forest of verticals in the region of the serlianas, the impression is conveyed of other minor spaces cropping up, in the contrasts of the black,

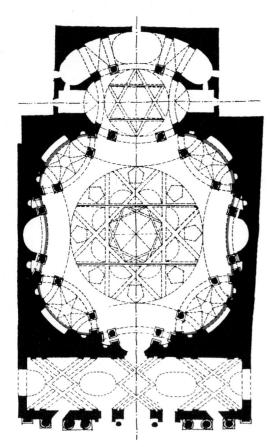

37. Turin, S. Lorenzo. Plan. The perimeter sinuosity counterpointing the eight projections.

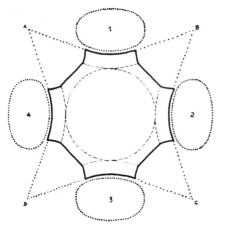

38. Turin, S. Lorenzo. Complex floor plan transformed into Greek cross at the lowest level of the pendentives.

39. Turin, S. Lorenzo. Nave. Chamfered pier changes from convexity to concavity in pendentive.

white and red marbles that Guarini has employed and in the dark shadows (Col. Pl. IV). This tendency to a deepening of space, where the eye is led past the arches to the real boundary of the church, ultimately finds its complete fulfilment in the one serliana that indeed gives on to deep real space – the elliptical presbytery, glittering in marble and gold – beyond which is a second serliana, through which one perceives a final hidden room, the retrochoir, more encumbered with shadows (Col. Pl. II).

But this penetration through into real space is insufficient to relieve the dynamic impulses generated by the undulating periphery. The only direction in which this pressure can escape is upwards, and that is where it goes. If we now look up and follow the development, in the next zone, of the entrance level convexities, we see that the diagonal features, those described above as 'jointed, with a central chamfer flanked by two curved components', change from convexities to concavities as their chamfers develop into pendentives (Fig. 39). Where this occurs, that is, at the lowest level of the pendentives, the complex ground floor plan is transformed into a Greek cross with very short arms (Fig. 38). The pendentives rise, and at their topmost level support the ring of a cornice,[12] which in turn appears to hold up the ribbed drum/dome and lantern.

To perform this function, it might be thought that an unbroken annular shape would provide the soundest structural answer, but Guarini interrupts his cornice ring with no fewer than eight horizontal oval openings (Fig. 40). If this creates unease, it is as nothing compared with what we feel when we bring our eyes down again to ground level, when we see to our consternation that each of the four pendentives appears to be transferring its mighty burden, via the chamfers of the diagonal convexities, onto the slender columns and responds of a serliana – in other words a hollowed-out pier (Fig. 43). Nor is this all. At the crown of each great arch embraced by the pendentives, where a keystone might seem imperative, Guarini has placed an oval opening. A comparable opening perforates the wall above the crown of each diagonal serliana arch, to disclaim functional responsibility, while the vaults to which these serlianas act as frontispieces feature an oculus in the centre through which the unnerved spectator beholds empty space. 'The stimuli to conflict and unrest which [Guarini's] architecture contains', remarks Wittkower, 'link it with the Mannerist tradition.'[13] The real mechanics of support are indeed elsewhere and will be noted later.

We return to the upper end of the pendentives, which support the 'fractured' cornice ring of the drum/dome, the latter pierced at its lower level by large oval vertical windows. Between these windows are eight piers from which spring hyperbolic vaulting ribs (Fig. 42). Instead of meeting at a central boss in the Gothic manner, they run in parallel pairs and thus form an eight-pointed star, with a regular octagon in the middle, before falling back on the two springers situated on the opposite sides (Col. Pl. III). Gazing at the centre, however, the spectator gets a view of pairs of parallel arches, so wide is the distance traversed. Thus, if he starts off from one springer and follows the trajectory of an arch until it comes down again on the other springer, and then sets out again along the twin arch and continues on in this way, he will find himself progressively relaunched from one springer to the other, without ever coming to the end of his course.

The impulse initiated in the zone of compression at the entrance level does not stop here; it continues upwards, since all the web between the flying ribs has been suppressed (Fig. 41). As the parabolic ribs ascend they thus create an openwork dome through which light progressively penetrates. On top of the

48

43. (*facing page*) Turin, S. Lorenzo. Nave. Pendentive appears to transfer burden to hollowed-out pier.

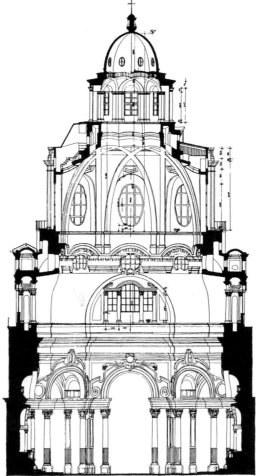

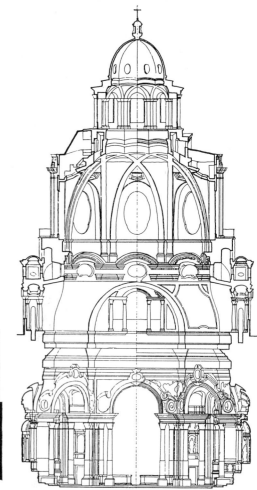

40. Turin, S. Lorenzo. Section.

41. Turin, S. Lorenzo. Section.

42. Turin, S. Lorenzo. Plan at cornice ring of drum, showing piers from which hyperbolic ribs spring.

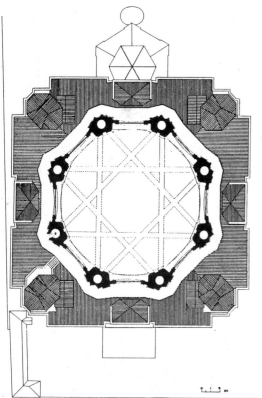

octagon which the interlaced arches form in the centre (Col. Pl. I), Guarini has placed a lantern through which daylight streams. Instead of a conventional Baroque inner dome with a secretly lit celestial scene, or a *trompe-l'oeil* apotheosis painted on a soffit (with a single optimum viewpoint), the dome is opened to skylight, an analogue for celestial illumination. In the lantern, space has no further visual limit. The vertical dimension has disappeared, to evoke an illusion of infinity.

This striving to express infinity is a characteristic seventeenth-century phenomenon.[14] As such, it is typical of the Southern European concreteness of approach to the problem, although it is far more abstract in its technique than the more sensational means employed by architects such as Bernini and the Asams to achieve the realization of an all-embracing oneness and a presence of the infinite. In Northern Europe, by contrast, similar goals were sought via a more cerebral path: Spinoza visualized a pantheism with God pervading all beings and all things while Newton and Leibniz discovered the infinite for mathematics in their conception of the calculus. A mid-point between Northern abstraction and Southern concreteness may perhaps be seen in the work of Rembrandt, who can be said to have discovered the infinite, for painting, in his treatment of light and the way it merges action into an undefined but live background.

We have already noted Guarini's use of the diaphanous dome in his church of the Padri Somaschi in Messina and of interlaced ribs at Ste Anne-la-Royale in Paris. Islamic prototypes for the S. Lorenzo cat's cradle of hyperbolic

50

44. A 'new maqsurah' dome in the Mosque of Al-Hakim, Cordoba, compared with the dome of S. Lorenzo, Turin (photographed before damage suffered in World War II).

arches were noted as far back as 1908 in O. Schubert's book on the history of the Baroque in Spain,[15] and have been the subject of several studies since.[16] Guarini may be presumed to have seen the 'prototype' of the S. Lorenzo arches in Spain,[17] notably in the Great Mosque in Cordoba, now the cathedral, completed under Caliph Al-Hakim II (961–76). It was Siegfried Giedion's publication of the cupola of S. Lorenzo and one of the domes in the Great Mosque at Cordoba in his famous book *Space, Time and Architecture*[18] that first popularized Guarini's achievements – and sources – with a wider public. Giedion reproduced his illustrations of Guarini's cupola and the Cordoban dome on facing pages (Fig. 44), in photographs of identical size, while readily admitting that 'the dimensions of these Moorish domes are humble in comparison with Guarini's daring masterpiece'. Guarini does not mention the Great Mosque of Cordoba in his Treatise, but he does refer to the great church of Seville in Andalusia and the cathedral of Salamanca in Castile.[19]

It has been suggested that 'with Naples and Sicily belonging to the Kingdom of Castile it seems unnecessary to speculate about Guarini's early contacts with Hispano-Moresque architecture'.[20] The exact implication of this remark is somewhat ambiguous, but it is certain that Guarini's stay in Messina would have allowed him to become familiar with Arab monuments of which far more were standing in the seventeenth century than today.[21] But at all events, as Paolo Verzone remarks, 'in reality Islamic art has had a catalytic effect on Guarini's fervent and gifted mind, since it was also permeated with geometrical stylizations'.[22] Thus, to take the most obvious example, none of the Islamic domes suppresses the web – the infill between the ribs – in the way that Guarini does, with the consequent diffusion of high-level light that converts his dome from one with a single continuous mural boundary into an aerial cage, opening onto an outer zone.

The star shape of Guarini's cage is a typical byproduct of Islamic geometrical art. It recurs with six, eight, sixteen or more points over the whole range of Islamic design, from ribbed cupolas to Quran covers; the open centre may enclose the oculus of a dome or a precious stone on a book binding. The star, in various forms, became a Guarinian motif: there are six in S. Lorenzo, as an examination of Guarini's plan will show,[23] while in the courtyard facade of the Palazzo Carignano it was to be reproduced in brick with an obsessive repetitiveness.

An attempt has been made to equip Guarini's building designs with esoteric *schemata*,[24] which, though drawn from an astounding array of sources running from Plato, via Rabbi Yehudah the Hasid, to Simon of Thessalonica, fails to convince in the case of S. Lorenzo; the insights afforded into the design of SS. Sindone are perhaps more suggestive. Who, looking at Giedion's matched photographs of the S. Lorenzo dome and the Cordoba maqsurah vault, could entertain the notion that S. Lorenzo's eight-pointed star might represent an astronomical chart of St Lawrence's day – 10 August 1557, when Emanuele Filiberto, Duke of Savoy, vowed to build a church to the saint if he won the battle of St Quentin – or even St Lawrence's gridiron itself? We may indeed accept that the Islamic prototype of the S. Lorenzo dome might have had an astrological significance; but that Guarini, at Cordoba, could have received detailed information on this significance, a century and a half after the Reconquest, seems improbable.[25]

There are, in fact, solid structural reasons for using interlaced ribs in the way Guarini does. Arches of great loadbearing capacity, however perfect their shape from the statical viewpoint, however well adapted they may be to transmitting loads, are always subject to the danger of buckling. This means that their size in cross-section often has to be much greater than that demanded by longitudinal compression. Guarini was quick to see that the apparent miracle of the Spanish domes was due to the interlacement of the arches, thanks to which, without reducing the span of the vaults, the arches were effectively divided into shorter segments, thereby eliminating the danger of buckling.

There is another source of inspiration for the aspiring verticalism of Guarini's design, and for the way he manipulated his interior effects to make it seem that, amongst other things, the whole weight of the superstructure is borne on a series of serliana columns. This is Guarini's interest in, and understanding of, Gothic architecture. There is a famous chapter of the *Architettura civile* (III.xiii.1) that deals with 'the Gothic Order and its proportions'. In contrasting Roman architecture with Gothic, the author says that the latter 'had as its object to erect buildings that were in fact very strong, but would seem weak and as though they needed a miracle to keep them standing'.[26] A little further on, Guarini implies that the same Gothic urge lay behind the construction of the leaning towers of Pisa and Bologna, 'which, if they do not actually delight the eye, nevertheless amaze the intellect and terrify the spectators'. If bad foundations, rather than cunning design, are generally recognized nowadays to underlie these effects, we may nevertheless reflect that they are in reality part and parcel of *baroque* art, where amazement,

IV. Turin, S. Lorenzo. Nave. 'Amid the forest
of verticals in the region of the serlianas.'

surprise and wonderment are essential factors invoked to 'persuade' or 'convince' the beholder.

A taste for the Gothic was rare in a seventeenth-century Italian. Filippo Baldinucci, for example, described Gothic architecture as 'altogether barbarous in its fashioning . . . just putting one thing on top of another, without any rule, order or measure'.[27] In France, however, there was a flourishing school of revival Gothic under the Jesuit architect Etienne Martellange, developed as 'local cover' in the Counter-Reformation's campaigns in France, the Low Countries and Germany, where the local bourgeoisie had been impressed by Lutheran agitation against 'Roman taste'.[28] The many books on stone-cutting (stereotomy) that Guarini refers to in his own Treatise are byproducts of this Gothic revival. Guarini's introduction to Gothic architecture in the first instance may have been through this literature, or he may even have seen some of Martellange's schemes in Rome, where the designs were always sent for approval, and where they may have been disseminated.

To judge from Guarini's own words in his Treatise, he would appear to have admired Gothic architecture for its boldness and lack of pedantry, while deprecating its failure to abide by classical proportionality. In this connection, he attempts to explain the vertical trends of Gothic architecture in anthropomorphic terms: 'and because the men of those times had, in their remarkable grace, a slender appearance and were small, as may be seen in the old portraits, this is the kind of thing they accordingly liked to do in their churches, which they made very high in proportion to their width; whence, pursuing the style in other matters, they made their columns very slender'.[29]

But it is not only in the matter of proportions that Guarini saw the great contrast between Classic and Gothic art. A few lines later, in a passage that has already been briefly excerpted above, he goes on to say:

> and besides this much-coveted slenderness, it also appears that they desired another end totally opposed to Roman architecture. Because where the latter had strength as its main aim and made a great display of it, including the solid disposition of the buildings, the former had as its object to erect buildings that were in fact very strong, but would seem weak and as though they needed a miracle to keep them standing. Whence you will see an enormous spire on a bell-tower stably supported on extremely slender columns; arches which seem to hang in the air; completely perforated towers crowned by pointed pyramids; enormously high windows and vaults without the support of walls. The corner of a high tower may rest on an arch or a column or on the apex of a vault.[30]

Whether this acute analysis of Gothic structural prodigies is given in the *Architettura civile* because it coincided with Guarini's natural bent, or whether it was the study of such Gothic effects that inspired him to emulate them in Baroque/Mannerist terms, would (to borrow a phrase of the Master) indeed be 'a problem worthy of an ingenious academic'. But the fact that he could use an Islamic structural device in pursuit of anti-classical 'Gothic' aims, is consistent with the open-mindedness of Guarini towards architecture and the rules which govern it. Thus, he speaks in his Treatise of the beauty of buildings being derived from 'a well-proportioned harmony of the parts',[31] to secure which the ancients laid down rules, some of them so firm and dogmatic that departure from them was not to be tolerated 'by so much as a fingernail's breadth. But I, using my own discretion, and by analogy with what goes on in every other profession, consider that one can both amend some of the old rules and add new ones.'[32] The Romans did not always follow Vitruvius, nor the moderns the ancients. Architecture changes as custom changes. And hence 'the symmetries of architecture can be varied between themselves without discord'.[33] Tastes change: Roman architecture displeased the Goths, and Gothic architecture displeases us.[34] Some like architecture fancy, and others like it plain.[35]

In the light of the foregoing we must finally confront the problem of how Guarini achieved his disturbing 'static acrobatism' in the lower level of S. Lorenzo.[36] The sectional elevation published in the *Architettura civile* (Fig. 46) reveals nothing of the means required to achieve the result displayed. The graphic difficulties of doing so are indeed formidable, not to mention the physical constraints involved.

The task was attempted by Luigi Denina and Alessandro Protto in an article published in 1920.[37] Their large isometric drawing of a section through S. Lorenzo (Fig. 47) has never been superseded and has been reproduced many times since, at varying scales, in every consideration of the problem. Unfortunately Denina, who supplied some brief notes to accompany the drawings, had no more than this to say in explanation:

> The structure of the building is clear enough from the annexed drawings to make it unnecessary to go into a detailed examination. We may be allowed to note that it has not been possible for us to define with certainty the springers of the four great arches which make up the main framework of the whole building. Basing ourselves on some extrados surfaces which we traced on the interior of the structure, we consider that these imposts are constituted by four quarter-sphere vaults, each located in a corner of the building. It has not been possible up to now to determine the accuracy of this supposition, as the Royal Administration has not granted the requisite scaffolding to reach the points of control.

Two further graphic studies have been made of S. Lorenzo, with the help of students from the Turin School of Architecture. One appeared in 1961,[38] the other in 1968.[39] The latter, in particular, has some excellent drawings of the altars and of flooring patterns, but neither tackles the deep structure of S. Lorenzo. Mario Passanti, in his study of the geometrical bases of the church's design,[40] reproduces Denina and Protto's isometric drawing to illustrate his own brief remarks on the subject.

In 1957, however, Dr Augusta Lange reported to the X Congresso di storia dell'architettura[41] in Turin the discovery in the Archivio di Stato of that city of an unsigned copperplate engraving, tentatively assigned to the year 1677, entitled 'Key to the Dome of S. Lorenzo in Turin' (Fig. 45). This shows a simpler scheme than was actually built. The two lateral master arches are thicker than they are in reality, and to judge from the black rectangle inscribed in them, hollow inside, or else serving to encase timber beams acting as ties. A timber truss resting on massive brick corbels supports each major arch. The lateral system of counterthrust, simplified into two rampant arches, seems to be inspired by Gothic architecture. It may have been these discrepancies that led Passanti to attribute the existing deep structure to the architect Bonsignore, who carried out repairs to S. Lorenzo at the beginning of the nineteenth century,[42] but Bonsignore's work was restricted to the fitting of metal ties and some refacing.[43]

The interior of S. Lorenzo has in effect two structural systems: a deep, hidden one, and a superficial, visible one. The real business of loadbearing is performed at the deeper level. In essence, four great brick arches originate at

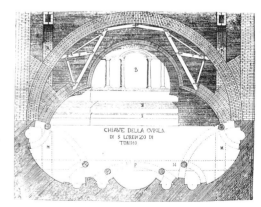

45. Turin, S. Lorenzo. 'Key to the dome.'

57

FACIES INTERNA   S. LAVRENTII TAVRINI

46. Turin, S. Lorenzo. Section.

47. Turin, S. Lorenzo. Axonometric view.

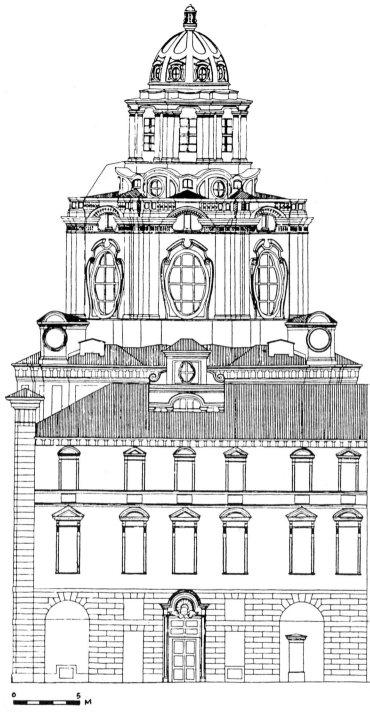

FACIES EXTERNA   S. LAVRENTII TAVRINI

high level in the four corners of the real structure, to wit, the 'chamfered' diagonal serlianas. These sweep over the circular oculi that interrupt the cornice ring at the four cardinal points (not the diagonals); the highest point of their intradoses touches the top of the intradoses of the oculi (Fig. 47,a).

Across each corner, where a pair of great arches sweeps out, four squinch arches are inserted (Fig. 47,b), braced against the major arches at about a third of the way along their haunch. Diagonal arch thus hits normal arch eight times, and the point where this happens corresponds on the inside of the church with the springers of the pairs of interlaced dome arches, and on the outside with the angles of the eight dished faces of the drum. Thus each loading point of the dome rests more or less on a third of the great arch

48. Turin, S. Lorenzo. Elevation as designed by Guarini.

49. Turin, S. Lorenzo. Elevation as executed.

59

below, and to avoid deformations this requires the base system to be stiffened by a series of metal tie rods. Of those currently in situ, some were inserted at the outset and others have been added since. Guarini's 'key' also shows a curious scaffolding of huge timbers placed under each of the four major arches and directed right onto the intrados at third points along. Taken as a whole, these huge triangular prisms constituted by each corner are the embodiments of vertical loads calculated to reduce to within acceptable limits the horizontal component of the thrust from the interlaced arches of the dome, on which, it must not be forgotten, the not inconsiderable weight of the lantern also rests.

Up to this point the system, though of bold proportions, does not present any particularly exceptional structural features, but complications set in at the lower level (Fig. 47,c), where the lines of the four major arches, as they die back into the wall (that is, in effect, at the corners of the parallelepiped they form), correspond, in each case, to the axis of the empty arches on the vaults of the four corner chapels. Their weight has to be sustained by powerful conical squinches resting on the four vaults in question,[44] and actually supported in their turn on the side walls of the chapel. What we have therefore is a repetition at a lower level of the legerdemain which up above contrives to channel the weight of the dome onto eight points.

This, in outline, is the inner structure. The outer structure, which is the one we see, and which was analyzed earlier, though it may appear to defy statics, also intervenes to a limited degree to stiffen the hidden loadbearing frame and facilitate a more thoroughgoing subdivision of the loads from the dome on the entrance-level zone.

Conversely, reading the design from below, all the visible articulation, in illusory tension upwards between the enormously wide serlianas, seems to spread out to expose ever more ample spaces to the sunlight that pours down to enliven it. As this light penetrates to the lowest levels, it invades the peripheral chapels, attenuating the otherwise deep shadow of their vaults, or setting them off by the luminosity reflected through the circular oculi that perforate the front and sides of the arches (Col. Pl. V).

Once we have passed the level of the cornice ring, the confusing 'surface' structure that masks the real mechanics of support ceases, and what we see beyond, namely the openwork dome and the lantern it supports, is 'true' structure – sufficiently amazing in itself to need no cover-up. There is accordingly a striking contrast between the pressures and 'deceit' of the lowest zone, and the stripped clarity and truth of the 'celestial' regions, which may in itself have theological or rhetorical implications.[45]

The main facade of S. Lorenzo, as illustrated in Guarini's *Architettura civile* (Figs. 48 and 49), features a giant Order of Corinthian columns at the lowest levels, which, when seen from the opposite side of the Piazza Castello, would have acted, in typical Baroque fashion, as the plastic realization of the flat pilasters that articulate the angles of the dished faces of the drum. In deference to the uniform facades of the immediate urban context, designed by Vitozzi at the beginning of the century, this was not executed, and a bland town-house type of elevation masks the church up to the level of the (internal) cornice ring. Above this, however, the drum and lantern of Guarini's original scheme were allowed to soar. The effect of this, at the time, has been well imagined by Andreina Griseri: 'the dome is grafted on to the tapered and, at that time, simplistic profile of the centre of Turin, like an organism in metamorphosis, on the piazza where Vitozzi's houses were isolated and isolating'.[46]

60

8   SANTISSIMA SINDONE

WHEN GUARINI ARRIVED in Turin in the autumn of 1666, it was to leave behind a scene of contention in Paris and to assist the Theatines in Turin with the building of S. Lorenzo. By the end of the year, Louis XIV was demanding Guarini's recall to justify his accusations that Sanseverino had falsified the accounts, while the Duke of Savoy was appealing to the Father General of the Theatines in Venice to allow Guarini to stay in Turin. We know this from two letters in the Archivio di Stato, Turin, conveniently printed in the second volume of *Schede Vesme*.[1] The first one, from Padre Maraviglia, the Father General of the Theatines, to Duke Carlo Emanuele II, dated 31 December 1666, reveals that he has received the Duke's request to let Guarini stay, but that the French foreign minister has transmitted Louis XIV's order to send Guarini back. The second letter, a week later, is from Count Bigliore, the Savoyan ambassador in Venice, to the Marchese di San Tomaso, a government minister in Turin. Bigliore has called on the Father General in his convent in Venice, and reports that Padre Maraviglia 'is between Scylla and Charybdis'.

In the event, Guarini stayed in Turin and on 19 May 1668 was appointed Ducal Engineer for the Chapel of the Holy Shroud. The patent is worded as follows:

> We, Carlo Emanuel, by the Grace of God Duke of Savoy, Prince of Piedmont, King of Cyprus &c., reflecting how it may be helpful to Our service to have a person of integrity and capability particularly applied to directing the construction of the Chapel of the Holy Shroud, have deemed that it cannot be better assured than by entrusting its charge to Father D. Guarino Guerini, Theatine. Wherefore by virtue of these presents, of Our own certain Knowledge, full power, absolute authority and in conjunction with the advice of our Council we create, constitute and depute the above-mentioned Father D. Guerino Guerini our Engineer for the said Chapel of the Most Holy Shroud, with all the honours, authority, preeminences, prerogatives and every other thing pertaining and belonging to this Office with the salary of a thousand silver lire of twenty soldi a year, to start at the beginning of January of the present year one thousand six hundred and sixty eight, & during his service & at Our pleasure, providing that he swears the customary oath. We direct as much and command &c.[2]

It is to be noted that Guarini is appointed engineer specifically for the Chapel of the Holy Shroud, not as an engineer in general.[3] The titles of Ducal Engineer and Architect were held by Count Amedeo di Castellamonte, who inherited them from his father in 1637[4] and retained them till his own death six months after Guarini's. More exclusive in nature was Guarini's subsequent appointment as theologian to the Prince of Carignano.[5]

The Holy Shroud of Turin is a stout piece of linen, about 4 by 1.4 metres, for which the claim is made that it is the actual 'clean linen cloth' in which Joseph of Arimathea wrapped the body of Christ (Matt. 27:59). It first surfaced at Lirey, in the Diocese of Troyes, around 1360, equipped with an elaborate provenance ('given to the King of Cyprus in 1087 by the Patriarch Heraclius when he was expelled from Jerusalem').[6] It held its own against the rival claims of the Shrouds of Besançon, Cadouin, Champiègne and Xabregas, etc., until in 1900 Canon Ulysse Chevalier, one of the greatest medieval bibliographers of the nineteenth century, and professor of history at the Catholic University of Lyons, turned up a series of documents dated 1389, the authenticity of which is not disputed, in which the Bishop of Troyes appeals to Pope Clement VII to put a stop to the scandals connected with the Shroud preserved at Lirey, which he asserted had been painted by a local artist with the likeness of a supine Christ some years before.[7] The Pope decided not to prohibit the Shroud from being exhibited, but directed that in future, when it was shown to the people, the priest should declare in a loud voice that it was not the real Shroud of Christ, but only a picture made to represent it. This directive evidently fell into disuse.

In 1430 the Shroud was brought to Savoy by Princess Marguerite de Chamy and given to the Dukes of Savoy in 1452. Duke Ludovico built a chapel in Chambéry to receive the relic, and this building was subsequently enlarged by his son Amedeo VIII.[8] Thereafter, in the words of Midana, 'it suffered quite a few vicissitudes'.

In 1578 Emanuele Filiberto learned that the saintly Bishop of Milan, Carlo Borromeo, wished to do something to bring the plague in his city to an end, and was proposing, as his contribution, to make a pilgrimage on foot to Chambéry, there to venerate the Shroud. To facilitate this pious endeavour, the Duke had the Shroud brought to Turin, where it arrived on 15 September, and was laid up in old S. Lorenzo.[9] The Shroud was subsequently moved to a rotunda (possibly designed by Palladio) in the old Royal Palace of Turin.[10]

Carlo Emanuele I, anxious to house the relic in a worthy setting, at first commissioned Carlo Borromeo's architect, Pellegrino Pellegrini, to design a special church that would be built on the Piazza Castello. He changed his mind, however, and opted for the cathedral, where in 1587 a *tempietto* was erected in the presbytery, standing on four tall columns. Four gilt seraphim supported the dome beneath which the Shroud was lodged. This structure underwent several transformations. Its final form may be glimpsed in the background of Giovenale Boetto's engraving of 1634, showing a ceremony in the cathedral to celebrate an alliance between Savoy and the Catholic Cantons.

Working his way through the State building accounts in the Archivio di Stato, Turin, G. Claretta found a reference under the year 1607 to four columns in black marble supplied by a stone cutter 'in conformity with the design of Count Carlo di Castellamonte for the Chapel of the Holy Shroud'.[11] This is the first indication of a new scheme for a building to house

62

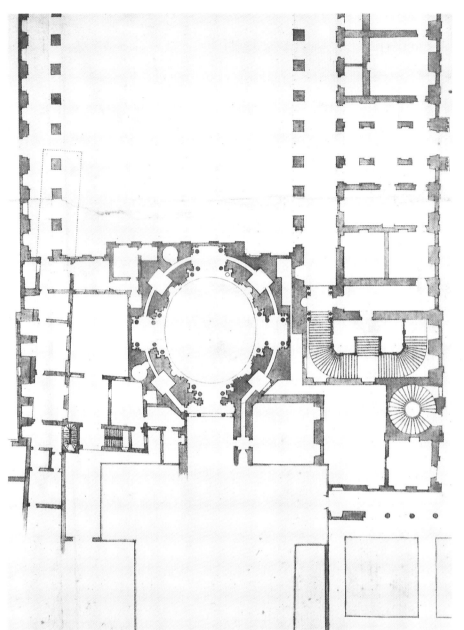

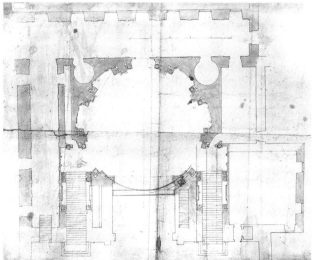

51. Turin, SS. Sindone. Quadri's plan, 1657.

50. Turin, SS. Sindone. Castellamonte's plan, early seventeenth century.

the Holy Shroud, which (to judge from the building accounts in the Archivio di Stato for the subsequent years) only gathered momentum from 1611 onwards. The site of the chapel was carved out of the west wing of the new Royal Palace, still under construction, as it passed behind the cathedral. It had an elliptical plan that reached from the rear wall of the presbytery (of which it was, in effect, a continuation) to an internal court of the palace, which seems to have been turned into a mason's yard. The layout is shown in Fig. 50, reproduced from a plan, or horizontal section, preserved in the National Library, Turin. Access from the cathedral is up a few central steps. Three quadrangular chapels ring the walls. In the vertical section that Licia Collobi saw in the 1930s, but which can no longer be traced, a low dome surmounted by a *cupolino* covered the building.[12]

Despite the drawings that were made for it, and the yard full of black marble columns waiting to be used, this scheme languished. Provisions were still being made for it in 1621,[13] but then nothing for another thirty-five or six years. Carlo Emanuele I's wish, expressed in a letter of 1620 to his ambassador in Rome,[14] to see the chapel finished and fitted out before he died was never realized.

Carlo Emanuele I was succeeded by his son Carlo Emanuele II in 1638. Half-way through the latter's reign, ecclesiastical rumblings portended the next burst of activity on the Chapel of the Holy Shroud. They emanated from the Prince-Cardinal Maurizio,[15] at whose instance a new plan was to be drawn up by Amedeo di Castellamonte, the son of Carlo Emanuele I's architect Carlo di Castellamonte, who had designed the first scheme. Yet another design was to be procured from the Swiss-Italian architect Bernardino Quadri, which the Cardinal helpfully suggested might be placed beside the schemes of Castellamonte father and son, 'to see all three of them together, pick the best of them, and put it into effect'.

Quadri's design was adopted; an official warrant exists, dated 5 June 1657, authorizing its construction.[16] A model of the scheme was prepared by the sculptor Pietro Botto,[17] but neither this nor Quadri's drawings survive. There is, however, a plan (Fig. 51) in the Royal Library in Turin which seems to correspond closely to such verbal descriptions as do exist.[18] This shows a circular chapel, not an oval one, reached by two flights of straight stairs flanking the altar at the east end of the cathedral, and accessible behind from the 'galleria nuova' of the Royal Palace. Thus, whereas Carlo di Castellamonte's plan had involved a rise of only two steps at the end of the cathedral, with a chapel that was distinct from the church and yet still a part of it wedged in between the blocks of the Royal Palace, Quadri's scheme was raised high above the level of the cathedral presbytery, and connected directly through to the royal apartments, at *piano nobile* level. A new conception is realized here, heavy with symbolic implications: Church and State meet under the shadow of the Holy Shroud, a relic not of a saint, but of Christ himself, and one that derives not from some random incident in his life, but from his sacrifice of it for the redemption of Humanity.

Three main features of the pre-Guarinian chapel remained as permanent constraints when Guarini eventually took over: its circular plan; its elevation, with access from the cathedral by two flights of stairs flanking the high altar; and the connection through to the *piano nobile* of the Royal Palace.

The minutes of the Building Committee, preserved in the Archivio di Stato, Turin,[19] together with two books of accounts,[20] cast light on the planning and building activities carried on up to the appointment of Guarini as the Duke's engineer for the scheme. There were two architects at first, Amedeo di Castellamonte, 'who must supervise the affairs of the above-mentioned building', and Bernardino Quadri, 'who has done the design of it [and] has to look after its execution'. They were joined later by a surveyor (*misuratore*) named Antonio Bettino, who acted as an assistant.

The foundations of the 1611 chapel were demolished by the builder Bartolomeo Pagliari, who was appointed in 1657 to do this, and to proceed with the new construction 'up to the *piano nobile* of the Royal Palace'. In fact he was responsible with his team for all the subsequent masonry work.

Although the floor of the new chapel was elevated high above that of the cathedral, its interior was meant to be visible from the nave through a large window giving on to an upper level of the presbytery. This feature was already completed by the end of 1662, when there is a note of the waxed cloth to be provided to close it off for the winter.[21]

The minutes of the Building Committee record a special site meeting that took place on 10 September 1665, when engineers, architects, builders and

surveyors foregathered to check whether the quality of the materials and the works that had been completed to date were adequate to support the structure of the chapel dome, 'which must be built to a great height, and exceeding that of St John's Cathedral'.[22]

The meeting presaged a good deal of doubt and uncertainty about the stability of the structure and the problems that were impending, so that its members must (says Carboneri)[23] have heaved a sigh of relief when, two years later, Guarino Guarini, at the behest of the Duke,[24] produced a new design for the chapel and in 1668 was appointed engineer for the project. By that time, the walls had reached the second tier: on 13 December 1666 they had the waxed sheets out again for the winter, but this time it was to close off the aperture over the cornice.[25]

Viewed from the archives, Guarini's arrival on the scene is signalled by an order given to a joiner for making a model commissioned by the Duke for the new design of the Chapel of the Holy Shroud.[26] Later references specifically mention Guarini's name in this connection. From then on, building was pursued vigorously, under the direction, and to the designs, of Guarini. The documents that survive chronicle the arrivals of material and the commissioning of subcontractors. We shall not pursue them.[27] The construction of the chapel continued for the rest of Guarini's life and beyond: mention has already been made of the urgent letter sent by Madama Reale – the dowager Duchess – to the Duke of Modena, less than two years before Guarini's death, requesting the architect's earliest return to Turin, to supervise the completion of the dome 'which simply cannot be done without the presence of the aforesaid father, who is the only one to have the direction of these works'.

Guarini took over a work that was substantially advanced, with a number of features which, while they might be modified, could not be dispensed with: the circular plan, the side stairs 'laid out with anonymous vagueness',[28] an opening towards the palace, and the big window looking into the cathedral, not to mention quantities of black marble, both in position and on site. Guarini did in fact dismantle part of the topmost existing structure – down to the level of the first Order[29] – and radically redesigned the rest. But it is time to emerge from the archives and examine the building on the ground.

—————

Meo da Caprino's Early Renaissance cathedral at Turin, built between 1491 and 1498, has a cool restraint of facade, no less than of interior, that bespeaks influences from Tuscany and Emilia. The quiet nave of the basilica, with its cross-shaped piers and coved ceiling, gives little hint of the Baroque apotheosis that lurks in its furthest reaches. But as the visitor proceeds down the length of the church, he catches an intermittent glimpse, there at the back where the apse should be, of something dark and glittering with gold, through a great window behind and above the high altar. At the end of each aisle a huge portal in shiny Frabosa marble confronts the visitor, framed by giant Corinthian columns, the harbingers of a major Order above (Fig. 52).

The portal is surmounted by a window, likewise framed in black marble, and flanked by curious herms with scrolled features.[30] A glimpse at the section (Fig. 53) will show that wherever the cathedral's light is being transmitted through this window, very little of it is directed to the stairs.

52. Turin, Cathedral. Approach to stairs of SS. Sindone.

53. Turin, SS. Sindone. Entrance to stairs.

Such natural light as does penetrate filters in from above in such a way that the climbing pilgrim does not notice where it comes from. The photograph (Col. Pl. VI) showing an electric candelabrum lighting the top of the stairs may reveal a concern for the visitor's safety; it also signals the fact that the architect's intentions have been betrayed. The shade, says Griseri, should be pierced, if at all, by the light of a (flaming) torch.[31] She is undoubtedly right.

I have only mounted these stairs alone, or with few companions. To do so, however, in a dense crowd, and by natural light, must be a daunting experience; an ascent, which may in any case be full of the presentiments of passion and death, is imbued with further overtones of awe by the mechanics of Baroque drama. The curved steps, which Guarini substituted for such plain ones as he may have found there, impart to the flight a slow forward motion, and although the stairs themselves continue in an uninterrupted flight, the side walls are articulated by successive pairs of pilasters supporting arches, which, as they are disposed in successive planes normal to the axis of the route, also tend to slow it down.

In each bay, between the ascending pilasters, are empty wall niches,[32] with soft curling frames, of the type Guarini used again at the grand portal of the Collegio dei Nobili. There is no view out to the sides, nor is it possible (*pace* the Archbishop of Turin's electric chandelier) to discern clearly what lies ahead. It is motion forward in a crowd, under these circumstances, which doubtless gives the sensation of 'being in an autonomous space derived from within a continuous mass', as Passanti puts it,[33] or, in plain English, of being underground. On reaching the end of the flight, however, the visitor is suddenly aware that he is indeed high up (there are stars in the floor to confirm this symbolically), but 'one steps out into the light of the dome hallucinated, not liberated'.[34] Where one does step out is not into the main space of the chapel, but into a lobby, a device that has served to mask any view of the main space from the pilgrim toiling up the stairs (Fig. 54). At *zona terrena* ground level it acts as a transition between the stairs and the main hall. A comparable device is used at the Palazzo Carignano, where twin stairs ascending to a great hall debouch not into the hall itself, but into an interposed space.

The circular vestibule in which the visitor arrives – the right-hand one nowadays – is one of three that Guarini has intruded into Quadri's innocent cylinder. There is another at the head of the left-hand stair, and a third marking the entrance from the palace. The first two are on the axes of the cathedral aisles; the palace one is on the axis of the nave. In fact the palace vestibule only exists for the third of it that projects into the main space, but the spectator extrapolates the rest, which he assumes is buried in the palace gallery.

These vestibules announce an obsessive triadism that pervades the design. There are three of them, dividing the periphery of the main space into three equal stretches. Each one of them penetrates the main space for a third of its own periphery, and each one, or rather each of the two fully realized ones, is articulated within by three sets of three columns.[35] Flat arches span between these sets of columns and divide the ceiling in an equilateral triangle. The sides of these triangles preface respectively the head of the stairs (Fig. 55), the entrance into a sacristy and the entrance into the main space.

Once through the vestibule and into the main space, the visitor finds himself displaced to the periphery, as the centre is occupied by the towering mass of the altar and the Shroud case. The walls are faced in black Frabosa marble; a major Order of nine pilasters, their capitals gilded and displaying a

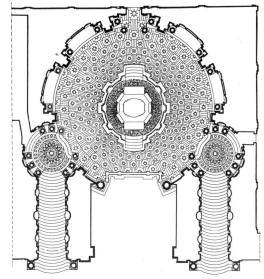

54. Turin, SS. Sindone. Plan.

69

crown of thorns above the acanthus leaves, articulates the periphery – a legacy, at least in the layout, from the Castellamonte/Quadri design. If we look at the plan, starting from the right-hand vestibule where the visitor emerges today (the left-hand staircase is kept closed), the pattern of bays runs as follows: right-hand vestibule, serliana, serliana, vestibule to palace, serliana, serliana, left-hand vestibule, blank, blank. The two blanks are caused by the omission of the ninth pilaster, and the broad aperture thus created is filled with the window to the cathedral. The pre-Guarini plan (Fig. 51) shows that the serlianas are a legacy from Castellamonte/Quadri, and in fact the modified form in which they are built is infrequent in the work of Guarini, who prefers (as in S. Lorenzo) to accept the usual form and then to inflect it in a curve. The omission of the ninth pilaster is also inherited, and the three entrances – entrances, but not vestibules: the latter, with their convex intrusions and triadic articulation, are Guarini's innovation.

Whatever had been built above the trabeation of the major Order was taken down in preparation for a radically· new design (Fig. 56). The trabeation itself has clear traditional resonances, which bespeak its pre-Guarinian origins, as compared, say, with the significant deformations of the analogous feature in S. Lorenzo. The second Order, which Guarini dismantled, had been a straightforward continuation of the *zona terrena* cylinder, destined to be capped, no doubt, by a spherical dome. Its replacement is something vastly different.

In the next zone upwards, between the *zona terrena* trabeation and the cornice rings at the base of the drum, Guarini flings three great inward-leaning arches across the space. They rise, in each case, from the pairs of pilasters flanking the vestibules, and if extended on plan, would give an equilateral triangle. The idea of inscribing an equilateral triangle in a circular plan may have been suggested to Guarini by the plan he inherited, with its three points of entrance and an omitted pier;[36] its schema is repeated like a logo on the ceilings of the two complete vestibules.

The arches, rising from the pilasters flanking the vestibules, 'skip' an intermediate pilaster. In the segment of periphery between the two stair-head vestibules, there is of course no pilaster to skip: it has been omitted to facilitate the window. The other two intermediate pilasters, each below the centre of an arch, remain without any evident statical function to perform. They are compensated by being crowned by decorative segmental broken pediments (Fig. 57). Between the arches (that is, over the circular intrusions of the vestibules), three great pendentives lean forward, truncating the cylinder below and reducing the span of the cornice ring of the drum which they support by a quarter in relation to the diameter of the cylinder.

The whole conception abounds in statical and stylistic paradoxes. A pendentive, in essence, is a concave spandrel which leads from the angle of two walls to the base of a circular dome; in other words, it is a device for ensuring the transition from a square chamber to a round one. The usual complement of pendentives will thus be four. But at SS. Sindone, Guarini is using spandrels to effect the passage from one circular space to another circular space. He therefore has to drop one of the pendentives and use a set of three, an unprecedented procedure.

The usual manneristic ducks and drakes are played with the evident statical functions of the major structural components. Under the arches, where openings might be expected, walls are found, that is the walls at the back of the shallow serlianas. Under the pendentives one expects walls, and finds the penetration of the vestibules, a usage comparable to the hollowed–out piers at

55. Turin, SS. Sindone. Stairs from cathedral.

71

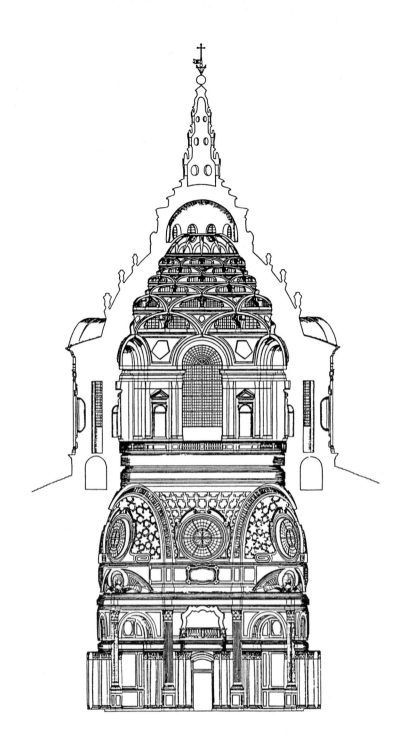

56. Turin, SS. Sindone. Section.

57. Turin, SS. Sindone. Intermediate pilaster.

S. Lorenzo. The same large circular windows are let into the pendentives as into the arch-bowls, suggesting that both these features perform the same function, whereas the opposite is really the case.[37]

The soffits of the pendentives and arch-bowls are decorated with coffering whose patterns modulate constantly as the natural light changes above (Fig. 58). The pendentives feature rows of hollow crosses distantly reminiscent of one of the motifs used by Borromini on the soffit of the dome of S. Carlo alle Quattro Fontane. The arch-bowls, however, are decorated with an Arab pattern where the circular disposition of six hexagons forms a six-pointed star in the centre.[33] In both cases, a decisiveness of plastic incident appears that is unknown at the lower level of the *zona terrena*.

Nothing in the canon of Renaissance, Mannerist or Baroque architecture

58. Turin, SS. Sindone. Pendentives and arch bowls.

would lead one to expect the shining black and gold proprieties of the first Order to be succeeded, in the next zone upwards, by the manifestations that have just been described. These are, however, but the prelude to further autonomous zones of even greater idiosyncratic originality.

The cornice ring supported by the three pendentives marks the limit of the area of darkness in the chapel. Above it we have crossed another frontier, into a zone of increased light: the high drum. Maintaining his conversion of the *zona terrena's* nine bays into six, which has been achieved, almost surreptitiously, by the three arches and three pendentives, Guarini articulates the drum by the use of six high windows with arched heads, their centres coinciding with the centres of the arches or pendentives below; between them are six piers that feature Borrominesque convex tabernacle niches. This steady rhythm establishes some semblance of traditional calm after the strange prodigies achieved below. Perhaps a culmination might still be achieved with a spherical dome? Far from it: we are now on the verge of one of Guarini's famous 'specialities'.[39] The crowns of the six arched windows serve as the springers for a series of segmental ribs, which span from crown to crown. The crowns of the first series of ribs perform the same service for the next

74

series, of lesser height, and this process is repeated six times, producing on plan a series of staggered hexagons projecting progressively inwards (Fig. 59 and Col. Pl. VII). Three-dimensionally, a nest of thirty-six arches is created, of which three are always on the same vertical axis. The continuity of the movement is accentuated by the torus mouldings that, gradually winding along the arch lintols from the springers to the crowns, alternately move away from and near to each other without ever touching, thereby accentuating the feeling of instability produced by the staggered superimposition of the arches, the thrusts of which seem to be resisted only by the tie-beams that subtend them.

In fact, as is usual with Guarini, the mechanics of support lie elsewhere. Each rib is seen from within to be bisected by a vertical spine, which cuts each amygdaloid window (for that is what these openings are) in two. These vertical features, which from inside read as individual consoles or spines, prove on the outside to be powerful buttresses that transfer the weight of the dome and the superimposed lantern to the outer drum, which, as shown in the section and plan (Figs. 56 and 59), is of double thickness, with a passageway between the inner and outer shells. From the outer drum the thrusts continue on down to the outer walls at the lower level, while the cornice ring, main arches and pendentives appear to be doing the real work.

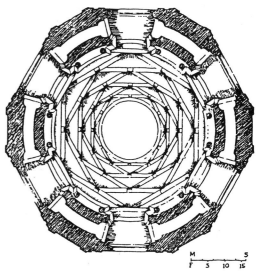

59. Turin, SS. Sindone. Plan of dome, looking up.

The view on looking up at the dome from the floor of the chapel is an extraordinary *coup de théâtre* (Col. Pl. VIII). An illusion is produced of almost endless distance, an infinite shimmering recession where architecture is suspended in space. At the summit the system opens up into a twelve-pointed star, at the centre of which hovers the holy dove, strongly lit by the twelve oval windows of the lantern.

A reference to the section will show that the rib-system of the dome is not in reality very high: it is not even as high as the drum. The optico/geometrical basis for the illusion has been examined by Passanti,[40] but it should be stressed that the effect of infinite recession is enhanced by the fact that the stone used in the dome network is a dressed but unpolished grey marble. The spectator who looks into it unconsciously contrasts the softened tonal values he perceives with the polished black marble and gilding of the *zona terrena* where he is standing and assumes that the impression which it conveys is due to the great distances involved.

The perceptual psychology employed to contrive this illusion was neither instinctive nor spontaneous, but was studied in the first place from ancient sources and developed by Guarini through his own researches. He says so himself. His views on the matter are tersely but pointedly expressed in the *Architettura civile*. The whole of chapter xxi in the third Tractate is devoted to the use an architect must make of perceptual psychology. His seventh observation is headed 'Objects that are white appear larger than those that are dark or black, and brighter.' Guarini, therefore, may be seen to be no less at home in theory than in practice.

When seen from the outside, the dome is dominated by the great arched windows of the drum, surmounted as they are by an undulating cornice (Fig. 60). Above and between them appear the twelve buttresses of the dome,[41] which are seen inside as individual consoles bisecting the windows. Between and behind the buttresses run the fascinating zig-zags created by the segmental window heads flicking in and out. Above this is the tambour of the lantern with the twelve oval windows that light the dove inside, and then four horizontal rings diminishing in size. These are capped by a little pagoda, which corresponds to nothing inside.

60. Turin, SS. Sindone. Elevation of drum and
    dome.

61. Rome, S. Ivo della Sapienza (Borromini).
    Dome and lantern.

There is a remarkable reminiscence here of the dome of Borromini's S. Ivo
della Sapienza in Rome (Fig. 61), which was begun in 1642 and finished in
1660. Guarini saw it under construction during his first stay in Rome, as a
novice. He could have seen it finished on his voyage from Modena to
Messina. The exterior of Borromini's dome is similar in its upper reaches to
Guarini's, and no less cryptic. The usual cupola cap at S. Ivo is replaced by a
spiral (of which Guarini's three rings are a horizontal version) that twists
round four times and then takes off into a wire sculpture. 'It can hardly be
doubted', says Wittkower, 'that this element has an emblematic meaning, the
precise nature of which has not yet been rediscovered.'[42] It may be worth recalling in this connection the interesting opinion that Borromini was making
an approach here to the interpenetration of inner and outer space, which the
spiral, with its inherent movement, characteristically embodies and which
was later notably re-evoked by Tatlin's tower.[43] A more likely source of

inspiration may perhaps be found in the drawings of the Milanese architect G. B. Montano (1534–1621) purporting to show reconstructions of ancient works.[44]

This is but one detail. If the full range of sources were to be investigated, a wider palette might be discerned, including the Islamic patterning already mentioned on the arch-bowls above the *zona terrena*, and the clayey forms of Buontalenti's Tuscan Mannerism in the drum.

In analyzing possible sources for the openwork dome of S. Lorenzo, it was not difficult to find Islamic prototypes, which Guarini might have seen in Spain. With the SS. Sindone there are no such obvious points of departure. The staggered superimposition of arches can often be met with in Eastern Europe. Professor Verzone has published a remarkable photograph looking up the conical chimney (of uncertain date) of the kitchen of Rila Monastery in Bulgaria,[45] where an effect comparable to the Sindone dome is achieved by the build-up of a series of staggered arches leaning progressively inwards. We may suppose it to be a vernacular coincidence. Better-known examples of this structural device are featured on the shorter towers of St Basil's, Moscow, where they may perhaps be regarded as a variant of the traditional Slavonic *kokoshniki* or *zakomary*, the stepped arches so characteristic of Russian churches, the use of which goes back to the twelfth century.[46] We know that Aristotile Fieravanti (1418–1486) was made to study the local Russian style when summoned by Ivan III to work on the Church of the Annunciation in Moscow,[47] but there is no record of his having published an account of his experiences when he got back to Bologna, nor was St Basil's itself built in his lifetime.

A more possible source of inspiration has been suggested as the church of S. Maria della Valle, 'La Badiazza', near Messina, where the pendentives that support the dome have their surfaces broken down into a series of little arches.[48]

With the volumetry of the church, we are confronted, as in S. Lorenzo, with a succession of apparently autonomous zones in vertical section, where the structure, style and incidents of one sector give no sure hint of what may be found in the next one up. Traditional and Mannerist elements are set off against the crystalline star-hexagons of the pendentives and the extraordinary geometry of the dome-nest.

All these stylistic and structural contrasts may perhaps be subsumed, in the Chapel of the Holy Shroud, under the larger conception of the contrast between a sombre and restless lower zone – extending in effect right back to the access staircases – and the bright ecstatic celestial zone which crowns the work.

The search for a *concetto* to explain Guarini's scheme, or even a *metafora acuta*, to borrow a term from Italian literature of the period, has led one scholar to scan the pages of Camillo Balliani's *Ragionamenti sopra la Sacra Sindone di N. S. Giesu* (Turin 1624) for possible theological programmes,[49] while another has interpreted a passing reference to *tenebrosa luce* in Guarini's play *La pietà trionfante* as foreshadowing an interest in the manipulation of light and shade which its author displays architecturally at SS. Sindone.[50]

These researches, albeit of profound learning and ingenuity, are more impressive for their abstruseness than for the understanding they afford of Guarini's schemata. As far as the SS. Sindone is concerned, all who have visited it and have experienced the building three-dimensionally (or perhaps, considering its use of light, four-dimensionally) will not doubt what message Guarini was striving to impart.

VII. (*following pages left*) Turin, SS. Sindone. Interior of drum/dome.

VIII. (*following pages right*) Turin, SS. Sindone. Interior of drum/dome.

77

9   PALACES

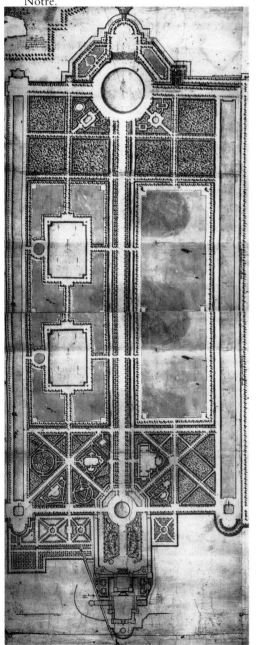

62. Racconigi. Plan of castle and park by A. Le Nôtre.

RACCONIGI

THE HOUSE OF SAVOY has a cadet branch, the Princes of Carignano.[1] Carignano is a small town, twelve miles south of Turin, which Duke Carlo Emanuele I ('the Great') erected into a principality for his third son, Tommaso Francesco, in 1619. Besides Carignano, the appanage included the fiefs of Racconigi, Casselle, Villafranca Piemonte and many others.

Racconigi, twelve miles south of Carignano, boasted a *castello* on a site that had been fortified from the earliest times.[2] Bernardino di Susa had built a stronghold there in 1004, on the ruins of an even earlier *fortezza*; it had four corner turrets and a glacis.[3] Four corner turrets were still in evidence at Racconigi, in a style, however, typical of the fourteenth century, when Carlo Morello surveyed it in 1650.[4] It was in fact substantially a medieval castle that Carlo Emanuele made over to his son Tommaso Francesco in 1619.[5]

Tommaso and his wife were unable, due to the cares of state, to spend much time initially at Racconigi, but the Archivio di Stato in Turin, so thoroughly ransacked by Dr Augusta Lange, reveals that considerable sums were disbursed over the years on upkeep and in acquiring more adjoining land.

The large plan, 1.72 metres long (Fig. 63), drawn up by the architect Carlo Morello around 1650 shows the park at Racconigi extending in length for over a kilometre.[6] The decorative beds laid out to the north of the castle, and covering part of the medieval moat, are *parterres de broderie* in the French style of the time. The castle itself is shown as having an irregularly built rectangular courtyard, and an irregular south front (towards the town of Racconigi), while the north front facing the garden has been recast, with a slightly inset central section enclosing a double staircase.

Carlo Morello was one of a series of architects, engineers and landscapers employed over the years by Tommaso Francesco and his son Emanuele Filiberto ('di Savoia Carignano'), who succeeded him in 1656.[7] All were engaged in pursuit of the Carignanos' ambition to convert the old *fortezza* into a 'palace and pleasure garden'. The most distinguished recruit was undoubtedly André Le Nôtre, who sent a detailed scheme, with annotations, from Paris in 1670,[8] aimed at providing Racconigi with a full-blown garden and park *à la française* (Fig. 62).

The most important architectural intervention was by the secretary to Duke Carlo Emanuele II, Tomaso Borgonio, identified by his handwriting and by the payments made to him in 1669 and 1670 as the author of a scheme for reworking the old castle.[9] It is set in the context of Le Nôtre's design for the grounds, and shows the central courtyard opened up to the south and covered over by a basket vault (Fig. 64). At the north end, the corner turrets have been reduced on their internal faces to make space for a broad terrace overlooking the garden, in place of the inset stairs on Morello's plan. From this new terrace, a great oval staircase descends to the garden, and two low-rise galleries extend east and west from the north towers, as part of a layout that embraces a formal garden with a fountain in the centre of four parterres. At the south end, the basket vaulting of the new central *salone* – the former courtyard – continues into a vestibule (corresponding to the terrace at the north) flanked by stairs leading to the upper storeys. Beyond this, a grand staircase like that on the garden front descends to the parvis. Basket-vaulted galleries are located on the east and west sides between the towers.

All these projects, however, or at least the architectural ones, got no further than the paper they were drawn on, so that when, in 1676 or thereabouts, Prince Emanuele Filiberto di Carignano eventually invoked the help of Guarino Guarini, the castle, in the words of Dr Lange, 'was still in essentially the same state that Bernardino di Savoia had left it in at his death in 1605, except perhaps for a staircase on the north which led down into the garden from a terrace between the towers, and various schemes of interior decoration'.[10]

Guarini was presumably recommended to the Prince of Carignano by the latter's cousin, Duke Carlo Emanuele II, who had retained Guarini for the SS. Sindone. That Guarini had only built churches hitherto in his architectural career was clearly no disincentive to the Prince, and what Guarini came

63. Racconigi. Plan of castle and park by C Morello, 1650.

64. Racconigi. Plan of castle by T. Borgonio.

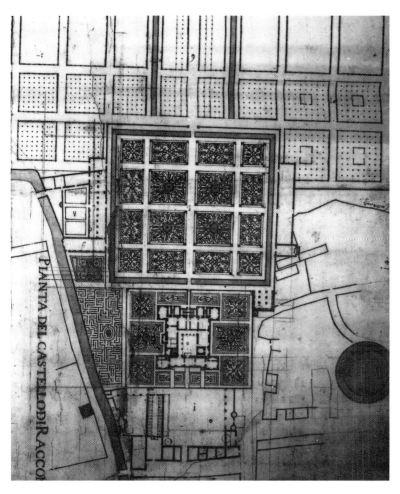

81

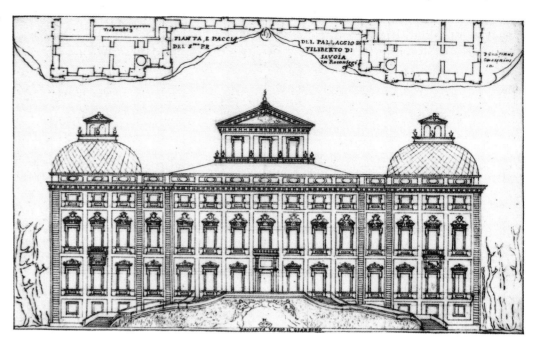

to plan for Racconigi evidently met with Emanuele Filiberto's cordial approval, as we know from a patent delivered in 1680 creating Guarini the Prince's theologian,[11] which is couched in the following terms:

> Emanuel Filiberto Amedeo di Savoia Prince of Carignano etc. The merit and the singular virtues of Father Don Guerino Guerini, Theatine Cleric Regular, both of which shine out in this metropolis, in which he has displayed his great ability in the majestic design of the Chapel of the Most Holy Shroud which is advancing towards completion under his care and supervision which he has indefatigably continued to bestow on it, meriting the commendation of Their Royal Highnesses, and of all the most distinguished architects who have seen and examined it with admiration; in that of his church of San Lorenzo, erected on ingenious and extraordinary principles, and then of our Palace, so singular and out of the ordinary, as that of the Castle of Racconigi, which is second to none in its *bizzarria* and inventiveness; besides those other parts which unite in him, of the highest philosophical and moral sciences which are proper to a zealous and worthy religious; have made us think of acknowledging with some appropriate award the affection he has ever displayed to our person. Wherefore, deeming that we cannot at present better satisfy our kind inclination, we appoint the same Father D. Guerino Guerini our Theologian, with an annual stipend of 400 livres. Turin, 9 June 1680.[12]

Guarini's scheme for Racconigi does not appear in *Architettura civile*, though there are two drawings in the Archivio di Stato, Turin, which are thought to have been prepared for engraving (Figs. 65 and 66).[13] Dr Lange, in the course of lengthy research in the archives of Turin, Rome and Karlsruhe, has brought to light a wealth of material showing Guarini's schemes, not so much in different stages of gestation, but in various 'states', the differences consisting mainly in alternative treatments for the south stairs and in dimensioning anomalies. It would be otiose to review these details, which may be consulted in her article in *GGIB*.I.[14] For the purposes of the present work, it will be sufficient to examine Guarini's intentions, as laid out in a carefully

prepared set of presentation drawings that were sent in 1682 to the Duke of
Bavaria, who had married Enrichetta Adelaide, a daughter of Duke Vittorio
Amedeo I of Savoy. It was she who had brought to Munich a taste for
architecture, an urge to build grand ducal palaces and to lay out gardens in the
modern French style. She was the initiator of the works at Nymphenburg.

Guarini's plan (Fig. 67) takes over from Tomaso Borgonio's scheme (Fig.
64) the courtyard covered with basket vaulting, the terrace between the north
towers, and the side arcading, though the latter feature was omitted in the
drawing mentioned above that he prepared for engraving (Fig. 65). He
omits, too, the lower wings to east and west, which in Borgonio's design set
out to enclose a formal garden, and instead he treats the main block as a free-
standing structure, with four large corner pavilions. For this purpose the
medieval corner towers are developed into more ample wings, three bays
wide and two bays deep, to help in building up a more formal composition
in the manner of the classical French châteaux. A special feature is made of
the great staircases that give access to the *piano nobile* north and south. On the
south a double stair with a lozenge-shaped plan descends to the parvis; on the
garden front two S-curves embrace a pool with a fountain and three jets.
Borgonio's utilitarian stairs to the upper floors are converted into oval flights
flanking an ample vestibule.

Guarini's intentions for the *gran salone* are illustrated in a drawing (Fig.

66. Racconigi. First floor plan by Guarini (drawing prepared for engraving).

67. Racconigi. First floor plan by Guarini. Later
proposal for south stairs.

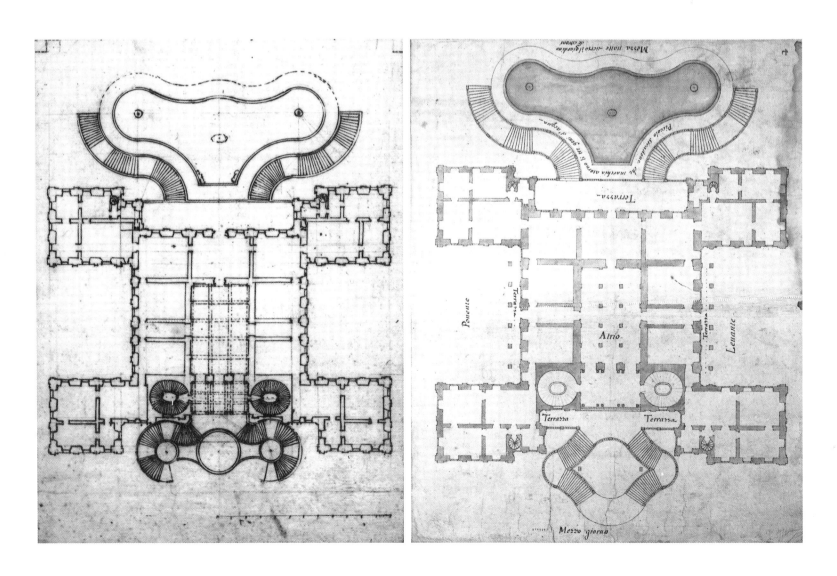

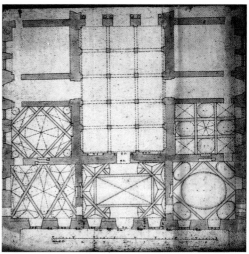

69. Racconigi. Plan of central part of first floor.

70. Types of vaulting (from *Architettura civile*).

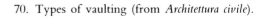

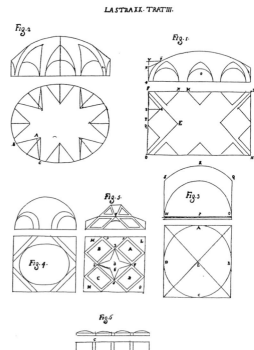

68) formerly (1942–71) preserved at the Quirinal in Rome but now back at the Archivio di Stato in Turin.[15] The *piano nobile* is shown as windowless, articulated by arches supported by piers and columns with Tuscan capitals. The system of vaulting is not clear. The basket vaulting (*volta a cestello*), referred to above in connection with the plan, had been pencilled in on a drawing in the Archivio di Stato, Turin,[16] of which the Munich version of the plan, illustrated here (Fig. 67), is otherwise an exact copy. This system was a legacy from Borgonio. Guarini's ultimate intentions in the matter of vaulting are more clearly indicated on another sheet also formerly in the Quirinal collection,[17] where a plan of the *piano nobile* (Fig. 69) shows a different system, the '*volte a fasce*', or banded vaults, dotted in. These are specifically referred to by Guarini in connection with Racconigi in *Architettura civile* (III.xxvi.9) and illustrated in Lastra XX, Fig. 6 (our Fig. 70); other types of vaulting on this plate seem to be employed in the side chambers of the *piano nobile*. They are likewise noted in Guarini's text (III.xxvi.10–11).

Returning to the section, we see that the upper floor is vaulted by a Guarinian 'special'. Corinthian columns support pendentives that enframe coved vaults, where alternating segments are omitted to let in clerestory light from the topmost level of the central block. This is the kind of treatment that

84

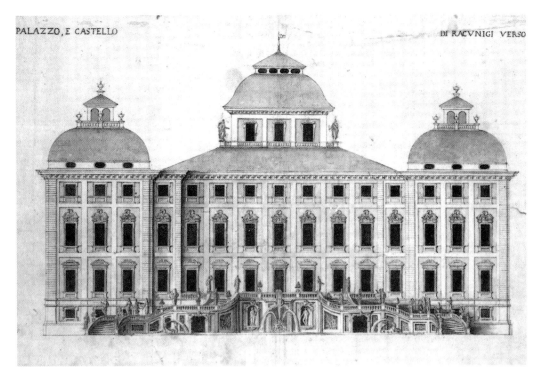

doubtless prompted Guarini's princely client, in the patent quoted above, to refer to the *bizzarria* of the design. It would certainly have afforded ample wall space for the display of art works, but later Carignanos disliked it and it disappeared in Giambattista Borra's reworking eighty years later. A similar scheme for transforming a medieval courtyard by roofing it over with Baroque top lighting survives in a sketch Guarini made for the Palazzo Madama in Turin.[18]

Guarini's red brick elevations (Figs. 71, 74 and 75) recall the image of French châteaux of the classical period in their massing and some of their details: the use of side wings in relation to the *corps de logis*, pavilion roofs and grand outside staircases. Guarini's scheme also parallels common French usage by inflecting the front elevation in deference to the *corps de logis*, while running straight through between the side wings on the rear elevation.

The individual bays at Racconigi are marked off with pilaster strips rather than *chaînages*, and the Baroque pediments over the windows (somewhat simplified in practice as compared to the ones shown in the drawing) make a stronger impact than French classical usage would consent to, recalling the effects met with in an Italian town palace; but Piedmont's French connections and Guarini's time in France are unmistakably signalled here,[19] though Professor Portoghesi detects 'a fidelity to a scheme that we might call Emilian',[20] as exemplified by the Pilotta in Parma or the Rocca di Scandiano.

Guarini refers to his design for the elevations of Racconigi in the *Architettura civile*. Chapter xxv of the third Tractate is devoted to the various ways of treating an elevation. There are six chief ways this can be done, of which the second 'is with strips (*a fasce*) which divide up the whole wall into various panels'. In the 'second observation' to the chapter, Guarini says of this method, 'and this is how I did the Palace of the Most Serene Prince of Carignano at Racconigi, where the vertical strips are only crossed by horizontal strips without any cornice, except the last, which is between'.

This radical simplification of the classical Orders was also applied by

72. Rome, Oratory of S. Filippo Neri (Borromini).

Guarini to the Villa di Govone (the penultimate scheme engraved in *Architettura civile*) and the Villa il Maggiordomo, a kind of pocket Palazzo Carignano at Gerbido, generally attributed to him on stylistic grounds. But it is not an invention of Guarini's. It was developed by Borromini forty years earlier, starting with the facade of the Oratory of S. Filippo Neri in Rome, where the ground floor pilaster caps are drastically simplified, and culminating in the clock tower he built for the same complex (Fig. 72), where the pilasters and stringers are reduced to mere strips in a manner that clearly foreshadows Racconigi.

This phenomenon is not confined to the Italian Baroque: it occurs in other countries where sophisticated practitioners of architecture have outgrown a long established classical style. The usages adopted by Sir John Soane would be the English equivalent.[21]

There is a discrepancy between the detailing of the tower roof in the Munich drawing and that shown in the one prepared for engraving (Fig. 65). That it was the Munich one which was followed is evidenced by a painting owned by the Prince of Piedmont (Fig. 73), and published by Brinckmann.[22] It shows Guarini's new facade around the year 1700, with the bell-like roof clearly outlined.

The Bavarian collection has designs for a side elevation (Fig. 74), with a terrace running between the towers, and a south elevation (Fig. 75), the latter replete with discrepancies vis-à-vis the plan and the other elevations.

Only Guarini's garden front and *salone* were carried out to his designs; an engraving from the year 1712 (Fig. 76) shows an untreated south front and sides, with Guarini's north front visible in the background. These areas, together with the *salone*, were done up between 1756 and 1760 by Giambattista Borra in what Professor Millon drily calls 'nascent neoclassic with Anglo-Saxon overtones',[23] and Jasper More, with greater fruitiness, 'the style of a pump-room in an English inland spa'.[24] Perhaps it was the

73. Racconigi. North elevation, about 1700.

86

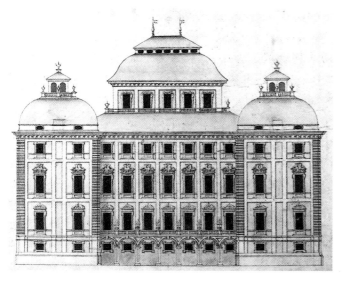 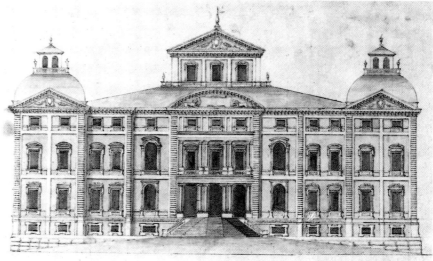

latter circumstance that evoked the rather baffled reaction in the fourth edition of Murray's *Handbook for Travellers in Northern Italy* (London 1852): 'The building, though handsome, offers only the usual features of palaces of this description.'

There exists in the Archivio di Stato, Turin, a complete scheme by Guarini for the entourage of the castle (Fig. 77).[25] A huge *cour d'honneur* bounded by a semicircular portico is struck on a radius of about 80 metres from a point at the foot of the entrance stairs. This portico conceals ranges of stables and coach houses that run out to the right and left, tangentially to the semicircle. The castle itself is flanked by two great *nicchioni* embracing *rond ponts* and fountains, and pairs of square pavilions. None of these were built. Had they been, says Professor Millon, 'Racconigi would have been the first full

74. Racconigi. Side elevation.

75. Racconigi. South elevation.

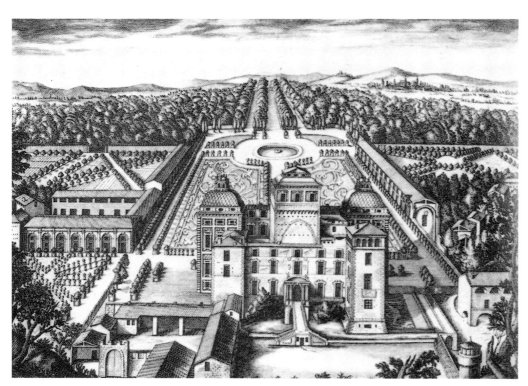

76. Racconigi, South front, 1712 (engraving by Tasnière, from Audiberti's *Regiae villae poetica descriptae*.)

87

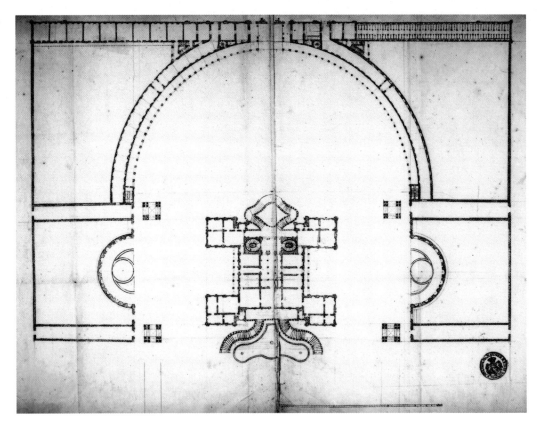

77. Racconigi. Complete layout of entourage.

78. The extensions of Turin.

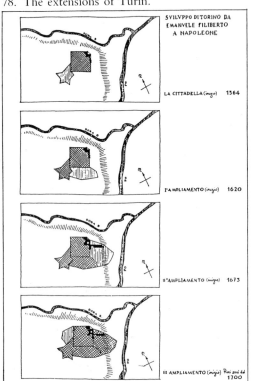

realization in Italy of the new French standards for integration of primary structures with outbuildings, garden and park'.[26]

But somebody saw all this, if only in the mind's eye. In the year 1712 the Jesuit priest Camillo Audiberti published a book of odes, *Regiae villae poetica descriptae*, with engravings by G. B. Tasnière, in praise of the villas of the House of Savoy. His ode on Racconigi ('Racconisum') is based on a reading of Guarini's proposals, including this layout, rather than what was on the ground. Tasnière, however, drew what he saw (reproduced in Fig. 76). The learned reader of Fr Audiberti's odes would have been hard put to match up the poet's lush descriptions with the quarter re-faced castle in unpretentious rustic surroundings depicted in the artist's engraving.

PALAZZO CARIGNANO

Why were Guarini's schemes for Racconigi never completed beyond the north front and the *salone*? The answer must be that from 1679 onwards the building owner, Prince Emanuele Filiberto di Carignano, began spending large sums elsewhere – also on a building, and also to a design by Guarini: the Palazzo Carignano in Turin.

We have seen that Turin was an old Roman city, which scarcely extended beyond its ancient limits till the end of the Middle Ages. When the Duchy of Savoy transferred its capital from Chambéry to Turin in 1563, the first extension of the city bounds was effected by the building of the Citadel on the angle of the city walls facing the open plain; the other sides were protected by the rivers Dora and Po.[27] The first non-military extension was begun, to the south of the Roman square, in 1620, and in 1673 a second

88

79. Prince Emanuele Filiberto Amedeo di Savoia Carignano, 'il Muto' (1628–1709) and his wife Maria Caterina d'Este (portraits by an unknown artist at Racconigi).

extension was decreed by Duke Carlo Emanuele II, who solemnly celebrated the start of the new city wall on 23 October of that year (Fig. 78).

Carlo Emanuele II died in 1675, leaving a son, Vittorio Amedeo II, aged nine, and a widow, Maria Giovanna-Battista di Savoia-Nemours, who assumed the regency under the now-traditional title for a Piedmontese dowager duchess, 'Madama Reale'.[28] She continued her late husband's policy of encouraging the building of grandiose palaces in the new quarter.

With a reigning Duke aged nine, the question arose of an heir apparent. The first in line was the eldest representative of the cadet branch, Emanuele Filiberto, Guarini's client for Racconigi (Fig. 79). Though a man of great intelligence and culture, he had been born deaf and dumb, and was looked down on by his mother, the acerbic Princess Maria di Soissons. Emanuele Filiberto's younger brother, Eugenio Maurizio, had died in 1673, but he had had a son, Luigi Tommaso, and it was on this grandson that the Princess set her hopes for the dynasty.

Luigi Tommaso, however, irretrievably damaged his prospects by secretly marrying in 1678 the daughter of an equerry to the Prince de Condé.[29] Maria di Soissons, mortally offended, transferred her favours, *faute de mieux*, to her elder son, then aged fifty, and proposed that he should now seek a wife.[30]

These two circumstances, therefore – the State policy of encouraging the embellishment of the new extension to the city, and the proposed marriage of Emanuele Filiberto, now uncontested heir apparent – conspired to suggested the erection of a palace of regal rather than merely noble proportions for the Carignano line. This would replace the 'Palazzo Vecchio', a modest complex of three old buildings,[31] hemmed in all round by other houses save for an entrance on the south, in Old Jews' Street.[32]

The social, political and dynastic conjunctures proving favourable, all that was needed were funds and a site. The Prince approached Madama Reale and

90

80. Turin, Palazzo Carignano. Main elevation.

81. Turin, Palazzo Carignano. Courtyard elevation.

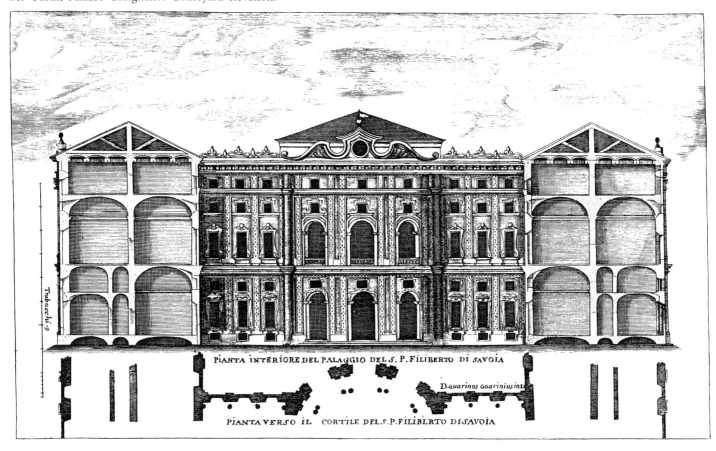

explained his financial situation,[33] including the loss of income that had resulted from the extinction, with his father's death, of the revenue from taxes on notarized deeds and the failure to materialize of certain legacies that had been intended for him. He came away with a grant of 50,000 ducatoni and permission to convert some of his appanage feus into cash.[34]

As regards the site, Emanuele Filiberto had most of it already in a piece of land given to his father, the first Prince of Carignano, by Duke Carlo Emanuele I, as part of his policy to encourage the development of Turin.[35] The first Prince, Tommaso Francesco, had used the site to build stables on. Although it was very ample,[36] another small piece of land was still required to ensure that the projected main door of the palace coincided with the centre of the piazza in front of it. This plot, which measured 43 by 12 metres (14 by 4 trabucchi), belonged to the Society of Jesus. A price of 'lire 12,000 ducali di argento a soldi 20' was exacted for it.[37] 'As always,' comments Professor Abrate, 'the good fathers knew how to do an excellent piece of business "ad majorem Dei gloriam".'[38]

The documents in the Archivio di Stato, Turin, relating to the building of the Palazzo Carignano include a folder with a number of drawings, and a ledger bound in parchment, running from May 1679 to April 1685, in which Carlo Raimondo, comptroller of the household of the Prince of Carignano, records all disbursements 'for the building of the New Palace'. This book actually gives a starting date for the building – 11 May 1679 – and on 6 August of that year notes a payment (the only one ascertainable) of 50 doubloons to Guarini for his design of the building.

It is possible, by close study, to derive from this ledger a complete building history of the palace, the names of Guarini's colleagues, the sub-contractors, stone dressers, brick burners, bricklayers, carpenters, sculptors and *stuccatori*; what they did, when they did it, who measured it and what it all cost. It is possible, and Dr Augusta Lange has done it, or a good representative sample of it.[39] I shall not duplicate her work, but content myself with noting the organizational powers of Guarini which it reveals. The work proceeds smoothly and expeditiously; the various labours are measured and paid for promptly, and this while the architect was also supervising S. Lorenzo, SS. Sindone and Racconigi; getting out a scheme for the Collegio dei Nobili; writing his books and preparing them for the press.

Guarini's intentions with regard to the design of the Palazzo Carignano are illustrated in two engravings in the *Architettura civile*. One shows the west front of the building facing the Piazza Carignano (Fig. 80); the other depicts the rear of the same block (Fig. 81), looking on to a courtyard, the side wings of which (represented by four-bay corner pavilions on the front elevation) are shown in section. Only strip plans of the front walls are given at the foot of each elevation. The implication is that what we are being presented with here is that part of the building devoted to *rappresentanza* or prestige, the living and service quarters being assigned to the side wings. This presumption is confirmed by a drawing in the Archivio di Stato, one of a set, previously referred to, that affords a unique insight into the development of a major design by Guarini.[40]

A complete palace scheme is presented (Fig. 82), not just the *corps de logis* with the prestige rooms. Instead of the usual U-shaped plan – usual for Turin, that is – with a courtyard opening on to a garden, we get a closed court, as a slender rear wing joins up the ends of the side wings. Each side wing projects forward in the centre in an *avant-corps*. At the heart of each of these central blocks is an inner court, connected in the case of the right-hand

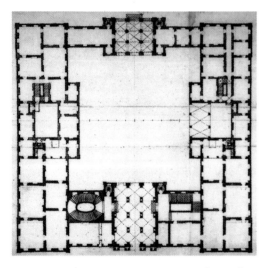

82. Turin, Palazzo Carignano. Complete palace scheme.

or south wing by a cross-vaulted open gallery to the main courtyard. If the left-hand or north wing is meant to represent the first floor, this open gallery may be reduplicated on the ground floor on this side, too.

At the rear of the main courtyard, the slender cross wing is penetrated by a vaulted portico in three bays, leading through to the garden. The counterpart to this on the west front is a major feature of the design: a rectangular atrium with three four-bay aisles, articulated by columns coupled longitudinally and bound by a single pedestal and architrave. Only the central aisle represents an actual way through; the side aisles end in facade windows.

The atrium represents the central, salient third of the *corps de logis*. The other two-thirds, on the courtyard side, are occupied by flanking staircases, oval on the left, rectangular on the right, and possibly intended as alternatives. A pair of elliptical stairs on such a transverse axis was featured in the French Palace (Fig. 26) and at Racconigi. A Parisian recollection may be evidenced by the atrium, too. Bernini's first plan for the Louvre – current in Paris when Guarini was working there – had a secondary atrium in three aisles, separated by coupled columns. It seems, however, superfluous in this context to pray in evidence the entrance vestibule of the Palazzo Farnese.[41] An atrium with cross-vaulted aisles was used at Racconigi and was to be proposed for the Collegio dei Nobili.

No elevational sketch exists for this scheme. It would have displayed the shallow rectilinear articulations of the three-bay central atrium and the projection of the side wings in two four-bay pavilions. But before the extra land was acquired from the Jesuits, there would scarcely have been room in front of the palace for a more *mouvmenté* treatment, nor indeed sufficient light for the *appartamenti d'onore*.[42]

From here on, though there are various treatments of the side wings in the Archivio di Stato drawings,[43] the main interest lies in the development of the central part of the west front. 'Here in fact', says Bernardi, 'the unitary conception of the entire organism was decided by the architect, while the other parts assume a quiet rectilinear development, obeying a criterion of simple functionality.'[44]

The next idea revealed in the set of drawings preserved in the Archivio di Stato represents a fundamental modification, which, through several variants, will persist to the end. (Fig. 83)[45] In the first scheme, the prestige rooms – ground floor atrium and first floor *gran salone* – are rectangular and run parallel to the main axis of the whole scheme. Guarini's second development shows the prestige block assume the form of an ellipse, a shape latent in one of the two staircases featured in the first project, and this block is placed transversely to the main axis of the palace.

The staircases are projected from their former exclusively flanking positions, and after two straight dog-leg flights in adjoining rectangular stair halls, wind themselves round the bulge of the elliptical block, on the courtyard side, until they join on a single landing on the main axis, at *gran salone* level. The opposite facade, looking on to the piazza, is correspondingly inflected, but the curvature is minimal, to avoid impinging on what was then a shallow piazza. The union of the centre block with the side wings is thus the same as in the first scheme. Access to the ground floor apartments at the front of the palace is through the atrium and an unoccupied bay of the stair hall; at first floor level it is through the vestibules flanking the *gran salone*.

In his book on Borromini published sixty years ago,[46] Eberhardt Hempel examined various sketch plans preserved in the Albertina, showing a number of solutions that Borromini proposed for the palace of Count Ambrogio

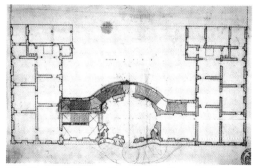

83. Turin, Palazzo Carignano. Second development of plan: prestige rooms elliptical.

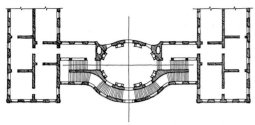

84. Turin, Palazzo Carignano. Preliminary design with oval atrium and stairs on piazza side.

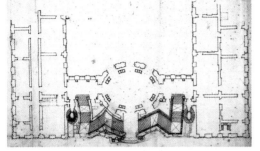

85. Turin, Palazzo Carignano. 'Disegni per refare le scale.'

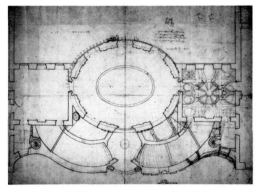

86. Turin, Palazzo Carignano. Penultimate design. Curvature of facade restored.

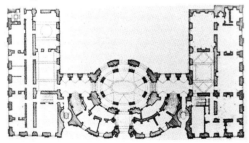

87. Turin, Palazzo Carignano. Definitive scheme. Ground floor plan.

88. Turin, Palazzo Carignano. Definitive scheme. Central block: *piano nobile.*

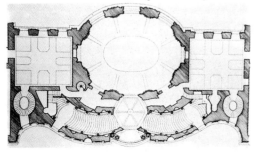

Carpegna near the Fontana di Trevi in Rome. The latest drawing in the series shows two flights of staircases ascending along the perimeter of an oval courtyard, and meeting on a common landing. 'The fact that only after him [Borromini]', Hempel wrote, 'were there similar structures in Rome, Turin and Bologna, shows how in this field, too, he was ahead of his time.' This linking of Borromini's Palazzo Carpegna device with Guarini's design for the Palazzo Carignano has been repeated by Wittkower (1958) and Passanti (1963), though it seems unlikely that Guarini ever saw Borromini's sketches, and very few of Borromini's proposals for this scheme were put into execution.

More certain points of comparison may be made with Guarini's own French Palace project, which features an entrance atrium with a salon above, projecting from the facade, with paired elliptical stairs behind, in a vestibule adjoining the courtyard.

On the same sheet as Guarini's design for an oval atrium with the stairs towards the courtyard, there is a pencil sketch, reproduced here for clarity's sake as redrawn by Passanti (Fig. 84), where the plan of the oval atrium has been rotated on its axis. The stairs now embrace the elliptical cylinder on the piazza side, and the whole central block has been slid back to avoid the exuberant curve projecting beyond the building line set by the end facades of the side wings.

On the back of Guarini's next scheme (Fig. 85) someone has written 'Disegni per refare le scale'.[47] The stairs are retained on the piazza side, but the vestibules they rise from are now centred on the main transverse axis, and the stairs themselves are twisted round so that each takes off, in imposing fashion, from the middle of a vestibule's long side. The flights are then subjected to three drastic zig-zag inflections, rectilinear on the right-hand variant, curved on the left, before reaching the first floor *salone* via three landings apiece. This rather muscle-bound design would have produced an elevation with deep angular flexions. The eight pairs of coupled columns, which in previous designs had been sited close to the curving walls of the atrium, are stepped forward in this scheme.

Guarini's penultimate design (Fig. 86) shows a symmetrical pair of stairs ascending from a hexagonal anteroom, placed just inside the entrance from the piazza.[48] The curvature of the facade is restored, and the junction to the side wings is now effected by swinging forward in a reverse curve.

In his definitive scheme (Figs. 87 and 88),[49] Guarini retains the hexagonal vestibule from the piazza, now adorned with six columns of 'pietra di Gassino' (Fig. 89),[50] but the stairs no longer start from here. From the limit of the hexagonal vestibule, where the guards would stand, there is a view of the elliptical atrium (Fig. 90) surrounded by eight pairs of Ionic columns standing out from the wall on common bases and supporting pieces of entablature from which pendentives rise, to support in their turn the oval flat vault in the centre, which reflects the ground plan at a reduced scale.

The visitor, on moving into the atrium, penetrates a room whose main axis is at right angles to the one along which he has so far proceeded. The level of lighting is subdued; there appear to be faint sources of illumination at each end of the transverse axis. In contradistinction to earlier plans, Guarini in his definitive scheme has contrived the overlap of several steps from the adjoining chambers to project into the atrium, at each end. The visitor feels himself drawn on, to left or right (Fig. 91), towards the source of light and the steps that will deliver him from this area of transition. He perceives from below, and to one side, a well-lit room beyond. Mounting six steps, he finds

90. Turin, Palazzo Carignano. Atrium.

89. (*previous page*) Turin, Palazzo Carignano. Vestibule. 'Giants with their bodies tangled in rope.'

91. Turin, Palazzo Carignano. Atrium. 'The visitor feels himself drawn to the source of light.'

himself in a rectangular vestibule. The visitor sees the beginning here of a curving flight of stairs (Fig. 93), its upper reaches bathed in light, its treads swelling out convexly to meet his foot. He begins to climb, and finds himself moving through a three-dimensional curve – up, forwards and around. The source of light which draws him on is a window at the single landing that occurs at the half-way mark (Fig. 94). From this landing, his eye embraces the curve of the last flight, and discovers that the treads are now curved back concavely, in opposite motion to the ones that have already been climbed;

96

they become welcoming and inviting.[51] At the top of the flight there is a richly ornamented hexagonal vestibule, reflecting the shape of the entrance lobby over which it stands, and where in effect the visit began.

The *gran salone* itself, which has been called 'the most spectacular late-seventeenth-century grand salon in Italy',[52] is unfortunately not illustrated in the *Architettura civile*, and in its existing state it has not proved possible for me to view the Guarinian vaulting.

At present the oval chamber is articulated by Corinthian pilasters of a giant Order, between which a minor Order is embraced, supporting a series of balconies below mezzanine height square windows (Fig. 92). The major Order reaches through to a balustraded ring above the architrave, and a vault with an oval oculus crowns, or originally crowned, the whole, filtering light through from large oval windows at clerestory level in the central ellipse raised to tower level (Fig. 95), though this arrangement is now concealed by a modern ceiling.

There is a good deal of doubt and ambiguity here about the development of the volumetry, as Guarini's elevations published in the *Architettura civile* show a much lower tower than was actually built. Professor H. Millon, who devoted the whole of his doctoral thesis at Harvard to a study of the Palazzo Carignano, has reproduced a drawing from this work, otherwise unpublished, in his little book *Baroque and Rococo Architecture* (Fig. 96), illustrating his concept of the original Guarinian interior. The major Order stops below

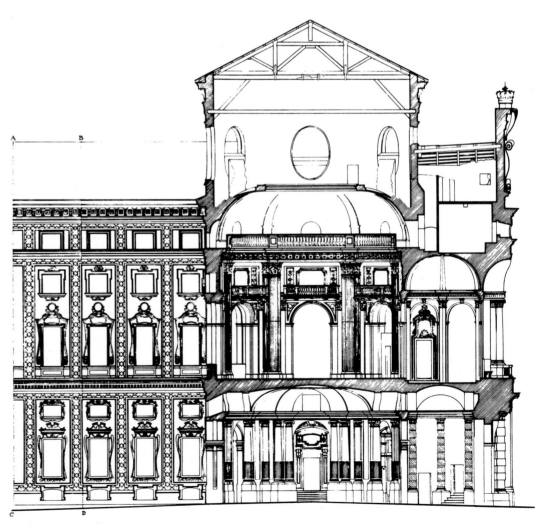

92. Turin, Palazzo Carignano. Section on main axis.

98

X. Turin, Palazzo Carignano. Main elevation.

the mezzanine windows, and the tower reconciles the low height shown on the Treatise engravings with the large windows as built. Most significantly, 'through the oculus, an apparently suspended domical surface, mysteriously lighted, contained a painted scene, the climax of the sequence of entry, stair and vestibule'.[53] The 'domical surface' was the underside of a plaster dome segment, suspended from wooden trusses in the clerestory space. Light filtered through from the clerestory windows, and was reflected as well from the top of the masonry vault.

From the palace entrance to the *gran salone* the visitor will have passed through a series of six rooms of varying size: the narrow hexagonal vestibule,

99

94. Turin, Palazzo Carignano. Light source on landing of stairs.

93. (*facing page*) Turin, Palazzo Carignano. Stairs leading to the *gran salone*.

XI. (*previous pages left*) Turin, Palazzo Carignano. Main elevation: central ellipse.

95. (*previous pages right*) Turin, Palazzo Carignano. View from courtyard, showing oval clerestory windows in central ellipse at tower level.

96. Turin, Palazzo Carignano. Section through *gran salone*.

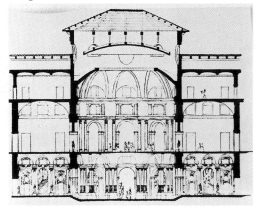

the great elliptical atrium, then the rectangular stair hall, followed by the curving stairs which deliver him into another hexagonal vestibule before he attains the *gran salone*: an astonishing variety of spaces disposed along a spiral, spaces that are revealed only bit by bit, in unexpected partial views.

All these spaces, until the *gran salone* is reached, feature Orders of columns that are detached, to a greater or lesser degree, from the mass of the wall. This has the effect of creating in every room a type of space that is independent of the perimeter walling and the openings in it. Each space thereby tends to become an autonomous organism, rather than part of a greater whole, retaining the visitor within itself, and making the route through the total sequence seem longer.

The use of freestanding columns – indeed of any kind of Order – involves problems when they are disposed along a staircase. Bishop Juan Caramuel de Lobkowitz, author of Guarini's least favourite book, *Architectura civil recta y obliqua*, would have made short shrift of such perplexities, by kinking both capital and architrave obliquely downwards to match the angle of going, as a plate in his book shows (Fig. 97). Guarini, who had the most cordial contempt for the theories of Caramuel (he refers to him acidly as 'a certain person, who has written in Spanish about architecture')[54] goes to great lengths to avoid using oblique details. Lastra XVII of the third Tractate (Fig. 98) is devoted to showing four ways of obviating this solecism, in illustration of observations 2 to 4 of chapter xxv. The bottom row of the plate, No. 4, shows how Guarini did it on the staircase at the Palazzo Carignano. The

97. Caramuel's treatment of a staircase, using the 'Oblique Order' (from *Architettura civil recta y obliqua*, Vigevano 1678).

98. Staircase treatments (from *Architettura civile*).

99. (*facing page*) Turin, Palazzo Carignano. Balusters.

architrave runs flat over the column capital, then curves gently down to the next one. It curves, in fact, two ways: down and sideways, in line with the gently spiralling stair. This can be seen in the photograph, Fig. 94.

By the same token, Guarini abjures oblique balusters. You can get round this, he says, by finishing the member off in leaves or volutes or flowers.[55] This is the explanation for the curious vegetable balusters flanking the stairs at the Palazzo Carignano, where the merest curve of a leaf is permitted to acknowledge the obliquity involved (Fig. 99).

The true significance of the Carignano staircase, however, does not lie in its being an exemplar of Guarini's more recondite theories about architectural decoration, but in the undoubted fact that it represents the culmination of all past developments in this field in Italy, while at the same time it is the harbinger of those developments in eighteenth-century Germany by the great continuators of Guarini, who would elevate the action of mounting a staircase, at palaces like Würzburg and Bruchsal, into an almost mystical experience.

In the main elevation of the Palazzo, that towards the Piazza Carignano, a new phenomenon appears in Italian Baroque palace design: the facade is inflected in the centre, as the elliptical prestige block displays its curved wall, swinging gently forward in curve and counter-curve between rectilinear end pavilions. Only church buildings had been treated like this before – facades such as S. Carlino – and never on such a scale. We have seen this type of plasticity employed by Bernini to dynamic effect on the Cornaro chapel, *inside* the church of S. Maria della Vittoria (see Fig. 35). The same architect produced a scheme for the elevation of a palace – the east front of the Louvre – which featured a great oval pavilion bulging out in the centre, flanked by two elliptical wings, ending in corner pavilions (see Fig. 29). This was never built, but it is possible that Guarini, whose time in Paris coincided with Bernini's visit, may well have known of the scheme or even have seen it.[56]

All the elevations are built in brick, which recent cleaning has revealed to be light brown in colour (Col. Pl. IX). Similar work would doubtless show the same colour on the nearby Collegio dei Nobili, now coated in three centuries of grime. Ingenious detailing by the architect exploits the nature of the brick to produce extraordinary effects of texturing (Col. Pl. X), in a manner pioneered by Borromini at the Convento dei Filippini in Rome.[57] At first glance, the lower of the two levels into which the elevation is divided appears to be rusticated, but the effect is in fact created by the special bricks, baked to a design by the architect, which give a rippled appearance at the least touch of sun.[58] These are used to fill in the shaft panels of the Doric pilasters that articulate the lower level of the facade and are doubled on the central curved portion as the entrance is approached.

The upper level of the facade changes the Doric Order of pilasters for Corinthian. Here the shaft panels are left blank, and, instead, ingenuity of design in brickwork is matched by impeccable craftsmanship in the astonishing pediment and architrave that are used to enframe the *piano nobile* windows (Fig. 100). The ensemble is said to represent the face and feathered head-dress of an Indian brave – a commemoration of the deeds performed by the Carignano–Salières Regiment against the Iroquois in Canada between 1665 and 1668.[59] In trying to come to terms with this extraordinary detail, Sandro Benedetti calls it 'a brutal return to objective nature'.[60]

106

100. Turin, Palazzo Carignano. 'Red Indian' *piano nobile* windows.

101. Turin, Palazzo Carignano. Appearance of central split, 1848 (from *Mondo Illustrato*).

The dynamism of the central bulge, where the prestige apartments seem to be in the process of extruding themselves from the core of the palace, is accentuated by the split that is contrived down its middle. This is shaped into a tall, narrow *nicchione*, where a declamation balcony surmounts the columned entrance (Col. Pl. XI). Guarini designed a monumental crowning feature, shown in the elevation published in the *Architettura civile* (Fig. 80 above), but this was never executed. The appearance of the central split in the first half of the nineteenth century is shown in an engraving from the *Mondo illustrato* of 15 May 1848 (Fig. 101). The present crowning feature is not too remote from Guarini's intentions. It was designed by Carlo Ceppi in the early 1880s to provide the setting for a bronze plaque commemorating the fact that Vittorio Emanuele II was born in the palace. The complementary pediments over the end pavilions, shown in the *Architettura civile* engraving, are still unrealized.

Some scholars have criticized the way in which Guarini has effected the junction between the curvilinear central block and the end pavilions. 'Although the executed solution is most fascinating,' remarks Professor Coffin, 'the relationship between the central part of the palace and its wings is quite perfunctory.'[61]

As always in Guarinian studies, there is someone on hand to defend the contrary view. Eugenio Battisti, in his recondite essay 'Schemata nel Guarini',[62] declares that it is perfectly obvious why the architect has acted in this way. The rectilinear wings are devoted to living quarters, while the curvilinear forms used in the centre denote 'almost violently' the part dedicated exclusively to *rappresentanza*. Guarini is disinclined, says Battisti, to reconcile circular and rectilinear movement in a fluid manner; it is a reflection of his anxiety to distinguish between sacred and natural.

In the chapter in *Architettura civile* devoted to pilaster stripwork,[63] Guarini describes how he used it on the elevations at Racconigi, where 'the vertical strips are only crossed by horizontal strips, without any cornice, except the last, which is between'. Then he goes on to say: 'Here at Turin the pilaster strips are not plain, but with the cornice, and carved with stars and divided not only by the strips that run across, but also by the cornices that interrupt them, which gives a superb appearance.'

By 'here at Turin' Guarini means the Palazzo Carignano, and specifically the courtyard side of the elevations (Figs. 102 and 103). His description is exact. Pilaster strips mark out every bay, from plinth to eaves, studded all the way up with eight-pointed stars in brick, standing vertically tip to tip in what has been called 'dynamic delirious repetition'.[64] And just as Guarini says, unlike Racconigi, they are crossed by moulded cornices and string-courses. These horizontal members run across the transverse stellate strips, half-masking the stars, which peep out unmistakably below. This is a carefully calculated effect, not an accident: it is shown this way in the *Architettura civile* engraving. The impact is brilliant: what might have been awesome, even oppressive, now becomes gay and sparkling – particularly when picked out by the sun or moon, 'vibrating in the air and light'.[65]

There are, to be sure, some scholars who have sought a profound symbolic or metaphorical meaning in these stars. Manfredo Tafuri, for example, asks 'whether it is not legimate to see in the obsessive reiteration of the eight-pointed stars ... the iconological translation of that postulated homogeneity of cosmic laws and laws of civil behavior, indicated to the "Governors of the provinces"?'[66] This is typical of the modern scholarly urge to look for *concetti* and hidden meanings in Baroque architecture. But, says G. C. Argan, no one

108

102. Turin, Palazzo Carignano. Courtyard detail.

more than Guarini has affirmed the non-symbolic, non-allegorical, non-metaphorical character of architectural form.[67]

These are negative characteristics, however. Do Guarini's positive trends give us any insight? Of the Vitruvian trio, *firmitas, utilitas, venustas* – Sir Henry Wotton's 'Commodity, Firmness and Delight' – Guarini was no niggard in the third category. He expresses himself in the first Tractate of the *Architettura civile*: 'Architecture, though it depends on mathematics, is nevertheless a flattering art' (I.iii); 'Commodity, to be perfect, must be agreeable and alluring' (I.iii.5); and 'architecture has as its purpose the gratification of the senses' (I.iii.7). The conclusion to be drawn is that, for Guarini, decoration is not part of the superstructure, the adjective, as L. B. Alberti put it, to the structure's substantive, but an inseparable part of the whole scheme: everything is ornate, but nothing is decoration, which can be left off. 'Imagine,' says Contardi, 'imagine for a moment taking away, mentally, the starry decoration of the strips that frame the curtain wall of the Palazzo Carignano on the courtyard elevation. You would not get a simple reduction of the decorative effect: you would say that the whole palace would be bound to collapse, so closely do decoration and structure identify with each other.'[68] This is powerfully, if paradoxically, expressed, but its truth is self-evident. Guarini explains why his stars are there: not to point up some riddle of the universe, but 'to make a marvellous show'.[69] We may leave it at that.

The Palazzo Carignano has meant different things to different men. When Arthur Stratton came in 1927 to re-edit William J. Anderson's *The Architecture of the Renaissance in Italy*, first published thirty years before, he gave in his preface as one of the reasons for doing so his view that 'the architecture of the seventeenth century in Italy can no longer be dismissed as wholly decadent'. When it came to the Palazzo Carignano, however, Stratton's struggle to be polite was a hard one. The vaulted elliptical entrance hall, he affirms, 'justifies itself internally, but externally proclaims the restless mind of its designer', and he concludes his few lines on Guarini by allowing that he 'had the courage of his convictions, and if judged by the standard of taste accepted in his time, scored a success with this design'.

Enrico Guidoni, quoting from Guarini's own *Placita philosophica* – 'beating of the heart is the first act of life in animals' – goes on to maintain that the sense of movement in an organism, heartbeat and respiration, constitutes one of the fundamental motifs of Guarini's architecture and cites in evidence the concave and convex steps of the Palazzo Carignano, which, he says, suggest flux and reflux.[70]

Jean-Louis Vaudoyer, of the Académie Française, glad to be back in Italy after the war, found something else in the palace. 'Its great clay facade, swelling and rounded like a piece of furniture, might well make you think of some luxuriant, prodigious sideboard.'[71]

For the Englishman, therefore, it was something that was not quite cricket; for the Italian, a heartbeat; for the Frenchman, a sideboard. 'It is proved', wrote the Master, 'that there are not only various, but most contrary opinions, even in the gravest matters of faith, customs and interest; so how much more may Architecture be varied ... [when] no other reason governs it save the approval of a reasonable judgement, and a judicious eye?'[72]

103. Turin, Palazzo Carignano. Courtyard: stars and bars.

111

THE COLLEGIO DEI NOBILI

Attention has often been drawn to the two different styles employed by Palladio for the palaces he built in Vicenza: one adapted to open sites, where the spectator can stand back and take in the whole composition at once, as with the Palazzo Chiericati; and the other designed for mansions in narrow streets, such as the Palazzo Thiene.

A parallel phenomenon occurs in Turin, where the space of the Piazza Carignano permitted Guarini to mould the facade of the Palazzo Carignano in curves and counter-curves, a treatment hitherto reserved for Baroque churches. The counterpart to this, the equivalent to Palladio's planar treatment for restricted sites, is to be found in the Collegio dei Nobili, a college Guarini was commissioined by the Jesuits to design.

As has already been noted, the religious Orders were particularly active in building during the reign of Carlo Emanuele II and the regency of his widow, the Madama Reale, Maria Giovanna-Battista di Savoia-Nemours. The Theatines were at work on S. Lorenzo, the Filippini began the church of S. Filippo Neri, the largest in Turin, while the Missionarists constructed the Immacolata Concezione. All these works had designs by Guarini, and it is this activity which supplies the socio-religious context for the scheme under consideration.[73]

The Jesuits, like the Theatines, were keenly interested in education, and particularly in educating upper-class boys who in time might occupy positions of power and influence. They proposed to set up a college in Turin for the sons of patricians who lived in outlying areas of the Duchy, and who, in the absence of suitable provision at home, had habitually sought their education in neighbouring states; a favourite institute was the Collegio Farnese at Parma.

The Jesuits' proposal was approved by Madama Reale. The idea of an institute of higher education commended itself, she favoured the religious Orders, and there was a chance here to promote the development of the second enlargement of Turin. In 1678, accordingly, she gave the Jesuits a site for the college on the main piazza of the enlargement, and this was exchanged, the next year, for a larger one, extending north from the Piazza Reale (the Piazza S. Carlo) along the old ditch, all the way to Piazza Madama. The new site was very extensive, covering three city blocks. The intention was to build a house for the Order on the north block, a large church in the centre dedicated to St John the Baptist, and the college on the south block.

Guarini received the commission to design the college early in 1679, when the new site was acquired, and construction was begun in April.[74] The site was bounded by the grid system laid down by Castellamonte, and Guarini ran the main block of his ⌐ shaped plan to coincide with the building line of the 11-metre-wide street. Whatever treatment the main elevation was going to receive was bound, therefore, to be in the nature of surface incidents on a planar background, without recourse to major three-dimensional manipulation of the units (Fig. 104).

Guarini has achieved this in essence by the complex brick detailing of his window surrounds, which are picked out by the oblique rays of the sun and articulate the facade with animated patterns of light and shade. Most modern writers in referring to the Collegio dei Nobili use expressions like 'imposing mass' or 'gloomy pile'. Portoghesi talks about 'bricks dark as damp earth'.[75] This is, unfortunately, the impression the Collegio gives nowadays, obscured as it is with three centuries of incrusted grime. But the newly cleaned brickwork of the Palazzo Carignano, which was going up at the same

104. Turin, Collegio dei Nobili.

105. Turin, Collegio dei Nobili. Sketch articulation.

107. (*facing page*) Turin, Collegio dei Nobili. Ground floor detail.

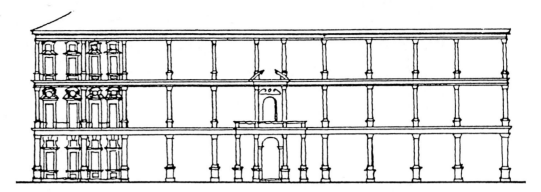

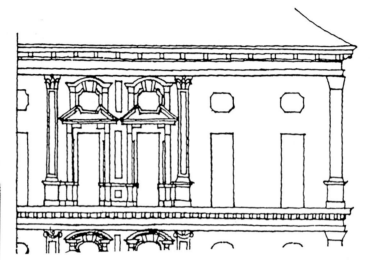

106. Turin, Collegio dei Nobili. Detail of elevation.

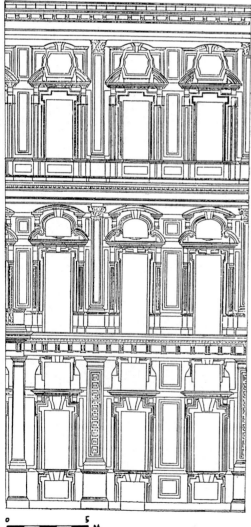

0   5
 M

time,[76] shows what a different effect must have prevailed when the college was new.

Although at first glance the building resembles a sixteenth-century town palace from the outside, the clients' brief envisaged a very different purpose. The life to be led within the college walls was not one of aristocratic pomp or mercantile affluence, but of Jesuit discipline.[77] There was thus no call here for a prestigious *piano nobile*, but for a regular series of dormitories and classrooms. Hence no use is made of a giant Order to emphasize the first floor, as at the Palazzo Carignano. There are three superimposed Orders, corresponding to the three floors of the building, each of the same height and importance, the only increases being with the plinth in the bottom Order and the cornice on the top one, crowning the whole building.

The three superimposed zones are divided by pilasters into uniform bays, each with two window units, save for the central bay, which is notably narrower, with a portal at ground floor level, and only one opening in each of the two floors above – a Mannerist form of inverted emphasis (Figs. 105 and 106).

Each window unit, on each floor, comprises one large window with a smaller window above. These units light storeys that are 9.5 metres high, and the smaller window enables intermediate floors to be constructed inside, if desired, while leaving the facade undisturbed.

Each storey has its own design of wall unit, and a gradual lightening in design may be detected, from the chunky proportions of the ground floor set, to the progressively more open formations of the two upper floors.[78] In

108. Turin, Collegio dei Nobili. Courtyard window: 'Gothic' colonnette.

the latter, the Borrominesque device is employed of enclosing the small windows – oval on the first floor, polygonal on the second – within the arms of the broken pediment of the large one.[79]

The designs of the window surrounds are Guarini specials (Fig. 107), carried out with consummate skill by outstanding craftsmen, using bricks of various dimensions, some specially made, others cut on site, and rubbed so as to appear sometimes like a moulded block, as in the curvilinear keystones over the ground floor windows.

109. (*facing page*) Turin, Collegio dei Nobili. Staircase.

116

110. Turin, Collegio dei Nobili. Ground floor plan.

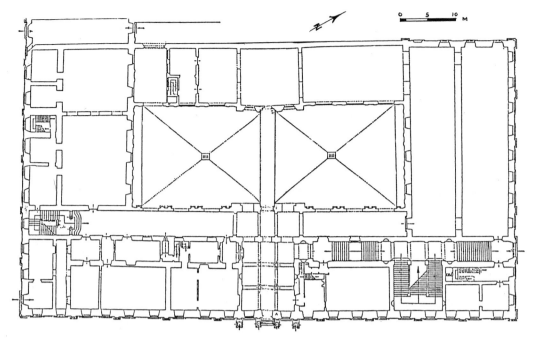

These designs are not illustrated in *Architettura civile*, but they must surely rank with the kind of detailing Guarini had in mind when he says, in another context: 'it could not be called Greek, but capricious, in the way I esteem and praise as beautiful, but not as proper'.[80] Even stranger features are used on the courtyard facade windows, including unmistakably Gothic colonnettes with shaft ring type capitals (Fig. 108), adopted later by Garove for the columns of the courtyard in the university.

The entrance gives on to a columned atrium, similar to that in the first scheme for the Palazzo Carignano (Fig. 110). This opens on to a long colonnade, terminating on the left – that is, at the south end – with a small stair that is one of Guarini's finest (Fig. 109).

At the outset of the scheme, Careri wrote, 'The Jesuit Fathers have started putting up a large building, but I don't know if their cash will suffice.'[81] His doubts were justified. Even with a grant from Madama Reale, funds ran out with no more than half the structure complete – not an uncommon Guarinian situation. It was finally completed in the nineteenth century by G. Talucchi, who built a new entrance portal and a monumental staircase. The building now houses the Academy of Sciences, and was the seat of the 1968 Guarini Conference.

Across the street from the main facade of the Collegio, the church of S. Filippo Neri was projected by the Filippini fathers, who sought a design from Guarini. Guarini supplied it, but the church was eventually built to other plans. Had Guarini's scheme been retained a third element would have been contributed to the architectural texture of what Umberto Chierici has called 'a determinant Guarinian block'.[82]

118

10 OTHER WORKS

GUARINI LIVED AND WORKED continuously in Turin from 1666 to 1681. 'Guarini in Turin', says Umberto Chierici, 'is like saying all Guarini.'[1] Turin is the scene of Guarini's longest single residence, his most fruitful activity and his burgeoning fame. It is also the site of his most important surviving buildings: S. Lorenzo, SS. Sindone and the Palazzo Carignano. We have examined these and certain other of Guarini's works in some detail. Before taking note, more briefly, of the rest of his oeuvre, it may be opportune at this point to look at some of the circumstances of the architect's life in Turin, so far as this is possible, in the light of the fortuitously surviving evidence.

Ever since the traumatic expulsion from his native city, Guarini seems to have nourished an intermittent desire to return to Modena. He wanted this most when it was the least possible, and when circumstances changed, he would go there and worry about his commitments in Turin. In the end, Modena won, though his final stay there, at the end of his life, did not exceed two years.

In 1670, when Guarini had lived in Turin for four years, and was held in great esteem by the court, he prevailed on the Duke, Emanuele Filiberto, to write to Laura, Duchess of Modena (then acting as regent for her son), seeking permission for him to return. The Duchess's reply, dated 15 November 1670, is categorical:

> It is just as necessary that Father Guarini should not return to his monastery here for the present as was the original resolution proper, that for various reasons he should leave it.[2]

Four months later, 'a good opportunity presenting itself',[3] Guarini secured permission for a short visit to Modena, and before leaving, wrote to the Duke saying that he would be back soon, if one may presume so to abridge the following obeisance:

> Fidelity, the obligations which I owe you, the extreme affection which binds me to your Royal service, my birth, the religious condition, the obedience which does not allow me to fall short in my duty, my reputation which will not permit me to leave so great an enterprise as is the Chapel of the Most Holy Shroud, and the gratitude which I owe to this House of S. Lorenzo, will oblige me to a sure and hasty return.[4]

The very next year, 1672, the Duke of Modena, Francesco II, while his mother was still acting as regent, wrote to Guarini, inviting him to return to his native land.[5] It is difficult to say for certain what caused this volte-face, but Sandonnini's conjecture seems not unlikely; namely, that the fly in the ointment all along had been the Cardinal d'Este, brother of Francesco I, who 'interfered a good deal in Theatine houses',[6] and may have preferred Castagnini to Guarini in the fatal appointment of provost of the Theatine monastery in Modena. The fact is that as soon as the Cardinal died in 1672, the Duchess permitted her son not merely to call Guarini back, but positively to urge him.

Guarini, now hard pressed with the work at S. Lorenzo and SS. Sindone, wrote to the Duke of Modena thanking him for his confidence but regretting that his royal master would not grant him 'the shortest absence'. He added, however: 'Your Serene Highness, to whose designs Fortune can place no obstacles, will know how to bend so rigorous a constancy.'[7]

The Duke of Modena wrote again, and Guarini, whose reply dated 26 August is preserved in the Archivio di Stato, Modena, suggests that Modena should write directly to Savoy, though he admits that he does not know 'how the Duke may take it', and suggests that it might be better to wait for some appropriate moment, 'such as a war',[8] when building work would stop and ducal architects be at liberty. Modena was impatient, however, and would not wait for a convenient war; he wrote at once to Savoy. Guarini was not sanguine, and expressed his misgivings in a letter to Modena, dated 26 August 1672, in which he said: 'a secret dread of my usual misfortunes speaks to my heart and makes me tremble [in anticipation] of an unfavourable reply'.

This striking phrase, slightly misquoted, is alluded to at the beginning of Portoghesi's little book on Guarini,[9] as a comment on 'the image of absorbed sadness' which looks out at us from Guarini's portrait (Fig. 1), and on the architect's life itself, 'a continuous incurable contradiction between aspiration and reality'. Henry Millon goes further than this, calling Guarini 'a tormented genius who suffered from near paranoia [and] constantly complained of being mistreated, misunderstood and unappreciated'.[10] This assessment is specifically challenged by Wittkower, who says, 'I do not know the documents to support this affirmation'.[11] There are documents, however. The circumstances connected with Guarini's precipitate flight from Turin in 1677 (see below) suggest a persecution complex. The Archbishop of Turin, in this connection, said that Guarini had 'a hypocondriac nature'.[12] And there is his outburst at a Buildings Committee meeting on 28 November 1679, in connection with a new city gate, the Porta del Po. When asked to supply futher technical details that were outstanding, 'the Reverend Father Don Guarino, Engineer of H.R.H., declared that he did not intend to apply himself any more on the City's behalf or to serve it, while for the many works carried out by him for it up till now, particularly for this gate, he had never received any recognition'.[13]

The paucity of this kind of personal record makes it difficult, at three hundred years remove, to be categorical about Guarini's temperament. Both Millon and Wittkower have a profound insight into Guarini's work and achievements; yet to Millon, 'he suffered from near paranoia', whereas to Wittkower, 'the personality which emerges from a study of his writings and his life, combines balance, moderation, constancy and breadth of view'.[14] At all events, whatever insight may be afforded into Guarini's character by the letter that has provoked this excursus, his secret dread proved well-founded, as the Duke of Savoy did not give his permission for the architect to move.

In 1677 another contretemps arose. On 19 April Guarini wrote to Monsignor Beggiamo, Archbishop of Turin, complaining of his treatment at the hands of Fr Virle, head of the Theatine house in Turin, where he had been 'receiving some pretty heavy sickeners (*non leggieri disgusti*) which oppress me and are driving me out of my mind'.[15] Since he does not think it likely that Fr Virle 'could change his style towards me', or at least convert his animus 'to a reasonable indifference', Guarini tells the Archbishop that he has asked the Marchese di San Tomaso to seek permission from Madama Reale, on his behalf, for him to return to Modena for the two years that have still to run of Virle's provostship of the Theatine house. While the Archbishop, the Marchese and the Regent were digesting the implications of this request, Guarini must have received another 'sickener', because three days later, having burned a large quantity of letters and deposited some clothes with a friend, he made off.[16]

General consternation ensued, as evidenced by the letters, notes and memos in the Archivio di Stato, all from the same week – four of them from the same day. The Prince of Carignano was alarmed, foreseeing that his new scheme at Racconigi would be adrift without a pilot, while Madama Reale was reported as saying 'several times in reply that she had more need of Fr Guerino than of Fr Virle'. In the meantime, the absconding cleric was last seen heading in the general direction of Venice, whence, the Archbishop of Turin observed drily to the Marchese di San Tomaso, 'the General himself[17] will have a job to chase him, as the nobles up there are keen to get hold of him'. In the end, Fr Virle was posted elsewhere, and Guarini was persuaded to return. 'This chap,' the Archbishop told the Marchese, 'if you deal with him gently, will do what you want of him. Any other way is a waste of time and labour.'[18]

In 1678 Guarini was back in Modena for a short visit. Writing to the Marchese di San Tomaso, he tells him he has been urged to stay and work for H.R.H. of Modena, 'whose entreaties I countered with the word I have given and my duty to Madama Reale to return quickly'.[19] He understands, however, that H.R.H. has written to Madama Reale. What has she decided?

A month later, he is writing to San Tomaso from Milan.[20] The Marchese's reply had been forwarded to him from Modena by his brother Giovanni Francesco, and from it he sees that he was right in what he had so often repeated, that Madama Reale would never let him stay in Modena. A week after this he is back in Turin, which he now seems to prefer: the Marchese's letter, detailing Madama Reale's intransigence, had given him 'no little consolation'.

In the next year, 1679, a communication from Cagnol, the Savoyan minister in Rome to the Marchese, refers to the fact that Madama Reale has undertaken to tell the Father General of the Theatines that she wants one of her own subjects to head the Theatine house in Turin, and, consequently, writes Cagnol, 'I shall advise, as Your Excellency commands me, that Father Guarini, who is at home in Turin, is one of H.R.H.'s subjects'.[21] Promptly on cue, Turin City Council, on 22 May, appointed as citizens 'Guerino de Guerini, ingegniere famosissimo', and D. Giacinto Boseggio, a distinguished preacher.[22] In fact, however, Guarini had already been appointed head of the Theatine house in Turin, as a letter of his dated 20 May to the Councillor of State, Francesco Bianchi, announces.[23] This promotion, while it must have involved Guarini in much extra administrative work, nevertheless freed him totally from the kind of annoyance to which he had been subjected under the Virle regime, and gave him the courage to accept a mass of architectural commissions, including the churches of S. Filippo and the Consolata, the Collegio dei Nobili and the Palazzo Carignano.

111. Racconigi. Pinacolo or garden pavilion.

On 9 June 1680 the Prince of Carignano, Emanuele Filiberto, appointed Guarini as his personal theologian, at an annual stipend of 400 livres, with a fulsome patent, the text of which was given on p. 82. The choice of title was probably linked to questions of protocol in connection with royal establishments. It was, of course, Guarini's architectural skill rather than his theological insights from which the Prince was anxious to continue benefiting.

At the beginning of 1681 Guarini was back in Modena,[24] working on designs for the Ducal Palace. A letter from Madame Reale to the Duke of Modena is preserved in which Guarini's presence is urgently demanded in Turin, so that work may continue under his supervision on SS. Sindone.[25] As the desired effect was not produced, Madama Reale wrote again on 8

122

May: 'the engineers here consider that there should be no further delay in resuming work, and this simply cannot be done without the presence of the said Father, who is the only one to have the direction of this work'.

Guarini duly returned to Turin, and Madama Reale, in a letter dated 5 August 1681, promised the Duke of Modena to send the architect back when work in Turin was finished.[26] There is an entry in the ducal accounts, Turin, for 15 April 1682 noting a payment of 1015 lire to Guarini for work on the high altar in S. Lorenzo.[27]

The final mention comes at the end of a letter to the Duke of Savoy from his Resident in Milan, telling him, with regret, of the death of Guarini on 6 March 1683. He had been in Milan in connection with the printing of his book *Coelestis mathematica* and had fallen ill there.[28] He was fifty-nine years of age.

Prague, S. Maria Ettinga

It would be possible, but unprofitable, to attempt a chronological treatment of Guarini's other works (that is, the buildings he designed during his time in Turin), besides those already described and analyzed in detail in the present work. Some of them are illustrated in the *Architettura civile*, some are not; some have complex archival documentation, others have none; some can be dated exactly, others can only be vaguely placed in time; some survive, some were built, but not according to Guarini's plans, some have been demolished, while others were never started. It may be more logical, therefore, to adopt another method, and start our examination of Guarini's remaining oeuvre with a look at three churches that are typologically comparable.

There is throughout Guarini's work a constantly recurring urge to design centralized buildings. An instance of a centralized secular building may be seen in the *casino* or *pinacolo* planned for dinner parties on summer evenings 'in the most delightful and huge garden of Racconigi', illustrated in the *Architettura civile* (Lastra XVI, Tractate III, our Fig. 111) and explained in III. xxiv.1. Mostly, however, Guarini's centralized buildings are churches. The rationale for this type of design is not specifically set out in the *Architettura civile*. It may perhaps be found in the general Renaissance context of the desire to build centrally planned places of worship, excited by a perceived affinity of such shapes with 'the vital force which lies behind all matter and binds the Universe together'.[29] Both S. Lorenzo and SS. Sindone are centralized structures, as are Ste Anne-la-Royale and the Padri Somaschi, which we have already examined, and S. Gaetano, Nice, S. Filippo at Casale Monferrato and the Sanctuary of Oropa, which have still to be considered.

This centralizing urge on the part of architects, seen at its zenith in Bramante's design for St Peter's, was resisted by the clergy, for whom the plan had no attraction due to its liturgical inappropriateness.[30] One Baroque response to this resistance was to elongate the circle into an oval or ellipse,[31] thereby lending the plan some feeling of directionality.

A variation on the theme of what may be called 'alternative centrality' is offered by a group of three churches designed by Guarini, where elongation, the key feature in liturgically favoured directionality, is combined with longitudinal symmetry about the cross axis (Fig. 112). This is achieved by making each end bay of the church, east and west, resemble the other on plan. Millon's unfortunate portmanteau word 'double-ended' is meant to express this concept in a nutshell, but tends instead to suggest the baffling notion of a church with one front and two backs.[32]

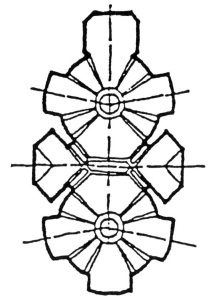

Turin, Immacolata Concezione

Turin, S. Filippo Neri

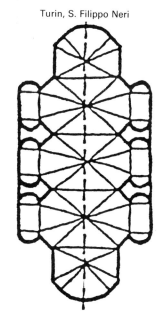

112. Diagram of three longitudinal churches displaying 'alternative centrality'.

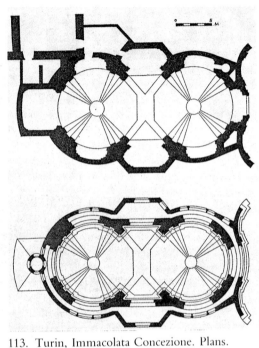

113. Turin, Immacolata Concezione. Plans.

114. Turin, Immacolata Concezione. Sections.

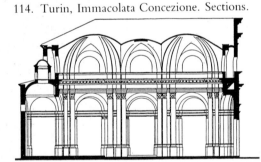

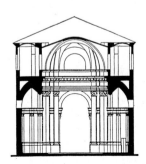

The church of the Immacolata Concezione, or the Arcivescovado, is not illustrated in the *Architettura civile*, nor is Guarini's name connected with it in contemporary documents: Giorgio Rigotti made a clean sweep through all the relevant papers in the Archivio di Stato, Archivio dei Preti della Missione, Archivio dell'Arcivescovado, Biblioteca Reale, Biblioteca Nazionale, Biblioteca Civica and Museo Civico, but the architect's name is nowhere mentioned.[33] Thirty years or more later, Luciano Tamburini examined a diary of some 267 pages in the Missionarists' archives, which goes into considerable detail about the purchase of the site and the building of the church, but is silent as to the author of the design.[34] The first attribution to Guarini was made in 1781 by O. Derossi, without stating his source for the ascription.[35] He has been followed, perhaps mechanically, by most writers since, with the notable exception of G. B. Ferrante, who contributed the article on architecture to the album *Torino 1880*. He assigned the building to Carlo Emanuele Lanfranchi, adding incidentally that it was not worth stopping to examine.

The church of the Immacolata Concezione was erected to a commission from the Missionarist Fathers, an Order founded in 1617 by St Vincent de Paul. The Missionarists were first invited to Turin in 1655 by General Emanuele Giacinto di Simiane, Marchese di Pianezza. They lived, in the first instance, scattered about in rented accommodation, but eventually built themselves a house between 1663 and 1667. In 1673 they were visited by Duke Carlo Emanuele II, who was moved to grant them a subvention to build a church of their own. Work began in the same year and, according to the diary, continued until 1677, when they ran out of funds. Nothing more was done until 1694, when a keen provost whipped in enough private donations to finish the job in two years, or at least to get it to the state where it could be used for services.[36] Eventually in 1776, when Clement XIV suppressed the Jesuits, the Missionarist Fathers took over the Jesuit church and monastery in Turin; their own house was then converted into an archbishop's palace, and the Immacolata Concezione was turned into the archbishop's chapel; hence the alternative name, the church of the Arcivescovado.

The church is laid out in three bays (Fig. 113). The west and east bays are circular, with ribbed domes, whereas the central bay is a narrow rectilinear unit, which acts in effect like a transept. It has a vault articulated by diagonal rib-bands which meet in the centre of the nave.

In a striking image, Richard Pommer pictures the church as a theatre, in which the laity, in a circular bay that is equal in size to that of the clergy's, look through the 'proscenium' of the rectilinear transept into the 'stage' of the sanctuary, dominated by a huge altar (Fig. 115).[37] But in the Immacolata Concezione, the emphasis is deliberately diffused: there is no crossing, no 'domed focus', as Millon puts it. None of the three bays is dominant, and space is interwoven in a way that looks forward to the exploits of J. B. Neumann at Vierzehnheiligen.

The circular bays contain lateral chapels, roofed by barrel vaults; the side chapels of the central bay, in contrast, are hexagonal. The remaining wall surfaces of the round bays are articulated by paired pilasters, which continue on up in the form of ribs which join in circular features that Guarini doubtless intended as oculi with lanterns over them (Fig. 114). Towards the centre of the church, the two circular bays lie open, and at ceiling level an uninterrupted vault surface runs through from the oculi to the rib-band of

116. Turin, Immacolata Concezione. Detail of vaulting.

the slightly depressed transept vault, so that the space of all three bays interpenetrates (Fig. 116).

A continuous gallery runs round the church at upper level, in a double wall construction reminiscent of Borromini's feature in the chapel of the Collegio di Propaganda Fide in Rome. Light from arched windows above the entrance, the side chapels and the main altar passes across this gallery and is filtered through the openings in the spandrels created by the dome ribs. The rectangular retrochoir placed behind the eastern bay is covered by an elliptical dome and a corresponding lantern, so that light can stream in behind the altar. In the central, rectilinear bay the vault is unlighted, but the vaults of the hexagonal chapels were to be left open to the high-level gallery, allowing light to seep down from above. These vaults, however, were closed when building was resumed in the 1690s, after Guarini's death. As the walls curve in their arcs of circles, and the ribs lean in and out, a spatial dynamic is created that would have been yet further dramatized if the architect's intentions had been respected regarding the modulation of light from its various indirect sources.

The facade has a central convexity that reflects the curved plan of the interior; it is continued on each side with the help of attached wings that reverse the central curvature into concavities (Fig. 117), in a way described by Guarini in his Treatise.[38] The diary explains that the detailing of the facade was greatly simplified from the architect's original designs.

Another example of 'alternative centrality' may be seen in the church Guarini designed for the Theatine Order in Prague dedicated to S. Maria Ettinga[39] and illustrated by three plates in *Architettura civile*. Little or nothing is known about the circumstances of the design. The engraving of the section bears the legend 'Guarino Guarini Auct. Anno 1679', Guarini's *annus mirabilis* for new commissions. Sandonnini suggested that Guarini might have been in Bohemia between 1657 and 1660, a period ascribed in the present work to his Iberian journeys. The Theatines, however, reached Prague only in 1666, invited by the Oberstburggraf, Bernard Ignaz Reichsgraf von Martinitz.[40] Though there are considerable lacunae in our knowledge of Guarini's whereabouts in his final years, it seems unlikely that he left Italy after his arrival in Turin. His design for S. Maria Ettinga was hence most probably sent to Bohemia without the architect having personally visited the site.

Like the Immacolata Concezione, S. Maria Ettinga has a three-bay layout that is symmetrical about the central cross axis (Figs. 118 and 119). But whereas the Immacolata Concezione has only a minuscule centre bay, at S. Maria Ettinga the centre bay is the largest of all. Each bay is an ellipse; those at the entrance and before the choir reflect each other closely, and are more compressed. These two compressed niches intersect on their inner face with the large central bay, the points of intersection being marked on plan by canted pier edges.

The two smaller bays are each bounded diagonally by four pilasters on angled piers. These pilasters continue up, beyond the cornice, in the form of ribs, which, as in the Immacolata Concezione, join in a circular feature that surrounds an oculus, above which a lantern is placed. In the central bay, however, the boundary features are paired columns on separate bases. Their projection onto the ceiling in the form of band-like ribs creates an elongated open hexagon, also capped by a lantern, a device that Guarini had used before at Ste Anne-la-Royale. The Borrominian antecedents of this basketwork feature have already been discussed.

Each of the three major units of the nave has an oval chapel niche on each

127

side, into which the major ovals of the bays powerfully intrude; a counter-penetration is effected in each case by the line of the altar rail, which mirrors in each case the line of the niche's wall.

A pair of inset columns on the entrance wall of the first bay is reflected by corresponding columns at the entrance to the retrochoir in the far bay, where they are linked up with a pattern of other symmetrically disposed columns that may have supported a baldachin-type feature over the altar.

The curved facade, with its central convex and lateral concavities, has affinities with Guarini's churches in Paris and Lisbon; the inspiration derives ultimately from Borromini's S. Carlino.

The Theatines built a church in Prague, but not to Guarini's design. The

117. Turin, Immacolata Concezione. Facade.

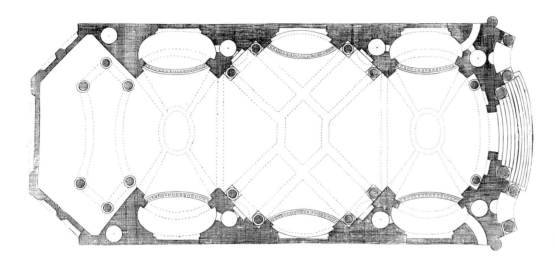

118. Prague, S. Maria Ettinga. Plan.

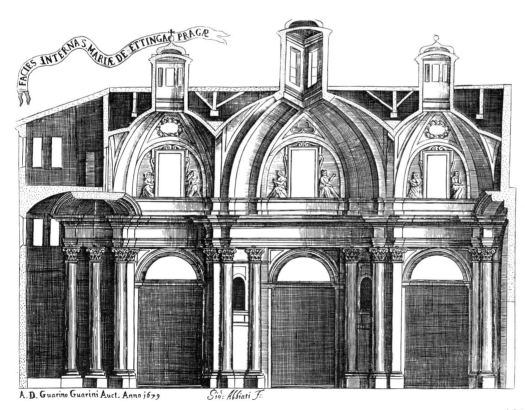

A. D. Guarino Guarini Auct. Anno 1679   Gio: Abbiati F.

119. Prague, S. Maria Ettinga. Section.

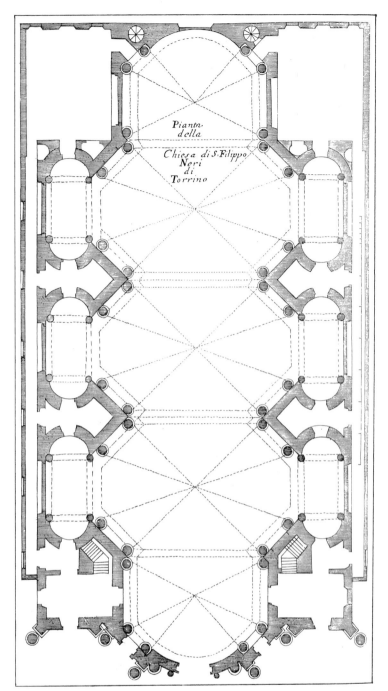

120. Turin, S. Filippo Neri. Plan.

121. Turin, S. Filippo Neri. Elevation.

Baroque church in Neruda Street which bears the name of Our Lady beside the Theatines (Kostel Panny Marie u Kajetánů) has a plan in the shape of a Greek cross, and an elevation that seems to owe a good deal to Flaminio Ponzio's Acqua Paola in Rome. It was built between 1691 and 1717. The architect's name is uncertain, but recent Czech research suggests the French architect, trained in Rome, Jean Baptiste Mathey.[41]

The third of Guarini's longitudinal churches, symmetrical about its cross axis, is that of S. Filippo Neri in Turin, illustrated by a plan, section and elevation in *Architettura civile*. Pommer calls it 'the end point in [Guarini's] development of the longitudinal church'.[42]

As is the case with S. Maria Ettinga in Prague, there is indeed a church of S. Filippo Neri in Turin, but it is not Guarini's either. The building history of S. Filippo is very involved, and has been examined in minute detail by a

130

number of distinguished scholars, whose work it would be pointless to duplicate. The most important studies are by Giovanni Chevalley[43] and Richard Pommer,[44] while Luciano Tamburini has devoted to S. Filippo two densely documented chapters of his book on the churches of Turin.[45]

The congregation of the Oratory of S. Filippo Neri was founded in Turin in 1649,[46] and after the usual period of struggle, discomfort and inconvenience, was granted a site in 1675 by Madama Reale for a church, convent and oratory, which were to form one of the grandest ecclesiastical complexes in the new enlargement of Turin.[47]

The Filippini examined a number of projects submitted for the proposed scheme, and chose that of Antonio Bettino,[48] a surveyor from Lugano who had worked on the pre-Guarinian scheme for SS. Sindone. Work was put in hand on Bettino's project for the convent and oratory, and the latter was opened for services by the autumn of 1678.[49] At this stage, little more than the substructure of Bettino's church had been built. It was of an old-fashioned design, a Latin cross, nave and transepts, with side aisles and chapels joined to the nave by low vaults.

'The choice of the Luganese', observes Tamburini, 'at a time when Guarini was intensely active in Turin – and a mere stone's throw from the new church – may cause surprise: clearly, however, the monks, attached at first to traditional modes, were conquered by the Theatine's ideas ... and turned to him for a more grandiose and audacious scheme.'[50]

Unlike the other longitudinal-symmetrical schemes – the Immacolata Concezione and S. Maria Ettinga – S. Filippo Neri's three bays are identical (Fig. 120): 'three identical elongated octagons follow each other down the nave, like scientific diagrams for a chain molecule'.[51] Here there are no curves, no interpenetrations and no variation in size between the centre bay and the other two. Does this make it early or late in Guarini's development? It is intriguing to study the reaction of the experts. For Anderegg-Tille, pursuing her path of rigid categorization by spatial type,[52] it must be early, because 'the interpenetration of forms has not yet begun'.[53] For Richard Pommer, the same facts inspire exactly the opposite interpretation.[54] For him, it must be the last in the series: all passion spent, all the major curves and contrasts eliminated, 'the church has become completely static'.

In my view, the attempt to plot a line of stylistic development in Guarini's work, or to date undocumented designs on the basis of style, is a delusion. As in the vertical sections through his centralized buildings where one zone gives no hint of what may be expected in the next above, so in Guarini's plans: one undated scheme can give no reliable hint as to its chronology or developmental context by relating it to another. This explains the wide divergencies in scholarly opinion that are occasionally to be met with. Thus, Portoghesi dates the Padri Somaschi in Messina to Guarini's mid-period, 1670;[55] Wittkower, on the other hand, places it at the outset of the architect's career, in 1660.[56]

S. Filippo Neri, which was designed by Guarini to stand on some of the existing foundation walls of Bettino's building, is almost completely symmetrical about its cross axis. The three main bays are identical, and the vestibule reflects the presbytery in shape. Nave bay is divided from nave bay by cranked transverse arches that spring from diagonal piers which thrust into the nave space, and which, together with the inclined arches, emphasize the distinction, even the autonomy, of each bay. The curious octagons, so strongly marked off from each other, would have produced a powerful visual effect: one of unrest and tension, in the opinion of Daria de Bernardi

131

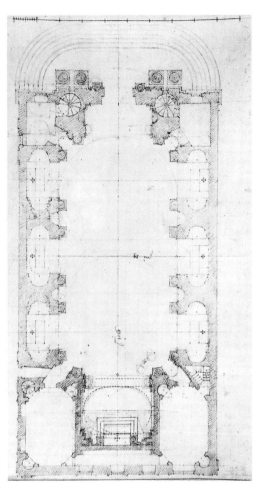

122. Borromini's first draft for S. Carlino, Rome.

Ferrero.[57] This is perhaps debatable. It seems likely, though, that the insistent repetition of these identical bays, however articulated, would have set up a strong impetus of movement towards the altar.

Each nave bay is flanked by a pair of side chapels (Fig. 123), rectangular in plan, as demarcated by four columns of a minor Order, and with a semicircular apse at each short end. It was the shape of these side chapels, linked to three identical nave bays, that provoked Sedlmayr into saying that Guarini had 'worked up' Borromini's first draft for S. Carlino (Fig. 122) to produce the plan for S. Filippo.[58] The suggestion is ingenious, but the thesis would be difficult to sustain. Borromini's draft is for a hall church with side chapels; Guarini's scheme is far more highly articulated, with its octagonal bays, diagonal piers and inclined transverse arches with their sharp edges contributing to the division between space and space. Besides, it may be asked, how would Guarini get a sight of this discarded draft, unless he was on intimate terms with Borromini? This relationship has in fact been postulated by Portoghesi,[59] but without the least evidence being adduced. In any case, why should an architect such as Guarini, at the height of his powers, need to fall back on the rejected design of an older architect? In this connection, it may be relevant to quote the remarks of Daria de Bernardi Ferrero, who observes that the curious shapes on Guarini's plan, 'carved out in the walling of the intermediate piers' between the side chapels, recall analogous chambers in late Roman buildings and fifth-century martyria; not that Guarini ever knew those structures, she adds, but they are 'the expression of analogous wishes in art, intent on seeking magical effects of space and light, anxious to overcome traditional values; equal creative urges, similar spiritual unrest, lead to comparable solutions'.[60] These 'analogous wishes in art' (*analoghe volontà di arte*) may perhaps be regarded as special cases of Alois Riegl's famous conception of *Kunstwollen*. At all events, Professor de Bernardi Ferrero's moderate views are far more reasonable in tone than Sedlmayr's abrupt and charmless dogmatism.

In the *Architettura civile* Guarini made the point 'that the facade and the main door shall not be less than the other parts' of a building.[61] The tradition of Emilia, however, which was Guarini's native province, was to have

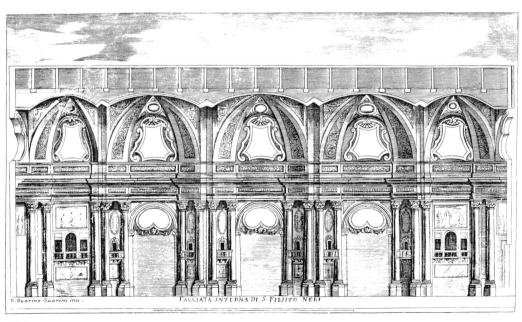

123. Turin, S. Filippo Neri. Section.

modest church fronts, with a restrained use of the major Order and without excessive display of pediments, statues and niches. This practice was followed by Guarini, 'perhaps in an unconscious recollection of his youth'.[62] The only degree of monumentality he achieved in this field is at the Annunziata, Messina,[63] and at S. Filippo Neri, Turin (Fig. 121). Here the minor Order of columns at the upper level seems to be organized on a different system from that below. It was this facade that Milizia singled out for special obloquy, in the venemous article on Guarini in his *Memorie*. He referred to it as 'most uncouth, hidden under a forest of columns and pilasters'.

The church of S. Filippo Neri is the subject of one of the most curious myths in art history, namely, that it was the church built to Guarini's design that had the misfortune to collapse before it was finished. This canard is repeated by the gravest authorities, starting with P. Toesca, who branded Guarini, because of it, as a 'somewhat inaccurate builder' (*poco accurato costruttore*)[64] who built the church in such a way that it was quickly ruined when the dome collapsed. Wittkower appears to say the same,[65] as does Anderegg-Tille.[66] That the church of S. Filippo Neri in Turin collapsed on 26 October 1714 there can be no doubt.[67] What is questionable is whether this was the church that Guarini designed. According to Soleri, what did the damage was the collapse of an enormous dome subsequently described in an early nineteenth-century guidebook as having been 'built to rival St Peter's in Rome'. This clearly has not the remotest connection with Guarini's scheme, whose modest tent-vaults were not even crowned with lanterns.

The trouble lay in the fact that, though Chevalley was able to turn up a mass of documents showing the intermittent pursuit of building activities between 1679 and 1714, he could find no reference to a change of plan or a change of architect.[69] Richard Pommer, however, working in the Biblioteca Nazionale, Turin, discovered a volume of drawings, attributed to Juvarra, and 'misplaced during World War II', which shows a series of drawings for a scheme for S. Filippo that evidently replaced Guarini's (Fig. 124). This was the project, dating from shortly after Guarini's death in 1683, which collapsed in ruins in 1714. On stylistic grounds, which Pommer sets out in detail, it seems likely that the author was the Swiss engineer Michelangelo Garove, who took over the site supervision of the works when Guarini left Turin.[70] In its turn, Garove's scheme, when the rubble was cleared away, gave way to Juvarra's, 'one of the coolest buildings of the Piedmontese Baroque'.[71]

Why Guarini's scheme was abandoned by the Filippini is a matter of conjecture. It may have been occasioned, Pommer hazards, 'simply by the desire – and the prospect of funds – to erect a grander church'.[72] Whatever the reason, it marks the early eclipse of Guarini's influence in Piedmont (except for lesser ornaments) in the half century following his death.

Guarini's longitudinal churches, which we have just examined, with their emphasis on the nave, derive from a traditional north Italian type with a sequence of domed units. What Guarini made of those quiet but stately interiors was something individual to himself. He employed jutting piers, 'like the prows of ships', as Chevalley puts it, as a dynamic substitute for the traditional use of static columns, to divide up the nave bays; while the latter are extended or inflated into complex polygonal shapes, remote from the placid volumetry of the source material. At the same time they are accompanied by the withdrawn spaces of the side chapels, whose restricted access and intimate atmosphere were designed to foster private devotion.

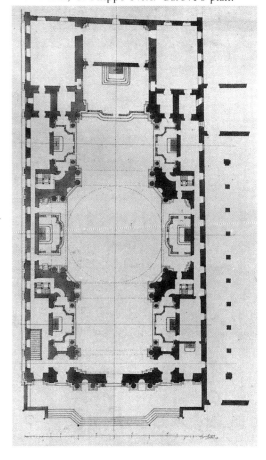

124. Turin, S. Filippo Neri. Garove's plan.

133

'Our Turin', wrote Pietro Buscalioni in 1938, 'would still be able to boast a good number of medieval churches, if the fury of demoliton had not caused a considerable part of them to disappear, and if the mania for innovation, which spread amongst us in the seventeenth and eighteenth century, had not completely de-natured and bastardized the rest.'[73]

One of the chief victims of this anti-conservationist spirit was the ancient church of S. Andrea, a place of particular devotion to the Torinesi, because of a shrine it housed to the Madonna Consolata. Founded in the year 942, S. Andrea survived as a complete, if somewhat decrepit, Romanesque basilica until the late seventeenth century, when its incumbent, D. Michelangiolo di S. Bernardo, noting the evidence of a building boom all round him (not least promoted by the religious Orders, as we have seen), determined to make his own contribution.[74] Approaching Madama Reale through the Princess Lodovica, whose confessor he was, he proposed a scheme, in the year 1675, for rebuilding the church in what he conceived to be a more fashionable style.[75] Madama Reale agreed with the idea of a rebuild, but her notion of modern architecture did not coincide with that of the abbot's. She turned to Guarini for a scheme.

The project that Guarini worked out for the Consolata was engraved, in the form of a plan and section, but the plate was not included in either the *Dissegni d'architettura* or the *Architettura civile*. Buscalioni first published it in his book in 1938 (Fig. 126), from a copy in the Archivio di Stato, Turin, and it has been reproduced several times since, from other surviving examples. The plan, basically a transverse oval nave abutting on to a hexagon, has four massive piers, housing stairs and other features, marked (via letter coding) 'part already built' (*parte già fatta*). In the absence of any relevant documentation, it is not possible to be categoric as to what this implies. All that remains of the medieval church is the apse (cut off by a wall from the present church), a crypt underneath it, and the campanile. These features, together with a sworn and signed written description of the old church made in 1705,[76] enabled Buscalioni to attempt a sketch-plan of the medieval church (Fig. 125), showing a long nave leading to a high-level presbytery ending in an apse. This was flanked by an aisle on each side, separated from the nave by the usual nave arcade.

If we impose the Guarinian scheme, or its early eighteenth-century development, on the site thus indicated, we may get some inkling as to what Guarini had to cope with. Fig. 127 shows Guarini's four great piers (marked on his own plan as already built) superimposed on the skeleton outline of a typical longitudinal Baroque nave, where they would constitute the dividers (with others of the same) between a series of side chapels. This Baroque nave represents the putative start made by the abbot of S. Andrea on his own scheme, peremptorily superseded, at Madama Reale's command, by Guarini's.

The abbot's long nave[77] was converted by Guarini into an oval by placing a hemicycle at each end of the rectangular central segment – the segment bounded by the ready-made piers. The rectangular centre bay is covered with a barrel vault pierced by lunettes, while the *nicchioni* at the ends are roofed by ribbed half-domes, likewise pierced with lunettes.

The walls which bear these roofs are not, however, the outer perimeter walls of the building, but an inner line of masonry which rises up some distance behind them (Fig. 128), borne on an entablature supported in its turn

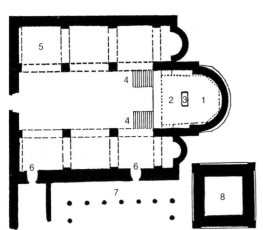

125. Turin, S. Andrea. Plan of Romanesque church. (1) Crypt. (2) High level presbytery. (3) High altar. (4) Access stairs to presbytery. (5) Chapel of the Consolata. (6) Doors towards cloisters. (7) Cloister arcade. (8) Campanile.

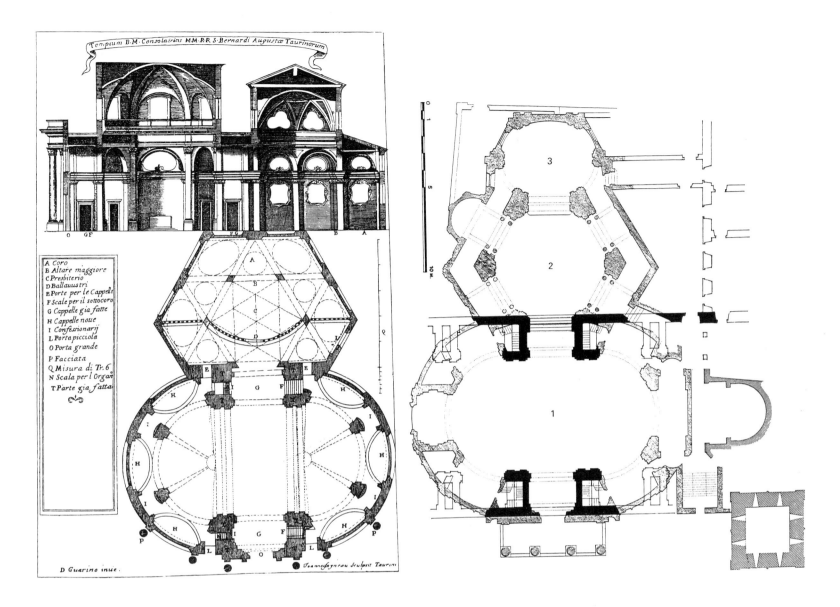

126. Turin, La Consolata. Section and plan.

127. Turin, La Consolata. Guarini's plan, plus Juvarra's 1729 choir, superimposed on Abate M. di S. Bernardo's 1675 baroque rebuild.

by a colonnade. In the straight stretch, the arches of this colonnade spring from pilasters·butting on to the two ready-made piers, but in the *nicchioni*, at each end, two intermediate wedge-shaped piers are provided to support the arches, and these arches therefore curve outwards as they rise, parallel with the perimeter walls at lower level. These wedge-shaped piers serve, in the *zona terrena*, as the rear walls of two radiating confessionals situated in the low-rise perimeter area of each *nicchione*, and these, in their turn, are inserted between three radiating chapels.

The medieval church, and the abbot's proposed Baroque successor to it, had their entrance in the west front, as tradition demanded. Guarini switched this entrance to the middle of the south side, between a pair of the existing piers. Directly opposite, on the other side of the straight central bay, is the entrance to the sanctuary, between the other pair of existing piers (Fig. 129). The sanctuary was designed by Guarini as a separate structure with a different roofing system: a kind of withdrawn space where the more esoteric rites of the Church were performed, a reserved space that would constitute a pole of attraction and spiritual concentration.

Whereas the nave of S. Andrea is oval, the sanctuary of the Consolata is laid out as a hexagon, again with a high-rise central section, borne on a

135

AUGUSTAE TAURINORUM CONSOLATRIX ET PATRONA

128. Turin, La Consolata. Facade.

hexagonal cornice supported by six arches rising from diamond-shaped piers, two of them abutting the great existing piers. As shown in Guarini's engraving, the high-rise hexagon had a complex panelled vault supported on six pendentives. Around the central hexagon, at *zona terrena* level, ran a low-rise ambulatory, roofed with an alternation of circular and oval domes, to correspond with the shape of the infill panels to be covered. The two major spaces of nave and sanctuary contrasted with each other in shape, directionality and lighting. The layout recalls in some respects the Mannerist church of the Annunziata in Parma (Fig. 130), which abuts a side-entered oval with an axially placed sanctuary on the other side.

Work on the Consolata began on 2 November 1678 and finished in 1703.[78] Augusta Lange has brought to light an unsigned, undated drawing of the plan, formerly lodged in the Quirinal archives, but since 1971 back at the

136

129. Turin, La Consolata. Entrance to Sanctuary.

Archivio di Stato in Turin, which shows a considerably beefed-up version of the structure, as compared with the engraved plate (Fig. 131).[79] The wedge-shaped piers of the *nicchioni* have been filled out, while in the sanctuary the slender diamond-shaped pillars have been encased in masses of masonry and flanked by pairs of columns. This transforms Guarini's delicate web of space into something far more stolid, with proportions that are more Carolingian than Baroque, let alone Guarinian.

Guarini left Turin a bare two years after work began on the Consolata, and died in 1683. We know, from the correspondence that has been quoted between Madama Reale and the Duke of Modena, that Guarini's personal supervision was regarded as a matter of urgent necessity when one of his 'specials' was being built. Antonio Bertola took over the direction of the work at the Consolata (and at SS. Sindone, S. Filippo Neri and the Palazzo

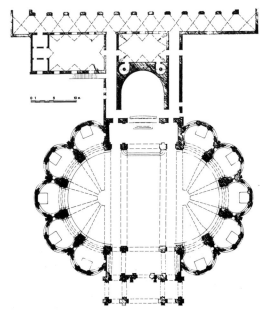

130. Parma, Annunziata. Plan.

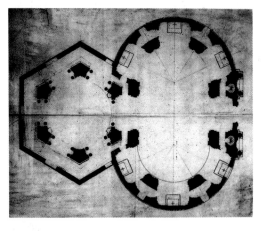

131. Turin, La Consolata. 'Fortified' plan.

132. Turin, La Consolata. Actual plan.

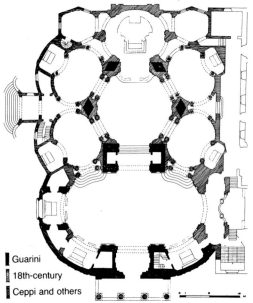

Guarini
18th-century
Ceppi and others

Carignano) after Guarini died. In the absence of the Master, it was perhaps he who produced the stolid details that could be relied on to hold the vaults up.

In 1729 Filippo Juvarra added a new oval choir to the sanctuary (No. 3 on Fig. 127), and between 1899 and 1904 Count Carlo Ceppi replaced the whole ambulatory of the hexagon with a ring of oval chapels (Fig. 132). The present florid décor is by Count Antonio Vandone, 'vaguely inspired by publications on Versailles and the French hôtels'[80] that were in vogue in his day.

Guarini's engraving does not show a facade. The plan indicates a portal framed by two great columns, with a further two spaced out on each side, following the curved line of the external wall. The portico shown in Fig. 128 dates from 1855.

The final group of churches that remains to be examined is one in which Guarini again explores the centralized theme. The Theatines of the city of Vicenza[81] invited Guarini to produce a design for rebuilding the church of S. Stefano, which was going to be rededicated to S. Gaetano Thiene, the founder of their Order. Guarini's plans, in the event, were rejected, and others sought from Rome, but the architect's intentions are recorded in two plates that are featured in *Architettura civile* (Figs. 133 and 134).

Guarini's scheme is based upon a Greek cross, built up of four ellipses that deeply intersect a central open space. Four circular satellite chapels fill in the corner spaces. Where the ellipses touch, four great piers stand, each consisting of a slender masonry core hidden by six free-standing columns that support a fully articulated trabeation and thence the four splayed inner arches of the oval arms of the cross. On these arches rests a cornice ring surmounted by a balustrade. The spectator, looking up from the floor of the church, would have perceived this tight ring fixed between the four splayed arches of the impost, and would have presumed that their projecting outline was designed to withstand the thrust from the spherical vault, seen through the ring. No such thing, however; the cornice ring is merely an oculus. The real weight of the drum and dome is revealed by Guarini's section to be resting on the vaults of the lateral spaces. The oculus frames the view of a frescoed inner dome, which in turn is opened up in the centre to reveal a vision of an even more remote heavenly glory, lit from concealed sources.

This use of a truncated dome was featured once before in Guarini's oeuvre, at Ste Anne-la-Royale, where, it was suggested, the inspiration may have been François Mansart's Church of the Visitation in Paris, and the stairwell at Blois. Guarini's contemporary Christopher Wren (who visited his site in Paris) drew on the same sources when designing the internal effects provided by the dome of St Paul's.

A more modest version of this 'nine spot' plan had been designed some years before[82] for the church of S. Filippo Neri at Casale Monferrato (Fig. 135), a small town forty miles east of Turin. In this design, the central space is not compressed by the others, as at Vicenza, but, on the contrary, it invades them. The four 'piers' that define it are also bunches of columns, but this time with no masonry infill behind them. They form part, in effect, of the central circular space, the oval arms, and the circular satellite chapels in the corners.

Elliptical chapels around a central space recur in the small church of S. Gaetano (Figs. 136 and 137), designed for the Theatines in the town of Nice, then a possession of the House of Savoy ('Nizza'). Guarini's church was never built: the times were inauspicious. For over twenty years, from 1691

138

133. Vicenza, S. Gaetano. Section and part plan.

134. Vicenza, S. Gaetano. Elevation.

135. Casale Monferrato, S. Filippo Neri. Section, part plan, etc.

136. Nice, S. Gaetano. Section and part plan.

137. Nice, S. Gaetano. Elevation and part plan.

onwards, Nice was at the centre of hostilities between France and Piedmont.[83] The church of S. Gaetano to be seen in Nice today was erected to the designs of Bernardo Vittone, on another site, in the eighteenth century. We have no date for Guarini's scheme; the most diverse suggestions have been confidently put forward, on stylistic and other grounds, from very early to very late in the architect's career.[84]

Guarini's centralized design is this time based on a pentagon inscribed in a circle, with one vertex pointed towards the entrance. In each side of this figure an arched opening is disposed giving on to a semicircular chapel niche, except for the side facing the entrance, where the arch frames the main altar, a breakthrough into real space involving a columnar screen, as at S. Lorenzo, though at Nice the retrochoir is a simple rectangle flanked by sacristies.

This zone is closed off at the top by a cornice that follows all the incidents of the perimeter. Rising over this feature in correspondence with the pilasters framing the niches in the *zona terrena*, five intersecting arches span in such a way as to frame a smaller pentagon, from the internal angles of which a further set of ribs takes off to create a five-pointed star dome. As these ribs intersect in their turn, they create an even smaller open pentagon at their centre, on which a five-sided lantern sits.

The piers at *zona terrena* level are located between the niches, where their angles are articulated as pilasters. They are real piers, not bunches of columns as in the previous two churches, and they carry out their traditional function without any statical sleight of hand.

The exterior of the church shows the relationship of the successive zonal polygons to each other with great clarity, in a characteristically Guarinian telescopic pyramid. The entrance is placed between two of the apsidal chapels, whose outlines produce an undulating facade.

The apotheosis of Guarini's centralizing pagodas is reached with the

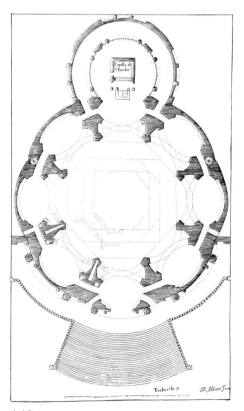

138. Oropa, Sanctuary. Plan.

139. Oropa, Sanctuary. Part elevation and section.

140

Sanctuary of Oropa, illustrated in two plates of *Architettura civile* (Figs. 138 and 139), one of them bearing the date 1680.[85] Its total geometrical regularity makes it the equivalent in the field of centralized churches to S. Filippo Neri, Turin, among the longitudinal ones.

Guarini appears to have been asked for a scheme to enlarge the old basilica built in 1600 at Oropa, the most frequented pilgrim resort in Piedmont. He advised against it, because 'you could never modernize that church',[86] and went on to produce his own scheme, which was not executed either.

The plan, described by Sacheverell Sitwell as 'only just not circular', is based on a series of superimposed octagons and rectangles. The *zona terrena* features eight oval side chapels separated by large triangular piers. One of the ovals serves as an entrance lobby; its counterpart on the other side of the nave acts as a link to the circular choir. The bulge of their rear walls produces the undulation seen on the elevation at its lowest level (Fig. 140).

The structure rises from zone to zone, sometimes octagonal in horizontal section, sometimes square, the transitions being achieved by trumpet squinches of idiosyncratic design. These internal changes are masked to some extent on the exterior, which shows a succession of diminishing octagons, ending in an eight-sided lantern.

Guarini's terse but packed plan has, needless to say, excited the metaphysicians. To Enrico Guidoni, the sight of it on paper reminds him of a fat man, or, as he puts it, shows latent anthropomorphism.[87] Marcello Fagiolo, on the other hand, points out that 'the presbytery corresponds by placing and significance, to the figure of the sun in the representation of lunar phases'.[88]

A different approach, mathematical rather than philosophical, is represented by Henry Millon's attempt to plot the geometrical bases of the Oropa plan, showing how 'a concentric series of squares and octagons constitutes the basic element that defines the central space, the position of the piers, their dimensions, the entrance of the chapels and the double order above the central space' (Fig. 141).[89] Neither universe of discourse precludes the other, and both conspire to prove that the study of Guarini's thought and creativity is a long and complex task.[90]

140. Oropa, Sanctuary. Sketch of exterior, based on Guarini's details, by Daria de Bernardi Ferrero.

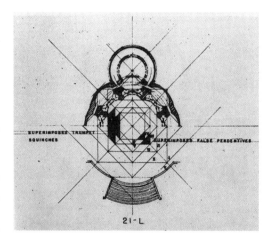

141. Oropa, Sanctuary. Millon's attempt at a geometrical analysis.

A set of drawings for the church of S. Maria d'Araceli in Vicenza was discovered in the Vatican archives by Professor Portoghesi and published in 1957.[91] These drawings (Figs. 142 and 143) were executed by 1695 by Gaetano Farine and bear the name of Guarini as the architect. The design is a Greek cross set in an oval, with the main space defined by four major piers. Ancillary spaces, high on the axes and low behind the piers, line the walls in parallel with the outer oval; they are defined by free-standing columns and roofed by cross-vaults. The nave itself is covered with a ribbed dome/drum, surmounted by a lantern. The actual building in Vicenza, fully illustrated and discussed by Portoghesi, departs in several details from Farine's drawings, with a consequent loss in tension between the direction of the axes.

Professor Portoghesi has also published a fully illustrated account of the Tabernacle of S. Nicolò, Verona, represented by a plate in *Architettura civile* that reproduces the monument 'with a few unimportant variations due to the engraver's lack of skill' (Fig. 144).[92] The three-tier structure is a 'diaphragm' type of high altar, which separates the choir and presbytery. It is concave in

142. Vicenza, S. Maria d'Araceli. Section.

143. Vicenza, S. Maria d'Araceli. Plan.

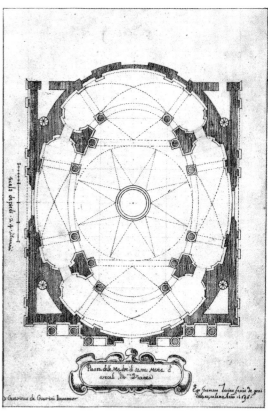

144. Verona, S. Nicolò. Tabernacle.

plan, with a convex *edicola* inserted at ground level in a manner reminiscent of Borromini's device on the facade of S. Carlino. Typical Baroque use is made of free-standing columns – spiral at the first upper level, smooth elsewhere – to frame statues and architectural features, and to articulate staggered projections at the lowest level. S. Nicolò of Bari, to whom the church is dedicated, gives his blessing from a niche at the first upper level. The general disposition and pyramidal build-up of the scheme is in some ways a more plastic realization of the Messina elevation, without the functional constraints involved in building a real church facade.

The church of the Madonna di Loreto in Montanaro, attributed to Guarini by Eugenio Olivero, lacks the ingenious planning and daring structures that are the mark of the Master.[93] According to A. Dondana, it was begun by a *capomastro* named Giovanni Battista Zanetto di Pralungo in 1677.[94] His designs were given to Guarini in 1680, who is said to have reworked them. There is a hint of the plan arrangement of the Consolata, but nothing in the scheme as a whole that would justify attributing it to Guarini.

———

In Guarini's *Dissegni d'architettura*, of 1686, there is a plate of a country house bearing a dedication to Count Francesco Solari, first equerry to Madama Reale (Fig. 145). This dedication, omitted in the version of the engraving published in *Architettura civile*, enables the building to be identified as the Castello di Govone. Govone was a fief of a branch of the Solaro family, and Francesco Ottavio Solari was invested with it in Guarini's lifetime.[95]

Unlike Racconigi, the house at Govone did not inherit any previous structures to which it had to defer. It is placed on the crest of a low hill and is

142

intended to be viewed from afar and from all sides. Although the most elaborate treatment is reserved for the courtyard front, all facades are regarded as important.

The plan is U-shaped, and may be regarded as a variation on the Piedmontese hollow square type, with wing ends returned forwards or outwards to make a greater impression, as at Racconigi. At Govone the vaulted *gran salone* gives immediately onto the courtyard, via a twin flight of stairs. The courtyard in its turn descends to the park by splayed ramps that enfold an ornamental pond and a fountain. These ramps are shown in elevation, but there is no room for them on the plan, which has been moved down uncomfortably near to the bottom of the sheet to make way for a large expanse of cloudy sky over the building at the top.

The courtyard elevation between the projecting wings is enlivened by a pair of serlianas, which front two little terraces flanking the *gran salone*. There appears to be some conflict in scale here: the serlianas, which open onto such small areas on plan, are inordinately large when compared with the fenestration of the adjoining bays. The other facades are articulated by the use of plain pilaster strips, in the way we have seen at Racconigi.

Guarini's involvement with the design of a new city gate, the Porta del Po, has already been noted. As shown in the *Architettura civile* (Fig. 146), it comprised two V-shaped receding walls, articulated with a Tuscan Order, joined by a central convex bay in which the gate was set. Bull-headed figures ('Taurini' – a pun on Turin) disport themselves on the attic and in a concave bay over the gateway that counterpoints the central bulge.

An engraving in *La sontuosa illuminazione della città di Torino* (1737) (Fig. 147) shows that in execution the design was considerably beefed up by banding the columns, pilasters and piers, in the manner of Sanmichele's city gates at Verona. The somewhat effete Taurini were replaced by an enlarged attic featuring historical reliefs. Whether Guarini was responsible for these modifications, it is not possible to say. The gate was demolished in 1813, during the second French occupation of Turin.

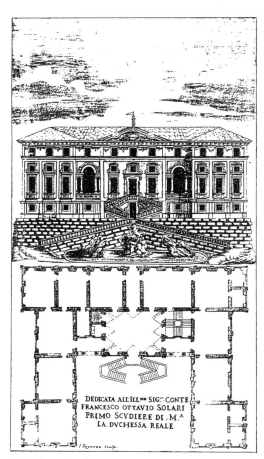

145. Castello di Govone. Elevation and plan.

146. Turin, Porta del Po. Elevation.

147. Turin, Porta del Po (detail from *Sontuosa illuminazione della città di Torino per le nozze di Carlo Emanuele III*, 1737).

143

11   OTHER WRITINGS

Guarini's literary activity began in 1660, with *La pietà trionfante*. It was continued with a book every other year, as he pursued his studies of geometry, astronomy, fortifications and architecture. Death overtook him in Milan, where he had gone to see *Coelestis mathematica* through the press.

Each of Guarini's books, says Wittkower, is a *summa*, an attempt to pour the whole of contemporary knowledge on a given topic into a single volume.[1] Thus *Placita philosophica* is a *summa* of philosophical learning gathered into a coherent system, while *Euclides adauctus* was an attempt to digest everything that could be known about mathematics. *Euclides adauctus & methodicus mathematicaque universalis*, a massive folio of over 700 pages printed in double column, was published at Turin in 1671, with a dedication to Carlo Emanuele II, Duke of Savoy. It was reprinted five years later.

The scientific climate of thought in seventeenth-century Europe had produced several universal compendia of mathematics in Guarini's lifetime – the *Cursus mathematicus*, for example, by the Belgian Jesuit Gaspare Scott – but these works were virtually unknown in Italy. Guarini expressly states in his preface that he intends *Euclides adauctus* to be for the use and convenience of the Italians, who have not hitherto had such a resource available. He also uses his preface, curiously enough, to express his regret at the action of a former pupil, Fr Bonifacio Bagatta, in attacking, rejecting or censuring, in a particularly insidious manner, various propositions in *Placita philosophica*,[2] though as far as unfavourable critics in general were concerned, he adds: 'Let them get on with it, I don't care. I've got used to that kind of thing.'[3]

Guarini's book contains thirty-five treatises on different aspects of geometry, theoretical and applied, including a new exposition of the twelve books of Euclid. As always, Guarini quotes his sources; his reference to Desargues, whose book on projective geometry was first published in Paris in 1639, reveals him as probably the only Italian architect who had studied this work.[4] The 32nd treatise of Guarini's work deals, in terms of descriptive geometry, with the projection on plan of lines that derive from the intersection with each other of the sphere, the cone and the cylinder, and the development on plan of curves of double curvature:[5] in a word, the theoretical exposition of the effects achieved in practice by Guarinian vaults. He was to return to the same theme in the chapters in *Architettura civile* devoted to *ortografia elevata* and *ortografia gettata*.

The 24th treatise of *Euclides adauctus* is devoted to conic sections. Chasles draws attention to an extremely simple demonstration Guarini uses, which applies to three conic sections at the same time: a demonstration of the property of constant ratio of the products of segments made on parallel chords, which had hitherto always demanded a knowledge of several preliminary proposals. Guarini was modestly proud of such contributions he was able to make to the actual advancement of mathematical knowledge: 'we too have raised a stone', he wrote, 'and have slightly advanced the old frontiers of mathematics'.[6]

In contrast to *Euclides adauctus*, a massive tome intended for the cognoscenti, Guarini brought out a small octavo volume in 1674, printed in Turin, his *Il modo di misurare le fabbriche*, which was of purely practical intent. It was to enable builders and subcontractors to measure up the work they had done, so that they could put in their accounts for payment, and to permit architects and builders' clerks to take off quantities from drawings, to enable them to prepare estimates.

The book, which is appropriately dedicated to Carlo Emanuele's minister of finance,[7] starts off with some instruction in elementary mathematics, and then sets out to deal with 'bodies and surfaces of all types, provided they have some sort of regularity'. Simple rules are set out to enable builders, tradesmen and craftsmen to cope with the measurement of parts of buildings of steadily increasing complexity,[8] some of which, the author claims, 'have hitherto boasted the title of being immeasurable'.

We have already noted the regularity with which work on Guarini's major schemes in Turin were measured and paid for, though the archives show only few instances of Guarini personally measuring the various labours. *Il modo di misurare* gives us some insight into how this was achieved. Overall supervision was in the hands of an architect who was a mathematician of great expertise and acknowledged innovatory powers, who was nevertheless able to distil a practical guidebook from this theoretical knowledge, intended for use on site and in the drawing office.

Guarini refers in his preface to 'our *Euclides*', but remarks that he did not wish to lumber his little book with the recondite instances worked through in the magnum opus, as this would do little to increase its utility, but much to inflate its price. He concludes his preface with typical mild irony: 'If therefore the kind reader finds the book agreeable, he will happily enjoy it, if not, as the expense has been small, he will have little occasion to regret having bought it, and it will always serve, like many others, to increase the numbers and esteem of his library.'

In the years between *Euclides adauctus* and *Il modo di misurare* Guarini had been working on a *summa* on astronomy, his *Coelestis mathematica*, which eventually appeared in two folio volumes a few months after his death. One of Guarini's friends, evidently keen on astronomy and knowing of this massive work in progress, paid for the publication of a brief compendium extracted from the major work.[9] This little book, in duodecimo, came out in Turin under the title of *Compendio della Sfera Celeste* in 1675. It was dedicated to G. B. Truchi,[10] who had succeeded Ferrari di Bagnolo as minister of finance. Like his predecessor, Truchi was responsible for passing the accounts for ducal expenditure, and Guarini evidently deemed it politic to flatter him.

———————

'In the latter half of the 17th century,' wrote Lt-Col L. C. Jackson,

> a prodigious output of purely theoretical fortification began, which went on till the French Revolution. Many of the 'systems' published at this time

were elaborated by men who had no practical knowledge of the subject, some of them priests who were engaged in educating the sons of the upper classes, and who had to teach the elements of fortification among other things. They naturally wrote treatises, which were valuable for their clearness of style; and with their industry and ingenuity the elaboration of existing methods was a very congenial task.[11]

This is exactly the context of the *Trattato di fortificatione che hora si usa in Fiandra, Francia et Italia, composto in ossequio del Ser.mo Prencipe Lodovico Giulio, Cavagliere di Savoia*, published over Guarini's name in 1677.[12] The young Cavalier of Savoy was a nephew of Guarini's patron Prince Emanuele Filiberto di Carignano, and one of the nine sons of his younger brother, the Conte di Soissons, whose early death in 1673 brought about the consequences we have discussed above. Emanuele Filiberto summoned the young prince to court, from Paris, in 1669, with his brother Emanuele Filiberto, Conte di Dreux, with the object of sponsoring their careers in the State service.[13]

Dr Lange has traced the brief careers of the two boys – di Dreux died in 1676 aged fourteen – and the various sums disbursed on their behalf, from the Fondo Savoia Carignano papers in the Archivio di Stato, Turin.[14] She has turned up a payment made by the Cavalier's tutor 'monsu' Point to Guarini on 15 October 1677 for 'things bought' for the young Lodovico. The sum involved was 3 lire 15 soldi. Dr Lange speculates that this small amount might have been for drawing instruments, to which Guarini actually devotes a chapter in *Architettura civile*.

This appears to be Guarini's first connection with the Carignano branch of the House of Savoy, a connection that was later to give rise to the designs for Racconigi and the Palazzo Carignano. The curious appointment as tutor for fortification, mentioned above by Col Jackson as a specialty of seventeenth-century Italian priests, is less strange in Guarini's case than in most, considering his skills as a civil architect; and the architect's occasional role as a military engineer is a tradition that goes right back to antiquity.[15]

Guarini did not boast any practical experience in the design of fortifications. He makes it clear in his introduction, addressed to the 'kind reader', that he is not putting forward new forms of fortification, 'not being able to offer them authenticated by experience, with which I have never yet tested them'. Nevertheless, he does expound his own views on what were known at the time as regular and irregular fortresses.

What Guarini proposes is a regular bastioned system, simplified and whittled down in its main interior elements. A 'regular fortress' is one in which curtain walls and bulwarks are constructed in such a way that artillery, placed on the flank of a given bastion, will be able to cover the curtain adjacent to it, and the face of the bulwark immediately opposite.

In this system, a clear position is taken vis-à-vis the flanking units and the additional ones inside. The effectiveness of a regular fortress depends, in Guarini's view, mainly on the additional outer works, while an irregular defensive system rests on three works alone: the middle ramparts, the tenailles and the flat bastions.

The Guarinian regular fortress is organized around a very simple terreplein covered by a parapet parallel to it (Fig. 148, a, d), which in its turn presents a slight rise at the rear, the *banchetta* (e), serving as an alure or *via di ronda*. The terreplein is faced by a rampart (b) sloping outwards, made up of a scarp wall (c) which is not reinforced on the outside by spurs or by relieving arches on the inside, to avoid reducing the compact texture of the terreplein in any way.

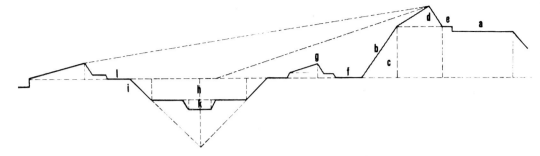

This deliberate simplification of the inner works of the fortress represents a fairly drastic revision of Italian military thinking, as represented by such early seventeenth-century theorists as Busca, Scala, Cataneo and Sardi, who were all for doubling up the terreplein parapets and the alures, and for strengthening the rampart by various kinds of buttresses and reinforcements. Guarini's approach reflects the influence of the more modern French theories advanced by writers such as Fournier, Goret, Pagan and de Bitainvieu, who in their turn were transmitting the views of Dutch military engineers, men like Marolois, Fritach and Dögen. These matters, touched on superficially here, together with many others, are treated in depth by G. C. Sciolla in the paper he presented at the Guarini Congress of 1968.[16]

Two interesting contrasts are revealed by this treatise, one internal and one external. The internal one is the amusing contrast in style between the cap-doffing euphuism of the dedication to the Most Serene Prince,[17] then all of seventeen years of age, who is hailed as 'already learned in every art of Mars and Minerva', whose eyes 'radiate martial vivacity, and flash, no less than arms, with warlike rays', though 'amidst these gleams of war are fostered the most temperate warmths of humanity and sweetness' – between this stately pomp, and the cordial bonhomie of the introduction to the *benigno lettore*, who is told that the humble author has striven to keep the price of the book down by obviating the weight of many folios and the parade of illustrations nicely engraved on copper; what he seeks is not fame, but only the instruction of the reader, having printed the book 'so as to have many copies for distribution to those who might deign to be instructed by my slight talent rather than for any other reason; and so I salute you from my heart'.

The external contrast, if we may call it that, is between Guarini's writings on military architecture and those on civil architecture; that is, his *Architettura civile*. It has been identified, with sympathetic insight, by Professor Portoghesi.

> There emerges from these pages an image, unexpected perhaps by many, of prudence and moderation which is the sign of the presence of the major Guarini as contrasted with the minor one, which may often be identified in the *Architettura civile* when, in contact with the ancient rules of the Orders, with the syntactical repertory of classicism, he reveals his dilettantish rage and his inability to understand, to penetrate the jealous heritage of professional architects.[18]

In 1678 in Turin the heirs of Carlo Ianelli published a slim folio with a lengthy title generally abbreviated as *Leges temporum et planetarum*.[19] It was in effect another spin-off from the still unpublished *Coelestis mathematica*, briefly

147

(56 folio pages) setting out the laws governing the passage of civil and astronomical time, followed by 78 pages of tables linking these laws with the motions of the heavenly bodies, as observed from Turin. In a word, it is a manual of gnomonics, or the art of dialling.[20]

No book is complete without a dedication, and Guarini humbly offers this one to Madama Reale. Maria Giovanna-Battista di Savoia-Nemours was a woman of a practical turn of mind, but ... a handbook of gnomonics? Guarini, however, is more than equal to the occasion. 'She will perchance be glad to see ambitious Heaven in its unalterable laws imitating those which she has so well assured ... she will see expressed in their equations her own justice; in the intermediate motions, her moderation; in the courses, the rectitude of her glorious undertakings, etc., etc.'

All this, of course, is rhetoric, the seventeenth-century *metafora acuta*. If Madama Reale ever actually got the length of reading Guarini's dedication, she would have been perfectly at home in that world of extravagant, courtly

149. Title-page of *Dissegni d'architettura* (reduced).

150. Title-page of *Architettura civile* (reduced from folio).

obsequiousness. But is there a hidden universe beyond this again, a different kind of metaphor? The metaphysicians think so. The very concept of *la gnomonica* is a provocation. 'The dome of S. Lorenzo', writes Marcello Fagiolo, 'is really a great solar clock, ready to register all the variations of the sun's course, whether along the arc of the day or the arc of the seasons.'[21] In one sense this is true, of course, as it is true of every centralized building whose drum or dome is pierced all round by windows. But the constant pursuit of metaphysical *concetti* in Guarini's buildings always encounters the circumstance that Guarini himself, who wrote about them uninhibitedly in the *Architettura civile*, never suggests any such thing. We repeat again the observation of G. C. Argan: no one more than Guarini has affirmed the non-symbolic, non-allegorical, non-metaphorical character of architectural form.[22]

The long-delayed *Coelestis mathematica* appeared at last in two folio volumes in Milan. Guarini had gone to the city early in 1683 to see the work through the press and to help with the proof-reading, but died there on 6 March. The publisher alluded to this when the book came out a few months later:

> You should know, dear reader, that our *Celestial Mathematics* has suffered a great misfortune on earth, not only because its author was too long away from the press, but because, borne off by death before printing was completed, that most learned man was unable to correct all the errors which have crept into it, or add any later thoughts. So I would simply ask you, friend: if, in your reading, anything appears obscure to you, either endure it with patient love, or correct it yourself. Farewell.

The first volume of Guarini's book deals, in greater detail than in *Leges temporum*, with the laws of time and the planets, the motions of the moon, the nature of eclipses and the trajectories of each planet. All this, of course, is expounded in the context of a firm belief in the geocentric nature of the universe: already in *Placita philosophica* Guarini had refuted the views of Copernicus and Galileo, that the earth revolved round the sun.[23] The second part of *Coelestis mathematica* is devoted to an extensive treatment of gnomonics and the relevant geometrical laws of sciagraphy, to assist in particular the designers of solar clocks.

Three years after Guarini's death a folio volume was issued in Turin under the title *Dissegni d'architettura civile et ecclesiastica, inventati & delineati dal Padre D. Guarino Guarini*. The book consists entirely of engravings, without any textual accompaniment; its publication was probably instigated by the Theatines, who were in possession of the engraved plates commissioned by Guarini on the basis of his own drawings for an intended publication he never lived to organize.[24] These illustrations were issued without the accompanying text because, according to a contemporary leaflet, 'the public was so anxious to see the designs and the printer to publish them'.[25]

The book is in two parts. The first, prefaced by the portrait of Guarini (our Fig. 1), contains various architectural details invented by Guarini: capitals, columns and the undulating Order. The second part illustrates Guarini's projected or built schemes in 33 plates.

The main difference between the plates in the *Dissegni d'architettura* and those which later appeared in the *Architettura civile* is the removal from the latter of the cartouches bearing the names of the dedicatees, and in many cases those of the engravers as well. As we have seen, the names of the dedicatees are sometimes important when trying to establish the date of a design – for example, the Divina Providenza – or even the identity of a building, as with the Castello di Govone.

The plates in the *Dissegni d'architettura* are, of course, in a more pristine state than those in the *Architettura civile*.[26] The book was reissued in facsimile by Daria de Bernardi Ferrero in an edition of 500 numbered copies in 1966.[27] The original owner of the copy reproduced (now the property of Professor de Bernardi Ferrero) was Antonio Bertola, a military engineer who took over the supervision of work on SS. Sindone, S. Filippo Neri and the Palazzo Carignano after Guarini's death.[28] It is Bertola's name that can be seen neatly inscribed on the vignette of the title-page reproduced here as Fig. 149.

Fifty years after the publication of *Dissegni d'architettura*, Guarini's buildings in Turin were still admired, and commented on favourably in locally published guidebooks. Although Juvarra's fame had to some extent obscured that of Guarini, his architecture reflected the influence in Italy of the international neoclassical movement. His star was on the wane, whereas beyond the Alps there were architects still susceptible of influence *from* Italy: from the last stages of creative Italian Baroque, in a word, from Guarini.

The Theatine fathers in Turin judged the time ripe to organize the publication of Guarini's last book, the *Architettura civile,* of which the *Dissegni d'architettura* represented only the graphic part, and not even that completely. The help was invoked of Bernardo Vittone, a young architect (b. 1704) whose own churches show the blended influence of Guarini and Juvarra. Vittone prepared Guarini's manuscript for publication in conjunction with the existing plates, and in 1737 Gianfrancesco Mairesse, at the sign of S. Teresa di Gesù, brought out *Architettura civile del Padre D. Guarino Guarini Cherico Regolare opera postuma dedicata a Sua Sacra Reale Maestà* (Fig. 150).

The extent of Vittone's intervention cannot be determined. Reference is made in the *Avviso a' lettori* to the task that was involved of touching up (*ripulire*) the work and getting it into a single volume. The nineteenth-century art historian Amico Ricci is said to have consulted two unedited (and hence uncut) manuscripts of the work in the Vatican Library, but Professor Portoghesi has been unable to trace them.[29] If Vittone modified Guarini's text at all, it was by cutting it, not by adding to it. His own prose style, as exemplified in his books,[30] is far more florid than Guarini's and would have shown up in any extended passage. As far as textual supervision is concerned, Vittone was not diligent. The text and plates are peppered with errors, the numbering of the plates has fits and starts and sources are quoted inaccurately in places.

If the illustrations of *Architettura civile* are compared with those of *Dissegni d'architettura*, it will be found that the illustrations of buildings have been increased by only one – the elevation of S. Maria Annunziata, Messina – whereas the technical plates (*lastre*), which in the *Dissegni* numbered only eleven, have been increased to forty-five, with a wealth of drawings illustrative of problems in descriptive geometry, surveying, etc. These technical figures are linked to Guarini's text, unlike the engravings of the projects, which are not alluded to directly.

Guarini's text is divided into five Tractates (*Trattati*). The first deals with architecture in general, the second with what the author calls *ichnografia*, i.e., surveying, levelling, laying out and general considerations that affect planning. The third Tractate concerns *ortografia elevata*: how to elevate buildings, and deal with the Orders. Its final chapter, on vaults, begins with the words: 'Vaults are the main thing in building'. The fourth Tractate explains *ortografia gettata*, the projection on plan of cylinders, spheres, elliptical bodies and the like, always linked to the requirements of architecture. The fifth and final Tractate, on what Guarini refers to as geodesy, is another geometrical excursus on the division of hyperbolas, the methods of increasing and diminishing triangular areas, and similar problems (Fig. 151). It shows a familiarity with the work of the French mathematician Desargues, which had aroused great interest in learned circles in Paris when Guarini resided there.

Each Tractate of *Architettura civile* is divided into chapters. A chapter for Guarini, however, means merely the brief statement of a topic in four or five lines. The main burden of the text is consigned to the 'observations' which follow. This approach separates Guarini from all the previous *trattatisti*, from Alberti to Vignola. On the other hand, it has a good deal in common with the way that C. F. Milliet Dechales laid out his *Cursus mathematicus*. Dechales was an exact contemporary of Guarini at Turin, and they must have known each other personally.

The prose style of *Architettura civile* is devoid of prolixity or bombast, though well capable of irony and insinuation. The book's field is a wide one, ranging from the choice of drawing instruments to the geometric quadration of the circle. It is perhaps Guarini's views on aesthetics and his attitude to the architecture of the past that are of the greatest abiding interest.

'Architecture,' says Guarini, 'though it depends on mathematics, is nevertheless a flattering art' (I.iii). 'Commodity, to be perfect, must be agreeable and alluring' (I.iii.5), and 'architecture has as its purpose the gratification of the senses' (I.iii.7).

A major criterion, therefore, for judging architecture, is the degree of pleasure it procures the senses. But what is pleasure? And whose senses? 'Pleasure (*l'aggradimento*) can be judged, not by everyone, but by those who, free of all passion and sufficiently capable in the art, can express competent judgement' (III.iii.1). 'Free of all passion' means free of prejudices, including the prejudice that the art of the past is better than the art of the present. 'Capable in the art' does not mean, as in the past, students of the antique, but sufficiently expert to assure the inexpert that the work in question is aesthetically sound.

What, then, is aesthetically sound? 'As for myself,' Guarini writes (III.iv. 4), 'I should say that proportion is a harmony (*convenienza*) of parts so disposed that none exceeds, or is lacking from another, so that it seems neither too big nor too small as compared with it; because the eye does not judge (*l'occhio non compasa*).' The eye does not judge: it relies on what it sees. Here is, perhaps, an echo of Alberti: 'I shall define beauty to be a harmony of all the parts, in whatsoever subject it appears, fitted together with such proportion and connection, that nothing could be added, diminished or altered, but for the worse.'[31] For Alberti, however, ancient precept was binding: his attitude to Vitruvius was one of adhesion, if not of acquiescence.[32] Guarini sees things differently. Tastes change from age to age and from nation to nation. 'Men change their fashions, and what was formerly admired as beautiful becomes abhorred as ugly, and what pleases one nation displeases another, and in our own subject we see that Roman architecture formerly displeased the Goths, and Gothic architecture displeases us' (III.iii).

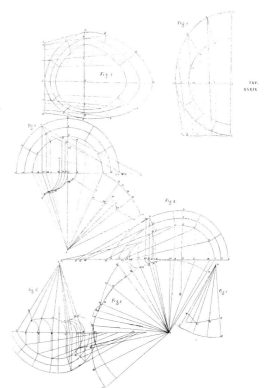

151. Methods of projecting and developing the surfaces of various types of cones (from *Architettura civile*).

Does this mean, then, that the rules can be changed? For Guarini, it does:

> The beauty of buildings consists in a well-proportioned harmony of the parts, to secure which, the Ancients, with Vitruvius, gave certain fixed rules, some of which are assertorial, so strict that they may not be departed from by even a fingernail's breadth; but I, judging discreetly and from what happens in every other profession, think that you can both correct some of the ancient rules and add others; and experience itself demonstrates it in the first place, because Roman Antiquities are not precisely in accordance with the rules of Vitruvius, or the proportions of Vignola or the other moderns who follow the ancient literature in every feature; but as may be seen, many new proportions and many new ways of building have been invented in our own times which the Ancients did not use. (I.iii.6)

These views were to some extent anticipated a century before, by Philibert de l'Orme, who in his book *Architecture* (Paris 1567) begged to differ from Vitruvius on several points, attacked those who blindly followed Italian models, and proposed to add a French Order to those of Greece and Rome; but they had never been so clearly expressed before.

Several consequences flow from this outlook. Most notably, Guarini necessarily rejects those proportional systems considered as tried and perfect: they merely provide the take-off point for the modern imagination. Tractate III of the book deals with the Orders, which still constituted the basic morphology of architecture in Guarini's day, but they are treated simply as units of vocabulary, not as the source of the basic modules of architectural proportion. Furthermore, Guarini adds other Orders, like the Gothic and the Atlantic, which turn the whole system upside down; and he quietly admits (III.viii) that once the form of the column has been determined, it can be altered to make it twisted, screw-like or wave-like. We have already considered the circumstances of Guarini's Supreme Corinthian Order.

When Guarini shed the historic systems of proportion, he furnished the impetus that was to spread the Baroque style north of the Alps in the next century. He also laid himself open to influences from Gothic and Arab sources. These circumstances have already been discussed in Chapter 7. Behind the static sleight of hand of S. Lorenzo and other Guarinian structures we may perceive the appreciation, expressed in Tractate III (xiii.1), of the contrast between Roman and Gothic architecture, where the latter was perceived as '[having] as its object to erect buildings that were in fact very strong, but would seem weak and as though they needed a miracle to keep them standing'.

Guarini devotes a chapter in his second Tractate to the nature of sites, but the reader who comes to it expecting sage advice on aspects, in the Albertian or Palladian manner, or how to insert a building into an urban context, will be disappointed. The chapter is another astronomical excursus, relating the lines of the site plan to the 'angles of the world'. Guarini's detached, closed, centripetal forms react to their ambience rather than coordinate with it. To judge from his built works, as the *Architettura civile* is silent on the matter, Guarini sees the urban grain as a neutral element in which he does not strain to integrate his buildings.

'The principle ornament in all architecture', wrote Alberti, 'certainly lies in columns.'[33] Two hundred years later columns were *vieux jeu*, and Guarini began chapter xxvi of his third Tractate with the words 'Vaults are the main thing in building'. The vaults Guarini describes derive from six round bodies, which, when cut in half, give rise to six elementary vaults. Guarini refers to banded vaults (*volte a fasce*) with particular satisfaction: 'This sort of vault is my specialty, and I have used it in practice not without much variety and to general satisfaction' (III.xxvi.9). He refers in this connection to Racconigi, and supplies a small diagram of it (our Fig. 70). Another type of vaulting, the *volte piane*, described in a later observation (III.xxvi.11), is noted as in use at Racconigi and the Palazzo Carignano, but Guarini does not discuss the use of his 'specials' in church domes; even the curious 'key to the dome of S. Lorenzo' (our Fig. 45) was omitted from the plates of *Architettura civile*.

The original 1737 edition of Guarini's book was reissued in 1964 in a facsimile edition in two volumes by the Gregg Press, from a copy in the R.I.B.A. Library. In 1968 a completely new edition appeared as Volume 8 in the Trattati di architettura series published by Edizioni Il Polifilo, Milan. In this version, the text has been completely reset in modern type, some of the asperities of seventeenth-century orthography have been modified and the defects of the punctuation made good. The plates have been reduced to permit a more manageable format, while the crude lettering and faulty numbering of the technical illustrations have been blanked out and a consistent system of figuration discreetly introduced in the margin, to which cross-reference is made in the margins of the text. The whole is equipped with a critical apparatus by Bianca Tavassi La Greca, which sets Guarini's book into the context of seventeenth-century treatise literature.

12   GUARINI'S LEGACY

COMPARISONS HAVE SOMETIMES been made between Wren and Guarini. They were born within eight years of each other. Both men were mathematicians and astronomers, though Wren followed the new cosmology, Guarini the old. Both applied their mathematical knowledge to the solution of structural problems, albeit Wren's architectural expression was remote indeed from the exuberance of Italian late Baroque.

Wren lived to be ninety-one. After he retired, jobbed out of office by a court favourite, he would drive down once a year from his house in Hampton Court to St Paul's Cathedral, and spend the day seated beneath the dome contemplating his work.[1]

Guarini was overtaken by death at the age of fifty-nine, in the midst of his building and writing.[2] He never lived to be carried back, in extreme old age, to meditate, say, beneath the miraculous dome of S. Lorenzo. But, though Wren lived half as long again as Guarini, the latter enjoyed an experience that must have outdone anything of which Wren could boast, and which for him personally would have proved a consummation beyond the reach of any lay architect. It was Guarini himself who celebrated the first Mass in S. Lorenzo.[3]

The occasion took place on Sunday, 10 May 1680, in the presence of Madama Reale, the Archbishop of Turin,[4] the Father General of the Theatines and the whole court: the Knights of the Supreme Order of the Annunziata, the Master of the Hunt, the Falconer Royal, the ambassadors and all the nobility. Crepaldi needs a quarto page of small print to enumerate them. The architect, surrounded by the monks of his Order bearing flaming torches, celebrated Imperial Mass. After *that*, you might think, one could die happy . . .

We have seen, in the last chapter, that although Guarini devotes several pages of *Architettura civile* to vaulting, which he calls (III.xxvi) the main thing in building, he refers only to the vaults he has used in his palaces. He does not refer to church domes.[5] But Guarini's openwork diaphanous domes were his unique contribution to architecture. All his predecessors, from the architect of the Pantheon to Borromini, had maintained the continuity and solidity of the domical surface, however they might have patterned it or inflected it. It was left to Guarini to pierce the dome – to build it from ribs, as the Arabs had done, but then to suppress the infill, which they had never ventured to do.

Although, in the words of G. C. Argan, 'no one more than Guarini has affirmed the non-symbolic, non-allegorical, non-metaphorical character of

154

architectural form',[6] the feeling comes across very strongly that in the extra-ordinary domes of S. Lorenzo and SS. Sindone we are in the presence of a striving to express the infinite, in architecture. In architecture, but not in words: there is no mention of this kind of thing in *Architettura civile*. On the contrary, that treatise is full of allusions to architecture as a sensuous art, among whose chief aims must be that of giving pleasure. Let the metaphysicians turn this way and that to find a symbolical meaning: Guarini says quite simply that he puts his stars and bars on the Palazzo Carignano because they make 'a superb appearance' (*una superbissima vista*).[7] Between Guarini's avowed hedonism, and his implied mysticism, we may detect a creative tension.

There is a similar contrast between what Guarini owns up to in the domain of perceptual psychology, and what he actually *does*, without verbal comment. The whole of Tractate III, chapter xxi, of *Architettura civile* is devoted to various ways of manipulating the spectator's vision: 'white objects appear larger than dark or black ones, and brighter'; 'how to proportion a facade which appears defective by reason of the site'; and so on. But the real prodigies of spectator manipulation that Guarini *practises* – the vast super-structures that appear to descend into serliana columns at S. Lorenzo, for example – go unacknowledged. The *hint* is there, of course, in the assessment of Gothic architecture, which, in Guarini's eyes, 'had as its object to erect buildings that were in fact very strong, but would seem weak and as though they needed a miracle to keep them standing' (III.xiii.1).

Guarini's appreciation of Gothic, as we have seen, was unique for his time. There is no doubt that he admired its structural achievements, but whether he actually saw a parallel between the Baroque urge to 'persuade' the beholder and the way that the leaning towers of Pisa and Bologna 'amaze the intellect and terrify the spectators' is hard to determine. Can he really have regarded the lean at Pisa as a piece of premeditated structural brinkmanship? Was he inspired to his own *funambolismo statico* by the achievements of the medieval builders, or did his existing predisposition merely receive encouragement from what he saw at Seville and Salamanca?[8]

The paradoxes and apparent contradictions in Guarini's buildings and his deliberate incongruities – the way he places unrelated units one on top of another in his centralized structures, and creates interpenetrations of diverse spaces in his longitudinal ones – may perhaps be regarded as variants on the theme of architecture for amazement, common to Baroque and high Gothic. The manipulation of space and the disruption of wall boundaries by complex plastic treatments (which vary from S. Lorenzo's bulging serlianas to S. Filippo Neri's jutting piers 'like the prows of ships') have the effect of disorientating the visitor. No longer cradled by the anodyne interiors of Vittozzi or Castellamonte, he is disturbed. But this disturbance is remote from the Mannerist jokiness of Giulio Romano or Zuccari: it is the mani-festation of a spiritual urge, expressed in architecture, and resolved most successfully in the soaring openwork domes of S. Lorenzo and SS. Sindone.

Although Guarini's understanding of the strength of materials was prag-matical and limited by the state of seventeenth-century science, his mathematical knowledge was very advanced and, for Italy itself, on the frontiers of what was then known. It underlies all his architecture and explains his predilection for ellipsoidal sections and parabolic ribbing. It invades and bids fair to take over a large part of *Architettura civile*, more than a third of which is devoted (in contrast to all other Italian treatises) to the new science of descriptive geometry, in a way that has had to wait until the

152. Turin, Church of the Misericordia (F. di Robilant). Long section.

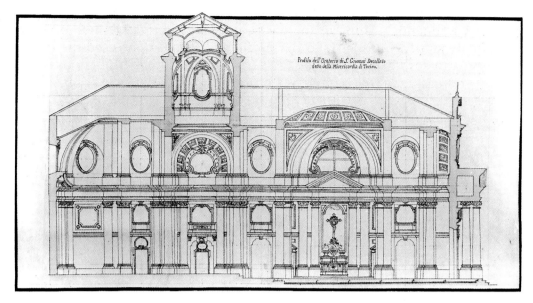

twentieth century for specialized scholars such as Werner Müller to evaluate.[9]

Whatever insights Guarini was eager to afford in those Tractates of his book that demonstrate the plane projections of spherical surfaces, and the transformation of the plane surfaces of a given shape into corresponding surfaces of a different shape, or how to relate the boundaries of a site to the 'angles of the universe', it is doubtful if there were many Italian architects who were qualified to benefit from them.

Guarini's death in 1683, coming as it did in the same year as that of the ducal architect Amedeo di Castellamonte, left a great void in the architectural life of Piedmont. Guarini's unfinished work was carried on by others, notably Antonio Bertola, with substantial fidelity. But Guarini himself was a hard act to follow, and architects of the next generation such as Carlo Emanuele Lanfranchi and Gian Giacomo Plantery could hardly cause surprise for opting to continue in the sober tradition of Castellamonte.

We shall look in vain, therefore, for local imitators of Guarini in the period immediately succeeding his death. S. Lorenzo was admired, but its structures were not taken up again – its openwork dome and its manipulation of light on the visible plane, or (even less) its concealed statics on the invisible one. Superficial features were sometimes employed, though. Count Filippo di Robilant used S. Lorenzo-type ribs to enclose a central hexagon in his church of the Misericordia in Turin, but only the hexagon is left open to admit light from a small chamber above (Fig. 152). Even less productive of imitations was SS. Sindone, which was generally perceived as a one-off project.

The Palazzo Carignano proved a more feasible exemplar: G. F. Baroncelli (Palazzo Barolo) and Plantery (Palazzo Cavour) both made use of Guarini's device of a vaulted atrium topped by the *gran salone*, though they moved their rooms over to the courtyard side of the block.

Of the architects actually associated with Guarini in his lifetime, mention may be made of Antonio Bertola and Michelangelo Garove. Bertola in his own works did not follow Guarini's more advanced spatial theories, but exhibits a certain verticalism, if it may be so called, in the Sanctuary of the Madonna delle Vigne and in his scheme for the church of S. Croce at Cuneo. Michelangelo Garove, an Italian-Swiss architect from Bissone, on Lake

156

Lugano, assisted Guarini at Racconigi, the Collegio dei Nobili and the Palazzo Carignano.[10] Some of the palace drawings in the Archivio di Stato are actually signed Garoue. Like Baroncelli and Plantery, he used the Palazzo Carignano device of a *gran salone* over a vaulted atrium in his design for the Palazzo Asinari di S. Marzano in Turin. His chapel of the Beato Amedeo in the cathedral at Vercelli, begun in Guarini's lifetime, is characterized by Nino Carboneri as 'pregnant with Guarinian spirit'.[11] He is referring to the way Garove used serlianas in the windows and tomb niches, and his handling of columns.

The twenty years that Juvarra worked in Turin (1714–35) bespoke a new golden age for Piedmontese architecture, but Juvarra was remote from the closed, intense world of Guarini. They meet head on, so to speak, in the schemes Juvarra was commissioned to draw up for a new cathedral in Turin, which would have reduced SS. Sindone to the status of one amongst many side chapels leading off from a blaze of centralized Baroque glory (Fig. 153).[12]

Two years after Juvarra left Piedmont for Spain, the Theatine fathers, with the help of Bernardo Vittone, brought out an edition of Guarini's *Architettura civile*. This had long-term effects further afield, as we shall see, while in the short term it gave rise to a modest Guarinian revival in Piedmont, first and foremost on the editor himself.[13] Vittone's architecture, while reflecting an appreciation of the achievements of Borromini, Bernini and Carlo Fontana, bears the unmistakable imprint of someone well familiar with Guarini's oeuvre. The vaults of his churches at Vallinotto (Fig. 154) and Bra (Fig. 155) borrow their structure from S. Lorenzo, but link this with the scenic effects derived from the double-shell domes proposed by Guarini for S. Gaetano, Vicenza. The Vallinotto church in particular is a remarkable tour de force. Its Guarinian dome is a shell of intersecting ribs. Through a large hexagonal opening in the centre no fewer than three more vaults appear, one

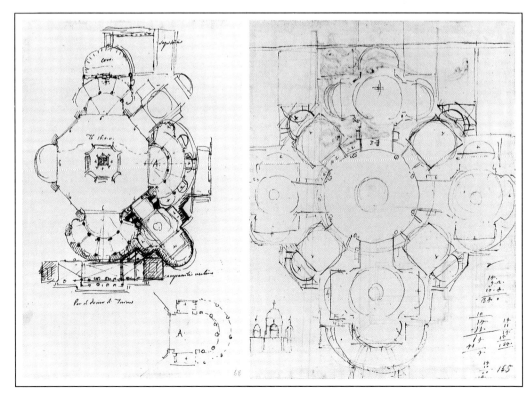

153. F. Juvarra: sketch plan alternatives for new cathedral, Turin.

157

above the other: two solid ones with circular openings, which diminished in size, and, beyond these, the hemisphere of the lantern.

Vittone achieved another Guarinian exaggeration at Corteranzo, near Carignano, where his church of S. Luigi looks like a mini-Consolata, pushed upwards to make a Guarinian pagoda (Fig. 156).

In speaking of the early post-Guarinian period, before the advent of Juvarra, it was noted that SS. Sindone, in view of its exceptional context, did not readily lend itself to any kind of emulation. In a drawing preserved at the Musée des Arts Décoratifs, in Paris, however (Fig. 157), we have evidence of an attempt by Vittone to get further mileage out of a scheme where three circular chambers abut, if they do not actually penetrate, a large central cylinder. These three chambers are interspersed with three rectangular chapels with curvilinear short sides.

Most of Vittone's non-ecclesiastical buildings were designed for a clientele fairly remote from Guarini's court circles, and short on funds for achieving *rappresentanza*. The delightful little town hall at Bra (Fig. 158) is a pocket Palazzo Carignano, which, in the apt words of Carboneri, it 'translates in village terms, fragrant as home-made bread'.[14]

To revert to Vittone's churches, the two parish churches illustrated in his *Istruzioni diverse*, with longitudinal plans, show inspiration from sources other than Guarini, but his project for a church for the Franciscans at Nice[15] shows a marked affinity in plan to the layout of Guarini's S. Maria Ettinga, Prague, with a large central bay and the other two reflecting each other, their points of intersection marked by canted pier edges (Fig. 159).

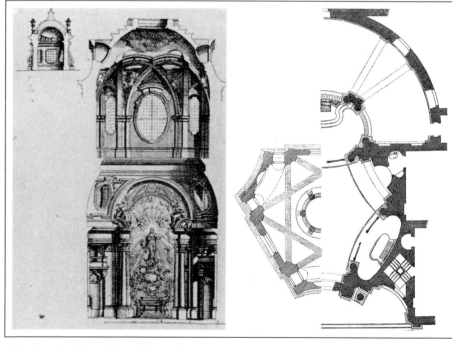

155. Bra, S. Chiara (B.A. Vittone).

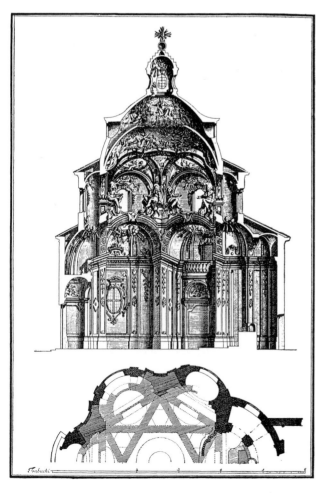

154. Vallinotto, Chapel of the Visitation (B.A. Vittone).

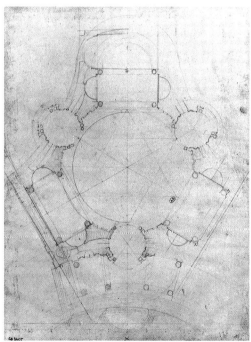

157. B. A. Vittone: sketch for a central plan church.

There is a Guarinian component in the whole of Vittone's work, explicit or implied. One of its most remarkable manifestations is to be seen in the unrealized scheme for the church of S. Chiara, Turin, published in *Istruzioni diverse*, which in some respects resembles a Guarinian anthology, culminating in a lantern that sits over the opening made by the interlacing ribs of a dome inspired by S. Lorenzo (Fig. 160). Had this dome been built, it would have joined the two by Guarini himself to make an impressive contribution to the Turin skyline.

158. Bra, Town Hall (B. A. Vittone).

There are other names besides Vittone's, architects such as Francesco Gallo, Antonio Felice Devincenti, Giuseppe Girolamo Buniva and Andrea Vaj, in whose works diverse interpretations may be observed of a number of Guarinian themes. There are followers of Vittone himself, men like Bonvicini and Quarini; and it is the work of Mario Quarini, 'Vittone's devoted pupil',[16] that marks the transition to Neoclassicism in Piedmont, most notably in the large cathedral he built at Fossano, forty miles from Turin, between 1779 and 1791.

But the reaction against Guarini was in evidence well before that. As a young man in 1737, Vittone had prepared Guarini's *Architettura civile* for publication. In his own book, *Istruzioni diverse* (1766), published towards the end of his life, Vittone makes little reference to Guarini, and when he does it is mainly critical. He speaks of the Master's domes as 'obscure and difficult and hard for a simple surveyor to understand'.[17] Two years later, F. Milizia launched his broadside on Guarini in the article devoted to him in his *Memorie*, ending with the words, 'whoever likes Guarini's architecture, much good may it do him, but he would be a nitwit', which is where we came in.[18]

160

The influence of Guarini had evidently run its course in Italy. But north of the Alps its leaven had worked still more powerfully, and we must now turn our attention there.

Germany, which had experienced such a brilliant high Gothic period, and had advanced on the path of Early Renaissance with the works of Elias Holl, took no part in the evolution of the Baroque style. Friedrich Sustris, a Dutch architect who had trained in Italy, built the great church of St Michael in Munich in the Mannerist tradition, and modelled in many respects on the Gesù, between 1583 and 1597, but the natural artistic development of the country was totally disrupted by the Thirty Years' War (1618–48), which virtually destroyed the German building trade.

When peace came, Germany was artistically isolated, fifty years or more behind the trend of things in the rest of Europe, and bereft of the craftsmen who could tackle the work of reconstruction. Architects and tradesmen from other countries flooded in: Italians in the south, French and Dutch in the west and north.

It was in this context that, when Princess Enrichetta Adelaide of Savoy, wife of the Elector of Bavaria, wanted to build a votive church for the Theatines in Munich in 1662, the proposal was made to send for Guarini.[19] Guarini, however, was already on his way to Paris and could not change his plans.[20] The architect eventually chosen was the Bolognese Agostino Barelli, who built the Theatines a Latin cross church with a high dome, still harking back to the Gesù. Time had stood still.

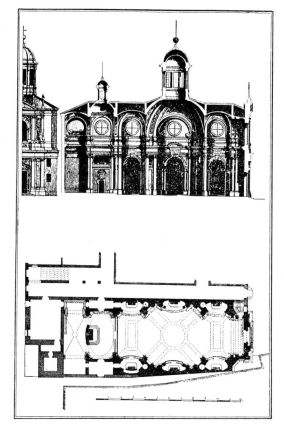

159. Nice, S. Francesco (B. A. Vittone).

160. Turin, S. Chiara (B. A. Vittone).

The political and spiritual regeneration of the German lands began after the defeat of the Turks at Vienna in 1683, and gathered impetus in the 1690s. It was Fischer von Erlach who initiated the German high Baroque. Fischer was trained in Rome under Carlo Fontana from about 1682 to 1685. He travelled extensively in north Italy 'making numerous studies and free renderings, in which he takes some recognisable building as a basis, but introduces such variations as his imagination suggests'.[21] Did he become acquainted with Guarini's architecture? Sedlmayr is doubtful,[22] and thinks that the only items Fischer took, probably from the *Dissegni d'architettura*, are the curvilinear crowning features on the campanili of the University Church in Salzburg (1694–1707) (Fig. 161), which seem to derive from the drum of S. Filippo Neri at Casale Monferrato (our Fig. 135) – in other words, a plastic motif, not a profound spatial impulse. But this was the way in which Guarini's message was received at first. Its assimilation begins in Austria with Fischer, continues in Bohemia with Dientzenhofer and culminates in Franconia with Balthasar Neumann. The possibilities for the emulation and further development of Guarini's space systems were not always grasped from the outset, particularly by those who had to rely for their information on engravings rather than personal experience of the buildings.

162. Weingarten, Benedictine Church (F. Beer, 1715–22).

163. Zwiefalten, Benedictine Church (J. Michael Fischer, 1738–65).

161. (*facing page*) Salzburg, University Church (Fischer von Erlach, 1694–1707).

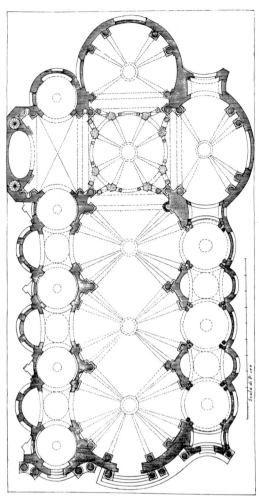

164. Model church, with alternative treatments of the tribune (from *Architettura civile*).

To revert to the University Church of Salzburg, however, there is a good deal more of Guarini in it than the campanile features. The whole disposition of the facade, where an elliptical unit is held between two rectangular wings, resembles the Palazzo Carignano. The same device is seen again at the Benedictine abbey church built to the designs of Franz Beer and (perhaps) J. J. Herkommer between 1715 and 1722 at Weingarten, north of Lake Constance (Fig. 162).

Instances of this kind of 'formalistic' borrowing can be multiplied without difficulty. Thus, Fischer produced a design for an altar at Mariazell that looks like a simplified version of Guarini's tabernacle for S. Nicolò, Verona, while Johann Michael Fischer's Benedictine church at Zwiefalten develops the theme of the Porta del Po (Fig. 163).

Eventually, however, Fischer seems to have become interested in a more inward approach to Guarini's architecture and in some of its motivating forces. There is in *Architettura civile* an untitled plan (Fig. 164) showing a kind of model church with alternative treatments for the tribune. It is entirely made up of ovals and cylinders which abut, interpenetrate, intersect and presumably create geometrical mayhem at vaulting level, though no sectional views are provided. The ultimate exploitation of this concatenation of curvilinear shapes was to appear at Vierzehnheiligen, but in the meantime Fischer was stimulated into some modest creative doodling, in a series of sketches of little pavilions made up of elliptical or angular cells, and in one case of ovals alone (Fig. 165).[23]

From these modest beginnings, the oval assumed for Fischer the role of a key component. His own specific contribution was to insert it crosswise in a static block, and from its first strange manifestation at the little palace of Niederweiden (Fig. 166), it grows to heroic proportions in the Imperial Library, Vienna, where the great longitudinal block, the Prunksaal, is penetrated transversely in the middle by an elliptical domed chamber, although seen from the outside this rounded hall is inscribed in an octagon.

The Imperial Library represents the pinnacle of Austrian Baroque, reached after forty years' development. Where Austria led, Bohemia was not far behind.[24] Guarini had sent a set of plans to Prague in 1679 for the church of S. Maria Ettinga, a longitudinal scheme where two compressed ellipses

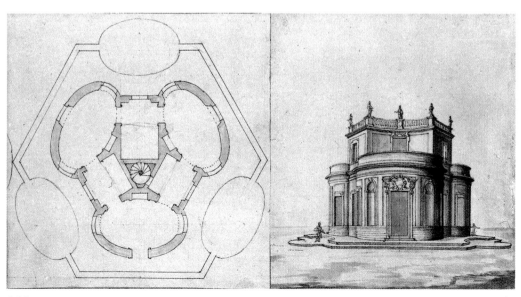

165. J. B. Fischer von Erlach: design for a pavilion.

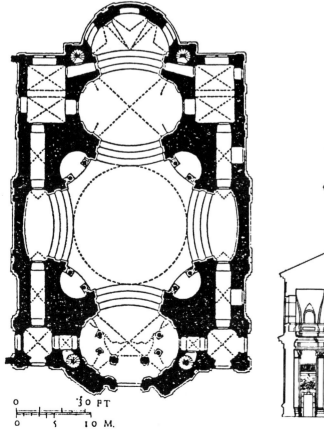

166. Niederweiden. Summer house (J. B. Fischer von Erlach).

interact with a central, larger one. This produces interesting consequences for the vaults, where diagonally placed pilasters are continued up as band-like ribs. Guarini's church was never built, for whatever reasons, but the plans for it made a profound impression, not least on Christoph and Johann Dientzenhofer, local architects whose family was of Bavarian origin.

Bohemia itself is the most westerly of the Slav lands. Less wedded to strict classic theory than the Latin and even the Germanic countries, it was backed by vast Slavonic territories reaching past Vilna and Lvov to St Petersburg itself, all 'only too willing to accept the more elaborate forms of the Italo-

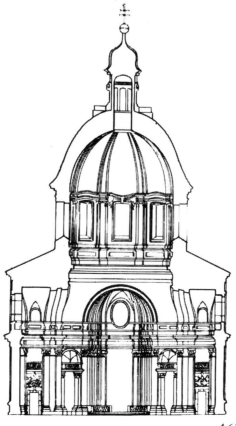

0   30 PT

0   5   10 M.

167. Gabel, St Laurence. Plan (J. L. von Hildebrandt, 1699).

168. Gabel, St Laurence. Section.

165

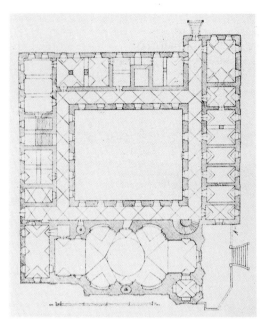

169. Obořiště, Pauline Abbey. Church by Christoph Dientzenhofer, *c.*1700.

170. Smiřice, Castle church (C. Dientzenhofer).

German Baroque, which suited their temperament and their innate preference for painterly qualities'.[25]

Guarini redivivus arrived in Bohemia in 1699, with a design by Johann Lucas von Hildebrandt, who despite his name was born and grew up in Genoa.[26] He trained in Rome under Carlo Fontana as a town planner and a fortifications engineer, subsequently accompanying Prince Eugene on his Piedmont campaigns of 1695 and 1696. Here he saw Guarini's buildings in their pristine glory, and experienced them three-dimensionally. The outcome was the church of St Laurence at Gabel, in northern Bohemia, which the Master would have found the sincerest form of flattery: an 'alternatively centralized' plan (Fig. 167) with two oval bays intersecting a middle circle. Hildebrandt levels the edges of the dome piers and continues the undulating rhythm vertically, through the arches and pendentives, to the concave surfaces of the dome vault (Fig. 168).

A year or two later, Christoph Dientzenhofer achieved a similar design for the Pauline abbey church at Obořiště, where two transverse ovals are overlapped in the centre by a third, narrower one, which expands above into the circle of a pseudo-dome, frescoed to depict a cupola. Along the side walls, the curves of the ovals produce diagonally placed piers, into which pilasters are inset on both sides (Fig. 169).

Although the church at Obořiště undulates inside, the outside walls are rectilinear. At Smiřice, however, the outside walls of the castle church by

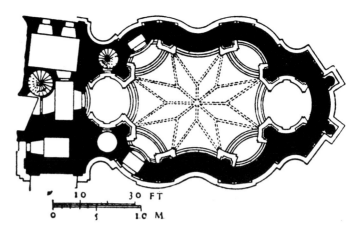

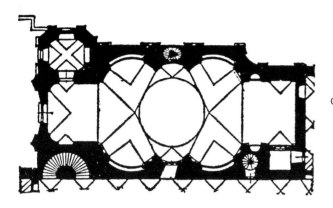

Obořiště

171. (*above*) Smiřice, Castle church. Plan.

172. (*left and below*) Plans of churches by Christoph and Johann Dientzenhofer.

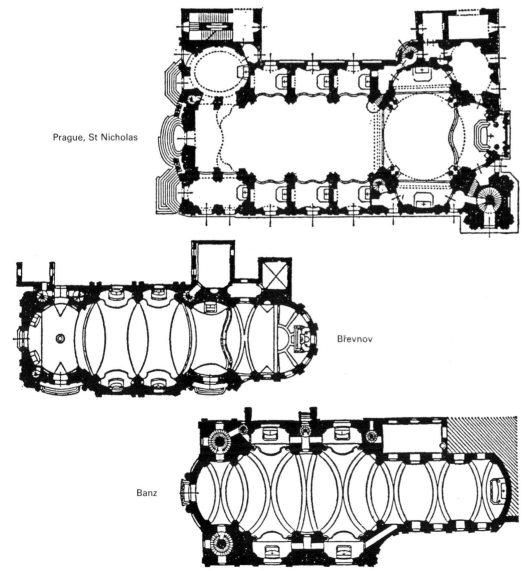

Prague, St Nicholas

Břevnov

Banz

167

Dientzenhofer undulate in sympathy with the internal movements, in a way anticipated by Guarini's model church (Figs. 170 and 171). The building, in effect, is a Bohemian hall church. The nave is a single longitudinal oval, with the long sides kinked inwards towards the centre to produce diagonally canted pilasters. An oval presbytery on the east reflects an identically shaped vestibule on the west.

The culmination of Guarini's influence in Bohemia is reached in the great church of St Nicholas (sv. Mikuláš) built in 1703–11 by Dientzenhofer in the Malá Strana quarter of Prague, 'the most ambitious Jesuit church of Bohemia, and perhaps of all Central Europe' (Fig. 172).[27] Here, the nave piers are

173. Prague, Malá Strana, St Nicholas. Plan and section.

set at angles, dividing up the nave into a sequence of three ovals. Their continuation, by means of banded groins touching one another crosswise at the apex, 'was ironed out by Kracker's splendid fresco',[28] but the intentions can be seen in a drawing preserved in the Groenesteyn Archives at Kiedrich (Fig. 173). To avoid blocking the upward thrust to the vaults, the entablature is not continuous, but each pier unit is equipped with its own segment of it. A usage rare in Guarini is the insertion of galleries,[29] with its resultant contrast of light levels between the shady ground floor vaults, laid out as concave niches, and the bright upper level, where pediments over the windows transmit the flowing movement set up by the piers (Fig. 174).

The type of planning used at St Nicholas was sharpened up some six years later at the church of St Margaret (sv. Markéta) at Břevnov, near Prague, which Dientzenhofer built for the Benedictine monastery there. Here the transverse ovals are packed in so tightly that they give the effect of 'syncopated interpenetration'.[30] There are no transverse arches, just vaulted

169

surfaces with curving edges. The overlaps between the ovals are treated as apertures, with a view through to the heavens appropriately supplied by frescoes. By the effect of syncopation, these 'apertures' are displaced with relation to the spatial zones below, so that where the wall opens the vault closes, and where the wall closes the vault opens.

This system was imported the following year (1710) to Banz,[31] in Franconia, southern Germany, by Christoph Dientzenhofer's younger brother Johann, who was commissioned by the Benedictine fathers to design a church for their monastery, built, in accordance with Benedictine practice, on top of a hill, which in this case overlooks the river Main.

The nave of Banz is made up of two transverse ovals, interlaced by a central one inserted between them. At vaulting level, unlike at Břevnov, the ovals are marked out by thick, emphatic bands, which act as transverse arches that swing forward towards the altar, or backwards towards the entrance. The whole system is generated from the hollowed-out masonry at the zone of the pilasters, but at ceiling level the rationale becomes overlaid, and where the three-dimensional arches touch, the illusion is suggested of a Gothic rib system, though in fact the conception is quite other (Fig. 172).[32]

Facing Banz, on the other side of the river Main, and likewise sitting on a hill, is the pilgrimage church of Vierzehnheiligen, the building of which began thirty years after Banz and continued for another thirty years. The architect was Johann Balthasar Neumann, born in 1687. Like Guarini, he was a mathematician; but whereas Guarini was a priest, Neumann's 'other profession' was soldiering. At the Residenz in Würzburg, Tiepolo has frescoed him in the uniform of a colonel in the Franconian army, sprawled astride a cannon. If Neumann also used geometry to achieve a transcendent sublimation of spatial form, he no longer did it with the religious impulse of the seventeenth century, though he certainly showed the urge to construct an infinite form as a symbol of eternity, albeit in the cooler climate of the Rococo.

Vierzehnheiligen has a difficult and complex building history, which it

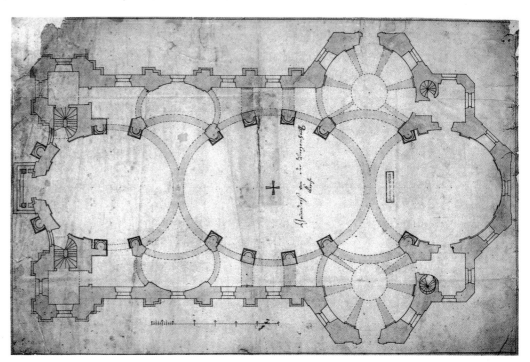

175. Vierzehnheiligen. Plan of B. Neumann's second scheme, 1744.

176. Vierzehnheiligen. Nave, looking east.

177. Vierzehnheiligen. Vault at crossing.

would be irrelevant to recite here. If we come to the heart of the matter at once: the plan (Fig. 175) consists of three longitudinal ovals placed end to end, with two transverse circles acting as a transept. A smaller pair of ovals is also worked in, west of the central longitudinal oval, where the high altar stands (Fig. 176). At the point of crossing, where, in a conventional structure, a dome might be expected, exactly the opposite happens: the vaults draw together instead of expanding, as binding arches in warped planes, consisting of curves of the third degree,[33] are driven together by the expanding oval fields of the vaulting (Fig. 177). The thrust into depth, and the upward thrust, are counteracted by the transverse ovals. The whole spatial concept of Vierzehnheiligen is one of great complexity: 'walls no longer enclose ... Columns do not order stable, comprehensible spaces; the spaces themselves are both separated and interwoven.'[34]

Neumann's church stands at the pinnacle of European Baroque, one of the supreme architectural monuments of the world. Nothing can detract from, or minimize, the supreme skill of its designer in creating the magical world that lies inside it. But the long path that leads to this achievement was undoubtedly illuminated by the genius of an earlier architect: Guarino Guarini.

NOTES TO THE TEXT

NOTES TO CHAPTER 1

1. Guarini himself wrote: 'we often see that people change their fashions, and what was once admired as beautiful becomes abhorred as deformed, and what one nation likes displeases another' – *AC* III. iii.
2. Quoted by G. M. Crepaldi, *La real chiesa di San Lorenzo in Torino* (Turin 1963), p. 52.
3. 'A chi piace l'architettura del Guarini, buon pro li faccia, ma stia tra pazzerelli.'
4. S. Giedion, *Space, Time and Architecture* (Cambridge, Mass. 1941 et seq.), p. 43. Subsequent landmarks in Guarini studies are outlined by S. Bordini in 'La critica Guariniana', *GGIB*.II, pp. 283–305. See also D. de Bernardi Ferrero, *Guarino Guarini e la sua arte* (Turin 1966), pp. 15–34, and L. Tamburini, *Le chiese di Torino dal rinascimento al barocco* (Turin [1968]), pp. 198–208.
5. The Da Capo Press. The double entendre of the imprint is evidently deliberate; the triple entendre (in this case) fortuitous.
6. See G. C. Argan, 'La tecnica del Guarini', *GGIB*.I, p. 42.
7. *AC* III.xiii.
8. 'Herr Frankl replied that Herr Weigmann was arguing about things that had never been asserted . . .' – Résumé of paper on Guarini's influence on Dientzenhofer. Sitzungen der Kunstwissenschaftlichen Gesellschaft in München, 1913–15. Sitzung am 1. März 1915. *Münchner Jahrbuch der bildenden Künste* (1914–15).
9. *Jahresgabe des deutschen Vereins für Kunstwissenschaft* (Berlin 1932).
10. 'Guarini e la diffusione del barocco', *GGIB*. II.
11. A. E. Brinckmann, *Theatrum novum Pedemontii: Ideen, Entwürfe und Bauten von Guarini, Juvarra, Vittone . . .* (Düsseldorf 1931), p. 11.
12. *AC* I.iii.6.
13. *AC* I.iii.9.
14. Argan, *GGIB*.I, p. 42.
15. (e), n. III.
16. U. Chierici, 'Guarini a Torino', *GGIB*.I, p. 359.
17. A. Griseri, *Le metamorfosi del barocco* (Turin 1967), p. 182.
18. In the Cassilla Collection.
19. Lettere di particolari; printed in *Schede Vesme*, Vol. II, pp. 552–3.
20. In the way, for example, that he puts down the eccentric scholar Juan Caramuel in his Treatise.

NOTES TO CHAPTER 2

1. T. Sandonnini, 'Il padre Guarino Guarini modenese', *Atti e memorie delle reali deputazioni di storia patria per le provincie modenesi e parmensi*, ser. 3, V (1888), pp. 483–534.
2. Ibid., p. 484.
3. 'Soprintendente ducale della fabbrica dell' ingrandimento di Modena.'
4. Abbreviated as CR; this is the explanation of Guarini's habitual manner of signing himself Don Guarino Guarini CR.
5. Pliny (3, 12, 17, § 106) called the inhabitants of this town Teatini, which is still the usual Italian way of writing the name of the religious Order. An illegitimate aitch crept into the sixteenth-century Latin form – illegitimate because the Greeks (as evidenced by Strabo and Ptolemy) called the town Τεατέα not Θεατέα. It was from this 'Modern Latin' version (as the *OED* calls it) that the English word 'Theatine' was coined in 1581. Thomas Goldwell, Bishop of St Asaph, was a Theatine in the reign of Henry VIII.
6. C. W. Currier, *History of the Religious Orders* (New York 1896), pp. 257–9.
7. Sandonnini, p. 487.
8. F. Ferrari, *Memorie storiche della regia chiesa parrochiale di S. Vincenzo Martire in Modena* (Modena 1924).
9. Quoted by Sandonnini, p. 487.
10. N. Carboneri, 'Guarini a Modena', *GGIB*.I. p. 47.
11. J. Summerson, *Architecture in Britain, 1530–1830*, 5th ed. (Harmondsworth 1969), p. 61.
12. Sandonnini, p. 487.
13. P. Portoghesi, *Guarino Guarini* (Milan 1956), p. [1].
14. Anonymous English writer (1620); quoted by J. Lees-Milne, *Baroque in Italy* (London 1959), p. 80.
15. L. Hautecoeur, *Histoire de l'architecture classique en France* (Paris 1948), Vol. II, p. 245.
16. From the *Journal* of Dubuisson-Aubenay for 22 December 1648, quoted by Hautecoeur, as above.
17. See H. Hibbard, 'The Early History of Sant'

Andrea della Valle', *Art Bulletin* XLIII (1961), p. 289.

18. Ibid.

19. See article in Thieme–Becker, signed B.C.K., and bibliography there.

20. Archivio di Stato, Parma, 'Libro delle croniche della Casa di S. Christina di Parma', under 4 November 1649.

21. Sandonnini, p. 491; *Bolletino d'Arte* (Rome 1909), p. 111.

22. Guarini was only responsible for the facade here.

23. See n. 20.

24. Sandonnini, p. 488.

25. F. Milizia, *Memorie dei più celebri architetti* (Rome 1768), s.v. 'Guarini'.

26. Sandonnini, p. 483.

27. Ibid., pp. 490–1.

28. H. Sedlmayr, *Die Architektur Borrominis* (Berlin 1930), p. 104.

29. The text was published posthumously (Turin 1737), conflated by Bernardo Vittone from two manuscripts of Guarini.

30. *Relazione del convento di S. Carlo alle 4° fontane di Roma*; reprinted in O. Pollak, *Die Kunsttätigkeit unter Urban VIII* (Vienna 1928), Vol. I, p. 48.

31. *AC* III.xxi.9.

32. S. Benedetti, 'Guarini ed il barocco romano', *GGIB*.I, p. 722.

33. 'It was at the suggestion of the Ticinese master that the young novice's work began' – Portoghesi, *Guarini* (1956), p. [1].

34. Archivio di Stato, Modena, Opera Pia, under 29 December 1647.

35. *AC* I.iii.3.

36. *AC* I.iii.11.

37. Archivio di Stato, Modena, Opera Pia, Teatini, 364. Document dated 13 October 1649.

38. Ferrari.

39. 'Whom Spaccini calls ignorant of architecture' – Sandonnini, p. 491.

40. "[The Provost] proposed Fr D. Guirino Guirini as superintendent of these Works and he was elected" – see n. 37.

41. Archivio di Stato, Modena, Giurisdizione Ecclesiastica, Regolari, b. 413.

42. Archivio di Stato, Modena, Opera Pia.

43. This subject is discussed in Portoghesi, *Guarini* (1956), and Carboneri, *GGIB*. I.

44. *Coretti* are private rooms giving on to a church, for the use of musicians or distinguished visitors. Fig. 35 shows a famous example in the Cornaro chapel. See I. Lavin, *Bernini and the Unity of the Visual Arts* (Oxford 1980). There are analogous features in St Martin's in the Fields.

45. Carboneri, *GGIB*.I.

46. Archivio di Stato, Modena, Giurisdizione Ecclesiastica, Regolari, b. 413.

47. Carlo Emanuele III, king of Sardinia, who had his court in Turin. His name is not mentioned.

48. Opera Pia, Teatini, Libro dei Partiti, 19 April 1650.

49. Marginal note by Fr G. Adimari to above entry.

50. Archivio di Stato, Modena, Opera Pia, Teatini, Capitoli fol. 116v.

51. Ibid., Libro delle cose più memorabili etc., p. 49.

52. Printed by Sandonnini, p. 495.

53. Libro de' capitoli della Casa dei PP. Teatini di Parma dal 20 Giugno 1650 al 31 Agosto 1801.

54. Archivio di Stato, Modena, Opera Pia, Teatini, Elenco di Prepositi.

55. 'Mercurio del nostro secolo.' The words are those of Filippo Pisciotta in the preface to Guarini's play *La pietà trionfante* (Messina 1660).

56. See n. 53.

57. Printed by Sandonnini, p. 495.

58. Archivio di Stato, Turin (c), Mazzo 5° (Anni 1657–94).

59. Archivio di Stato, Modena, Opera Pia, Teatini, 364; Atti Capitolari, May 1657.

NOTES TO CHAPTER 3

1. Argan, *GGIB*.I, p. 38.

2. R. Wittkower, *Art and Architecture in Italy, 1600–1750* (Harmondsworth [1958] 1980), p. 387, n. 22.

3. R. Wittkower. 'Introduzione al Guarini', *GGIB*.I, p. 31.

4. Printed by Sandonnini, p. 505.

5. *AC* III.xiii.1.

6. E. Guidoni, 'Modelli guariniani', *GGIB*.II, p. 238.

7. Antonio Carvalho da Costa, *Corografia Portugueza* (Lisbon 1706–12).

8. Ibid.

9. '. . . fue obrada por remedio' – Fray Agostinho de Santa Maria (1721); quoted by Ayres de Carvalho, *D. João V e a arte de seu tempo* (Mafra 1962), Vol. I, pp. 91–2.

10. Ibid.

11. R. C. Smith Jnr, 'João Frederico Ludovice, an 18th Century Architect in Portugal', *Art Bulletin* XVIII (1936), p. 275.

12. Fray Agostinho de Santa Maria; quoted by Carvalho.

13. J. A. Ramírez, 'Guarino Guarini, Fray Juan Ricci and the "Complete Salomonic Order"', *Art History* IV, No. 2 (1981), p. 181.

14. Smith, p. 276.

15. On the state of research in Portugal itself, I quote below the complete entry on Guarini from F. Marques de Sousa-Viterbo, *Diccionario historico e documental dos architectos, etc.* (Lisbon 1899), Vol. I, p. 467: '372 – Guarini of Modena (D). Here is a note about him that we find in Volkmar Machado: "D. Guarini of Modena, Theatine monk and architect of the Duke of Savoy, built the Theatine convent in Lìsbon: flourished in the middle of the 17th century" (*Memorias*, p. 162).'

Sixty years later, Antonio Terzaghi was reporting ruefully: 'Portuguese ideas on the Baroque enjoy a most exiguous bibliography, because it is a topic which arouses only very limited interest' (*Atti del X*, p. 378). When in 1962 Ayres de Carvalho's magisterial *D. João*

V e a arte de seu tempo appeared, it had to be published by the author at his own expense.

16. See, inter alia, the remarks of Sedlmayr (1930), p. 108; M. Passanti, *Nel mondo magico di Guarino Guarini* (Turin 1963), pp. 68–70; M. Anderegg-Tille, *Die Schule Guarinis* (Winterthur 1962), pp. 69–72; and A. Terzaghi, 'Origini e sviluppo della cupola ad arconi intrecciati nell'architettura barocca del Piemonte', *Atti del X*, pp. 369–79.

17. D. de Bernardi Ferrero, 'Chiese longitudinali del Guarini', *GGIB*.I, p. 418.

18. 'His little church of S. Carlo alle Quattro Fontane has in fact neither inside nor out any straight lines other than those on the window jambs, etc' – J. Burckhardt, *Der Cicerone* (Leipzig [1855] 1925), p. 353.

19. '[il] serrato repetirsi di quel motivo fra le due testate di queste' – Passanti (1963), p. 60.

20. 'Raumverschmelzung' – Sedlmayr (1930), p. 108.

21. 'Professor Portoghesi's sentences are a series of concatenations of polysyllabic abstractions – as he himself might write – and though in Italian they are resonant and at times impressive, in English they are only too often practically meaningless' – A. Blunt, review of the English translation of Portoghesi's *Roma Barocca*, in *Architectural Review* CL, No. 896 (October 1971), p. 259.

22. P. Portoghesi, 'Il linguaggio di Guarino Guarini', *GGIB*.II, p. 17.

23. M. Fagiolo, 'La "geosofia" del Guarini', *GGIB*.II, pp. 191–2.

24. Ibid.

25. *AC* III.viii.3.

26. See E. Mauceri, 'Colonne tortili così dette del Tempio di Salomone', *L'Arte* (1898), pp. 377 ff., and more recently J. B. Ward Perkins, 'The Shrine of St Peter and its Twelve Columns', *Journal of Roman Studies* XLII (1952), pp. 21–33.

27. Prepared for publication in 1930 as part of: *La vida y obra de Fray Juan Ricci. Fray Juan Ricci, escritor de arte y pintor de la escuela de Madrid por Elías Tormo y Monzó. Biografía del pintor D. Juan Andrés Ricci, monje de Monserrat, por el P. Celestino Gusi. Textos y juicios críticos sobre Fray Juan Ricci con el Tratado de la pintura sabia del P. Ricci. Edición preparada por Enrique Lafuente Ferrari* (Madrid 1930).

28. *AC* III.viii.3.

29. Ramírez, p. 178.

30. See the chronology in A. Lange, 'Disegni e documenti di Guarino Guarini', *GGIB*.I, p. 115.

31. *AC* III.viii.3.

Notes to Chapter 4

1. Sandonnini, p. 497.

2. See M. Accascina, 'Les soieries siciliennes du "Tiraz" normand', in *Actes du I. Congrès International d'Histoire du Costume* (Venice 1955), pp. 170 ff.

3. M. Accascina, 'La formazione artistica di Filippo Juvara', *Bolletino d'Arte* XLI (1956).

4. G. D. Gallo, *Gli annali della città di Messina* (Messina 1756), p. 149.

5. For a brief sketch of its building history, see W. Hager, 'Guarinis Theatinerfassade in Messina', in the Festschrift *Das Werk des Künstlers. Hubert Schrade zum 60. Geburtstag* (Stuttgart 1960), p. 232, n. 7.

6. Ibid., p. 235.

7. P. Portoghesi, 'Il tabernacolo guariniano dell'altare maggiore di S. Nicolò a Verona', *Quaderni dell'istituto di Storia dell'Architettura*, No. 14 (1956), p. 17.

8. G. Kubler and M. Soria, *Art and Architecture in Spain and Portugal and their American Dominions, 1500–1800* (Harmondsworth 1959), p. 24.

9. F. Sicuro, *Vedute e prospetti della città di Messina* (Messina 1768).

10. Portoghesi, *Guarini* (1956), pp. [2–3].

11. According to Thieme–Becker, s.v. 'Masuccio'.

12. Hager (1960), p. 240.

13. *AC* III.viii.3.

14. *Guida di Messina* (Messina 1902), p. 293.

15. Guidoni, *GGIB*.II, p. 236, n. 1.

16. Sandonnini, p. 497.

17. Portoghesi, *Guarini*, (1956), p. [3].

18. e.g. G. La Farina, *Messina ed i suoi monumenti* (Messina 1840).

19. Portoghesi, *Guarini* (1956), p. [13].

20. Hager (1960), p. 232, n. 6.

21. H. A. Millon, 'Guarino Guarini', in A. K. Placzek, ed., *Macmillan Encyclopaedia of Architects* (London 1982), p. 272.

22. Wittkower (1980), p. 386, n. 9.

23. Ibid., p. 268.

24. Interesting parallels to this rotation of superimposed features have been noted in late Gothic designs, e.g. Drawing 16889 at the Vienna Akademie der Bildenden Künste. See M. Tafuri, 'Retorica e sperimentalismo: Guarino Guarini e la tradizione manierista', *GGIB*.I, p. 683, with illustration.

25. P. Portoghesi, *Borromini* (London 1968), p. 8.

26. Cf., however, his scheme for the drum of S. Andrea delle Fratte and the adjoining campanile where he experiments with an aggregation of strata.

27. Portoghesi (1968), p. 5.

28. See G. B. Zander, 'G. B. Montano', *Quaderni dell'Istituto di Storia dell'Architettura* XXX (1959), XLIX-L(1962). A. Blunt's lecture on Montano to the Courtauld Institute in 1956 (referred to by Lees-Milne, p. 69) has not appeared in the *Journal of the Warburg and Courtauld Institutes*.

29. See R. Wittkower, *Architectural Principles in the Age of Humanism* (London 1962).

30. Demonstrated by Passanti (1963), pp. 110–11.

31. Wittkower (1980), p. 269.

32. By a Freudian error, Lees-Milne converts this title into *La pietra trionfante* when referring to it in passing (p. 167).

33. Guidoni, *GGIB*.II, p. 230.

34. The Theatines, like the Jesuits, were very interested in the use of theatrical and dramatic devices to promote religious observance. See,

for example, on their religio-dramatic activities in Paris, the contemporary observations of Oliver Lefèvre d'Ormesson (*Journal*, ed. M. Cheruel (Paris 1860), p. 598, n. 1).

35. The seventeenth century had the same difficulties with Scandinavian names that the eighteenth century had with Egyptian ones.

36. M. Fagiolo, 'La Sindone e l'enigma dell'eclisse', *GGIB*.II, p. 211. The expression *tenebrosa luce* derives from the neoplatonic concept of *lux tenebrosa*.

37. Sandonnini, p. 498.

38. Faculty dated 3 June 1662 in Archivio di Stato, Modena, Opera Pia.

39. Letter dated 13 November 1670 in the Archivio di Stato, Turin (c), 1657–1694.

40. Lange, p. 110.

NOTES TO CHAPTER 5

1. Lange, p. 106. Dr Lange's researches in the Registres capitulaires des Théatins in the French National Archives have cast much new light on Guarini's stay in Paris.

2. M. Dumoulin, *Etudes de topographie parisienne* (Paris 1929), Vol. I, p. 296.

3. The first reference to this sum is in the Registre capitulaire of 4 August 1661 (Raymond Darrican, 'Les Clercs Reguliers Théatins à Paris', in *Regnum Dei*, Collectanea Theatina (Rome 1954), Nos. 1–6, pp. 132–7). Later authorities vary the figure. Mazarin's most notable architectural legacy was the Collège des Quatre Nations (now the Institut de France) for whose contruction he also provided in his will.

4. Lange, p. 108.

5. C. Brayda, L. Coli and D. Sesia, 'Specializzazioni e vita professionale nel sei e settecento in Piemonte', *Atti e Rassegna Tecnica della società degl' Ingegneri e Architetti di Torino* No. 3. (1963), pp. 139–40.

6. Lange, p. 110.

7. Serving as chapels; the young Bolognese priest Sebastiano Locatelli, who visited the church in 1664, noted that the altars stood in the centre of the chapels, and not against the walls, a detail not indicated on the plan in Guarini's book, *Relation de Sebastien Locatelli* in A. Vautier, *Voyage de France. Moeurs et coutumes françaises, 1664–1665* (Paris 1905), pp. 141–2.

8. The plan of Ste Anne given in J. F. Blondel's *Architecture françoise* (Paris 1752), Bk ii, No. XXX, pl. 1, shows the crossing arches bent inward. R. Pommer in his book *Eighteenth-Century Architecture in Piedmont* (New York and London 1967), p. 8, considers this alteration to have been made not by Liévain, who completed the work between 1714 and 1720, but by Guarini himself. This seems unlikely, however. Work was suspended on Ste Anne already in 1668, and Guarini had no need therefore to let the engravings of this scheme (which first appeared in his *Dissegni d'architettura civile ed ecclesiastica* in 1686, three years

after his death) incorporate an outdated feature. It may be mentioned, nevertheless, that C. Bricarelli, in his article on Guarini in Thieme–Becker, *Allgemeines Lexikon der Bildenden Künstler* (Leipzig 1922), suggested that, as Ste Anne was not finished in his lifetime, Guarini may have altered the design for publication to conform with his later taste.

9. See the part plan at this level in the top left-hand corner of the general ground plan (Fig. 19). The plan suggests a pilaster and a quarter-attached column, but columns only are shown on the elevation (Fig. 25).

10. Pommer (1967), p. 5.

11. cf. Wittkower (1980), p. 269.

12. Pommer (1967), p. 10.

13. Ibid., p. 9.

14. See G. V. Arata, *L'architettura arabo-normanna e il rinascimento in Sicilia* (Milan 1925), pls. 4–5, 35, 38–40, 62.

15. e.g. by John Harvey, *Gothic England* (London 1947), p. 55 and pls. 72–3.

16. A. Blunt, *Art and Architecture in France, 1500–1700* (Harmondsworth 1970), pp. 124–5 and pl. 96b.

17. P. Smith, 'Mansart Studies II: The Val-de-Grâce', *Burlington Magazine* CVI (1964), p. 114, fig. 20.

18. A. Laprade, *François d'Orbay* (Paris n.d.), pl. VI–2.

19. Passanti (1963), p. 76.

20. A. Blunt, in 'Guarini and Leonardo', *Architectural Review* CXLVII, No. 2 (1970), p. 164, assigns a possible medieval provenance to this shape, which is 'basically contrary to any principles accepted in Italian architecture since the fifteenth century in that, instead of having a horizontal sill, they are symmetrical about a middle horizontal axis'.

21. It is present by implication only in the larger spaces of the Padri Somaschi. See Fig. 18.

22. Passanti (1963), p. 79, suggests that this may be to maintain in all four arms the same relationship between the width of the piers and the width of the opening.

23. This type of optical device, of course, is a well-known characteristic of the Baroque. Bernini's manipulation of the height and positions of the columns flanking the Scala Regia in the Vatican to suggest, by perspective implication, a standard height and width throughout, which they really do not have, is one of the most celebrated examples.

24. D. R. Coffin, 'Padre Guarino Guarini in Paris', *Journal of the Society of Architectural Historians* XV, No. 2 (1956), p. 6.

25. Wittkower (1980), p. 386, n. 12.

26. cf. ibid., p. 79.

27. pls. 9 and 10 (here Figs. 19 and 25).

28. H. Hibbard, *Bernini* (Harmondsworth 1965), ch. V, 'Le Cavalier en France'.

29. 'Without Guarini being present' – Wittkower, *GGIB*.I, p. 23.

30. P. de Fréart, Sieur de Chantelou, *Journal du voyage du cavalier Bernin en France*, ed. L. Lalanne (Paris 1885), pp. 33–4.

31. 1 May 1666. Wren Society, XIII (1936), p. 41. All the material relating to Wren's stay in Paris has been published by Margaret Whinney, 'Sir Christopher Wren visits Paris', *Gazette des Beaux-Arts* LI (1958), pp. 229–42.

32. P. Portoghesi, 'Guarini a Vicenza', *Critica d'Arte* n.s. IV (Fasc. 20, 21, 23) (1957), p. 115.

33. *Leges temporum et planetarum* (Turin 1678) and *Coelestis mathematicae* (Milan 1683).

34. C. Wren, *Parentalia* (London 1750), p. 261.

35. E. Sekler, *Wren and his Place in European Architecture* (London 1956), p. 47.

36. Ibid., p. 142.

37. Wittkower, *GGIB*.I, p. 30; Tafuri, pp. 685–7.

38. Blunt (1970), p. 146.

39. N. Pevsner, *An Outline of European Architecture*, 7th ed. (Harmondsworth 1963), p. 315.

40. Dancing, 1661; Painting, 1663; Science, 1666; Music, 1669.

41. Portoghesi (1957), p. 128, n. 5.

42. Hautecoeur, p. 757. He also (p. 247) cites a Chapel Royal designed by Fr Dubois in 1666 in the form of a helicoidal pyramid. It was not built. G. Cattaui, 'Guarini et la France', *GGIB*.II, p. 515, attributes the church at Asfeld to a Dominican, H. Romain. The connection with Guarini is discounted by R. W. Berger, 'The Church of St. Didier, Asfeld-la-Ville', *Architectura* (Munich) No. 1 (1973), p. 51.

43. Wittkower (1980), p. 374, n. 11.

44. *AC* I.iii.3.

45. Coffin, pp. 5 ff.; Lange, p. 107, n.

46. Letter from the Ambassador of Savoy in Venice, dated 8 January 1667, to the Marchese di San Tomaso, a government minister in Turin; in the Archivio di Stato, Turin (Lettere di Ministri: Venezia), now printed in *Schede Vesme*, Vol. II, p. 551.

47. Registres capitulaires, 13 October 1666.

48. *Schede Vesme*, Vol. II, p. 553.

49. Ibid.

50. Registres capitulaires, 3 March 1668.

51. Blondel, Bk II, p. 290.

52. Coffin, p. 8. Some surviving fragments of the eighteenth-century adaptations incorporated in later buildings are illustrated by Alan Boase, 'Sant'Anna Reale', *GGIB*.I, pp. 356–7.

53. To be precise, the engraver Feyneau has scaled the plan in palms (= 0.29 metre), and the elevation in Parisian feet. This would give a width of 116.58m to the plan, but 147.60m to the elevation. See Lange, p. 100, n. 1.

54. Guarini's church in Lisbon is scaled in *canne portoghesi*; in Messina he uses *palmi messinesi*; in Turin *piedi di Piemonte* and other local units.

55. Antoine Le Pautre, *Oeuvres* (Paris 1652).

56. Passanti (1963), p. 2.

57. Brinckmann, (1931), No. 112 (cf. our Fig. 63).

58. The side at the bottom of the sheet. The identification is Passanti's (1963, p. 14).

59. See L. Hautecoeur, *Le Louvre et les Tuileries de Louis XIV* (Paris 1927), pl. 33.

60. K. Noehles, 'Die Louvre-Projekte von Pietro da Cortona und Carlo Rainaldi', *Zeitschrift für Kunstgeschichte* XXIV (1960), p. 40.

61. Brinckmann (1931), p. 251A (our Fig. 83).

62. Passanti (1963), p. 15.

63. See Sedlmayr (1930), pp. 104 ff.

64. Plate 23 (our Fig. 26): 'A Atrium B Loggia D Galleries I Secret staircases + Chapels the rest [= 140 rooms!] are chambers and offices.'

65. Guarini discusses the effect of shadows in architecture in *AC* III.xxi.3.

66. Sandonnini, pp. 499–500.

67. The cosmology of Copernicus and Galileo is rejected in favour of a geocentric universe.

68. *Placita philosophica*, p. 214.

69. 'Ars est actus seu habitus, res simul applicans, iuxta illarum naturalem convenientiam.'

70. 'Ars naturae opera iuvare potest, perficere potest, sed non efficere.'

71. A point first made by G. C. Argan, *L'architettura barocca in Italia* (Milan 1957), pp. 61–3. The implications were subsequently explored in greater detail by the philosopher A. del Noce in *Il problema dell'ateismo* (Bologna 1964).

72. See C. C. J. Webb, *History of Philosophy* (London 1916), pp. 155–6.

73. See Bianca Tavassi La Greca, 'La posizione del Guarini in rapporto alla cultura filosofica del tempo' printed as an appendix to her critical edition of the *Architettura civile* (Milan 1968).

74. N. Malebranche, *Recherche de la vérité* (Paris 1674), Vol. VI, part 1, p. 4.

75. See, for example, G. C. Argan, 'Per una storia dell'architettura piemontese' in *L'Arte* XXXVI (1933), p. 396: 'typically baroque is the search in geometry . . . for stimuli to the imagination and paradoxical justifications for the fantastic judgements'.

76. *AC* I.iii.1. Over a third of the book is devoted to a study of the newly developed science of projective geometry.

77. Argan (1957), p. 63. See also the same author's *Europe of the Capitals* (London 1964), p. 123.

Notes to Chapter 6

1. See also Lange, pp. 111–16.

2. Quoted by Sandonnini, p. 500.

3. L. Schiedermair, 'Die Zeit des Barocks, der allegorischen Dichtung, des Einwirkens deutscher Musik, bis zum Anschluss Bayerns an Frankreich', in *Forschungen zur Geschichte Bayerns* (Berlin 1902), Vol. X, p. 108, where Guarini is referred to as 'der Theatinermönch Quarino'. E. Hempel, *Baroque Art and Architecture in Central Europe* (Harmondsworth 1965), p. 76, speculates on 'the novel situation that would have arisen for the whole of Southern Germany' if Guarini had accepted.

4. 'The history of this sub-Alpine region is not primarily a history of cities at all; it is a history of local chieftains ceaselessly engaged in wars of oppression or survival. Happy hours could be spent by the pedantic in tracing through the welter of centuries the striking and picturesque figures and families

of local fame, such as the Marquesses of Saluzzo and the Byzantine Marquesses of Monferrat; but for an appreciation of modern Piedmont it is easiest to consider, notwithstanding its present eclipse, a single family, the House of Savoy' – Jasper More, *The Land of Italy* (London 1949), p. 85. The welter of centuries is systematized, for the benefit of the pedantic and others, in the six volumes of E. Ricotti, *Storia della monarchia piemontese* (Florence 1861–9).

5. More, p. 86. See *Murray's Handbook for Northern Italy* (London 1852), p. 4: 'The Piedmontese dialect is much more like the Provençal than any other of the modifications of the *volgare* in the north of Italy. But this similarity is not the effect of mixture or corruption: it is an original language, holding a middle place between the two languages of Provençal and Italian, with some peculiar intonations and vowels.'

6. See L. Cibrario, *Storia di Torino* (Turin 1836), Vol. I, p. 317. The tag was adopted as a motto by Emanuele Filiberto's younger contemporary Francis Bacon.

7. G. L. Marini, *L'architettura barocca in Piemonte. La provincia di Torino* (Turin 1963), p. 14.

8. V. Golzio, *Seicento e Settecento* (Turin 1960), p. 217. The only early Renaissance building in the city is St John's Cathedral. See A. Ressa, 'L'architettura religiosa in Piemonte nei secoli XVII e XVIII', *Torino* XX (1941), p. 7.

9. L. Malle, *Le arti figurative in Piemonte* (Turin 1962). See also Wittkower, *GGIB*.I, p. 29.

10. See H. A. Millon, Review of Crepaldi [q.v.], *Art Bulletin* XLVII (1965), p. 531.

11. Crepaldi, pp. 18 ff.

12. Tamburini [1968], p. 94, n. 12; p. 199, n. 4 and the authorities quoted there.

13. Crepaldi, pp. 31 ff.

14. Ibid., p. 36, n. 15.

15. Archivio di Stato, Turin (h), Patenti, rig. LIII, 50.

16. The original church was subsequently called S. Lorenzo Vecchio.

17. Colonia Julia Augusta Taurinorum, a name bestowed in 29 BC.

18. 'Densely inhabited, since there are two or three families to a house' – Cardinal Bonelli, papal legate; quoted by Marini (1963), p. 27.

19. P. Abercrombie, *Town and Country Planning*, 2nd ed. (London 1945), pp. 40–1.

20. A feature that had characterized ancient Turin. L. Mumford, *The City in History* (London 1966), p. 227. G. C. Argan, *Storia dell'arte italiana* (Florence 1968), Vol. III, p. 371, points to the 'chronological coincidence' of this work with Domenico Fontana's in Rome.

21. M. Passanti, 'Le trasformazioni barocche nel tessuto urbano della Torino medievale', *Atti del X*, pp. 72 ff.

22. See Argan (1964), pp. 34–5, and L. Mumford, *The Culture of Cities* (New York 1938), Ch. 2. Already in 1566 the Venetian ambassador, Giovanni Correr, was reporting on Emanuele

Filiberto's vexation 'that in all his State, there was not one single city . . . worthy to be called the metropolis of all the others' – quoted by A. M. Brizio, 'L'architettura barocca in Piemonte', in *Annuario dell'Università di Torino* (1952–3), p. 25.

23. Argan (1964), p. 35.

24. Quoted by G. Craveri, *Guida dei forestieri per la real città di Torino* (Turin 1753): 'la più bella veduta che trovar si possa in Italia'.

25. e.g. by Griseri (1967), ch. 7.

26. Tamburini [1968], p. 198.

27. Griseri (1967), p. 180.

NOTES TO CHAPTER 7

1. Crepaldi, p. 43.

2. Archivio di Stato, Turin (e), Teatine – Memorie, etc., III.

3. Crepaldi, p. 44, thus interprets a contemporary document which refers to the site given for the church as 'no longer sufficient for the fabric as regards length and breadth'.

4. It was not till the last quarter of the seventeenth century that tax income increased notably in Piedmont, allowing the execution of major building works by outstanding architects. The change was wrought by the introduction of a military surtax and a thoroughgoing reorganization of the finances by G. B. Truchi. See Mario Abrate, 'Elementi per la storia della finanza dello stato sabaudo nella seconda metà del XVII secolo', *Bollettino Storico-bibliografico Subalpino* LXVII, Fasc. I–II (January–June 1969).

5. Archivio di Stato, Turin (h), Art. 205, Reg. 1659–63. See also Millon, Review of Crepaldi, p. 531.

6. See in particular Wittkower (1962), part I.

7. Ressa, pp. 14 ff.

8. Passanti (1963), pp. 128–9.

9. Brinckmann (1931), § 231.

10. J. Vanderperren and J. Kennes, 'De systematische ruimtelijke wereld van Guarino Guarini' in *A+*, No. 31 (September 1976), fig. 2, p. 74, and p. 89. A full-length manuscript with the same title as this article lies unpublished in Brussels, victim of the Flemish language in which it is written.

11. Wittkower (1980), p. 272.

12. 'The massive wall knows no rest until it reaches the round base of the dome; here the massive swelling material comes to a point of repose, the terminal point of the first "instalment"' – Vanderperren and Kennes, p. 89.

13. Wittkower (1980), p. 271.

14. 'The church interior . . . revealed a completely new conception of space directed towards infinity: form is dissolved in favour of the magic spell of light': H. Wölfflin, *Renaissance und Barock* (Munich 1888), English translation by Kathrin Simon (London 1964), p. 64.

15. O. Schubert, *Geschichte des Barock in Spanien* (Esslingen 1908), p. 176.

16. See in particular A. Florensa, 'Guarini ed il mondo islamico', *GGIB*.I, p. 639, and P. Verzone, 'Struttura delle cupole del Guarini',

GGIB.I, p. 401, and the illustrations in Bernardi Ferrero (1966).

17. En route to Lisbon in connection with the design of the Theatine church, S. Maria della Divina Providenza.

18. Giedion, pp. 58–9. The Cordoban dome is in fact not over a mihrab, as stated by Giedion: an example of it covers each of the lateral bays of the 'new maqsurah' in front of the third mihrab. See B. Bevan, *History of Spanish Architecture* (London 1939), fig. 14 and pl. XI.

19. *AC* III.xiii.1. Guarini's bête noire, the Spanish architect-bishop Juan Caramuel de Lobkowitz, also refers to these buildings in his book *Architectura civil recta y obliqua* (Vigevano 1678), p. 74, a book which Guarini read with the closest attention. This does not, of course, exclude the possibility of Guarini having seen them himself.

20. Wittkower (1980), p. 387, n. 22.

21. See on this point Eugenio Galdieri in the foreword to Florensa, pp. 637–8.

22. Verzone, p. 404.

23. Four six-pointed ones in the vaults; the eight-pointed one in the dome and a six-pointed one over the presbytery.

24. E. Battisti, 'Schemata nel Guarini', *GGIB*.II, pp. 107–77.

25. Ibid., p. 115.

26. 'ebbe per iscopo di erigere molto forti si, ma che sembrassero deboli, e che servissero di miracolo, come stessero in piedi'.

27. In his *Vocabolario toscano delle arti del disegno* (Florence 1681), s.v. 'Ordine Gotico'. See also R. Wittkower's Charles T. Mathews lectures, published posthumously as *Gothic vs. Classic: Architectural Projects in Seventeenth-Century Italy* (New York 1974).

28. See P. Moissy, *Jésuites de l'ancienne Assistance de France* (Rome 1958), and J. Evans, *Monastic Architecture in France from the Renaissance to the Revolution* (Cambridge 1964).

29. *AC* III.xiii.1.

30. Ibid.

31. *AC* I.iii.6.

32. Ibid. A similar attitude is expressed in *Placita philosophica* towards the views of the ancient philosophers: 'I have indeed deferred to, not worshipped, Aristotle, Plato, Galen and the other Masters of Wisdom; I have cherished their sayings as opinions, not venerated them as oracles.'

33. *AC*. I.iii.9.

34. *AC* III.iii.

35. *AC* III.iii.1.

36. 'l'acrobatismo statico' – Marini, (1963), p. 91.

37. L. Denina and A. Protto, 'La real chiesa di San Lorenzo in Torino', in *L'architettura Italiana* XV (1920), pp. 34–8.

38. G. Brotto and V. Todesco: 'S. Lorenzo a Torino', *L'architettura* No. 8 (1961), pp. 275–81.

39. G. Torretta, *Un'analisi della capella di S. Lorenzo di Guarino Guarini* (Turin 1968).

40. Passanti (1963).

41. This communication is not included in the *Atti del X*, but is alluded to in her listing of Guarini drawings in *GGIB*.I (p. 234 § 4).

42. Passanti (1963), p. 160.

43. Verzone, p. 402.

44. A device derived from Romanesque or Gothic crossings.

45. To G. L. Marini, an architectural writer who has little patience for either *concettismo* or semiotics, the church of S. Lorenzo as a whole nevertheless 'truly ... corresponds to a religious concept'; it makes him think of the description of the eternal light given by Dante at the end of the *Divine Comedy*: 'Within its depths I saw ingathered, bound by love in one volume, the scattered leaves of all the universe' (Paradiso, 33, 86–7) – Marini (1963), p. 92. For a sharp critique of Marini's view of Guarini, see H. A. Millon, Review of Marini (1963) [q.v.], *Art Bulletin* XLVII (1965), pp. 532–3.

46. Griseri (1967), p. 181.

NOTES TO CHAPTER 8

1. *Schede Vesme*, Vol. II, p. 551.

2. Archivio di Stato, Turin (j); excerpted in *Schede Vesme*, Vol. II, p. 551. A fuller version is given by G. Tiraboschi, 'Guarini', in *Biblioteca Modenese, o notizie ... degli scrittori natii degli stati del ... Duca di Modena* (Modena 1783).

3. As implied, for example, by P. Portoghesi in his articles on Guarini in *Civiltà delle Macchine* (January–February 1956) and in the *Encyclopaedia of World Art* (New York 1963), Vol. VII.

4. Confirmed by the Regent Maria Cristina di Francia. See Marini (1963), p. 73.

5. S. Cordero di Pamparato, 'Il Padre Guarino Guarini teologo del Principe di Carignano', *Il Duomo di Torino* II, No. 4 (1928).

6. A. Midana, 'La Real Cappella della S.S. Sindone', in *Italia Sacra* Fasc. VIII (Turin 1929), p. 420.

7. U. Chevalier, *Etude critique sur l'origine du Saint Suaire* (Paris 1900).

8. Midana, p. 420.

9. Ibid.

10. N. Carboneri, 'Vicenda delle cappelle per la Santa Sindone', *Bolletino della SPABA* n.s. XVIII (1964), pp. 95–6.

11. G. Claretta, 'Inclinazioni artistiche di Carlo Emanuele I di Savoia e dei suoi figli', *Atti della SPABA* V, No. 6 (1894), p. 351. Carlo di Castellamonte (?1555–?1639) entered the service of the Duke of Savoy in 1602, and succeeded Ascanio Vitozzi as Ducal Engineer and Architect in 1615 – C. Boggio, *Gli architetti C. e A. Castellamonte* (Turin 1896).

12. L. Collobi, 'Carlo di Castellamonte primo ingegnere del duca di Savoia', *Bollettino Storico-bibliografico Subalpino* XXXIX (1937), p. 244.

13. C. Duboin, *Editti e manifesti* (Turin 1846), Vol. XIII, pp. 916–17.

14. Published by Claretta, pp. 351–2.

15. Archivio di Stato, Turin (b), 1644 in 1657.

Maurizio Cardinale Mazzo 17, 14 and 23 September 1656. See also *Schede Vesme*, Vol. I, pp. 286 ff.

16. Printed in C. Rovere, *Descrizione del Reale Palazzo di Torino* (Turin 1858), pp. 70 ff.

17. Registro delle Sessioni del consiglio delle finanze per la fabbrica, 17 February 1659. Archivio di Stato, Turin, Art. 195, m. 1.

18. Listed by Carboneri (1964), p. 105, n. 34.

19. See n. 17.

20. (h), Art 179, n. 8, 1657 to 1666 and 1667 to 1669.

21. Ibid., Conti I, n. 179.

22. Referred to by Carboneri as 'the famous site meeting of 10 September 1665' – *GGIB*.II, p. 348. Tamburini calls them 'an impressive cast of celebrities' – (1968), p. 225.

23. Carboneri, *GGIB*.II, p. 348.

24. '... but we believe that that sovereign, having been very pleased with the church of S. Lorenzo, was eager to have for his architect him who had been the ingenious author of it' – Sandonnini, p. 501.

25. Conti I, n. 318.

26. Conti II, n. 8. The date is 30 April 1667.

27. See Tamburini (1968), p. 227, for various extracts.

28. Carboneri (1964), p. 108.

29. Ibid., p. 107.

30. 'headless, as in a nightmare' – Griseri, (1967), p. 197. For Battisti's esoteric interpretation of these features, see *GGIB*.II, pp. 142–4.

31. Griseri (1967), p. 198.

32. 'like abandoned tombs' – Tamburini [1968], p. 230.

33. Passanti (1963), p. 190.

34. Griseri (1967), p. 197.

35. Their Order is continued in the minor Order of the main space.

36. He may also have noted the way Vitozzi had inscribed a hexagon in a circular plan at his church of SS. Trinità, Turin.

37. Borromini sets oval reliefs into the pendentives over the nave of S. Carlo alle Quattro Fontane, but these do not read as voids.

38. In Islamic architecture the design occurs on both walls and doors. Guarini would have observed examples in Spain. See I. El-Said and A. Parman, *Geometric Concepts in Islamic Art* (London 1976), esp. ch. II, §3, 'The Hexagon and the Root Three System of Proportion'.

39. 'This kind of vault is my specialty' (Questa sorta di volta è mia particolare) – Opening words of obs. 9 ('Delle volte a fascie') in Guarini's chapter on vaults in his *Architettura civile* (III.xxvi).

40. Passanti (1963), p. 180.

41. '... to the largo of the drum succeeds the scherzo of the dome' – ibid., p. 185.

42. Wittkower (1980), p. 139.

43. Giedion, pp. 49–51.

44. See Fig. 18; and Benedetti, pp. 710–11.

45. Verzone, p. 413.

46. See R. Milner Gulland, 'Art and Architecture of Old Russia', in R. Auty and D. Obolensky, eds., *Companion to Russian Studies 3* (Cambridge 1980), pp. 18 and 55–6.

47. L. Beltrami, *Vita di Aristotile da Bologna* (Bologna 1912).

48. Portoghesi, *Guarini* (1956), p. [9].

49. E. Battisti, 'Note sul significato della Capella della Santa Sindone nel Duomo di Torino', *Atti del X*, p. 364.

50. Fagiolo, 'La Sindone', *GGIB*.II, p. 211; Guidoni, *GGIB*.II.

NOTES TO CHAPTER 9

1. It was from this branch that the nineteenth and twentieth-century kings of United Italy descended, the last member of the senior branch having died without issue in 1831. The last king of Italy, Umberto II (who reigned for a month in 1946), was born at the castle of Racconigi in 1904.

2. For a description of the town, see C. Merlini, 'Racconigi e il suo castello', *Torino* XIX (1941).

3. L. V. Bertarelli, *Guida d'Italia del T.C.I.: Piemonte, Lombardia, Ticino* (Milan 1914), p. 89.

4. Lange, p. 238, Scheda 2, and p. 291, Dis. 2.

5. It had devolved to the State, or rather had been confiscated by the Exchequer, when its owner Bernardino di Savoia died without issue in 1605.

6. First published in part by Brinckmann (1931), § 112.

7. Their comings and goings are documented in minute detail, on the basis of archival payment records, by Dr Augusta Lange. See also N. Gabrielli, *Racconigi* (Turin 1972).

8. Lange, Scheda 16.

9. Ibid., pp. 143–4.

10. Ibid., p. 149.

11. Duke Carlo Emanuele II had already made him 'Engineer for SS. Sindone' in 1668.

12. Archivio dei Principi di Carignano, Ordini. Printed in *Schede Vesme*., Vol. II, p. 555, and more fully in Cordero di Pamparato.

13. (g), Cat. 43, Mazzo 1, no. 3/3.

14. Lange, pp. 91–344.

15. (a), Cat. 95(1).

16. (g), Cat. 43, Mazzo 1.

17. (a), Cat. 95(1).

18. (g), Cat. 43, Mazzo I, no. 3/4; Lange, Scheda 7 and Dis. 7.

19. cf. A. E. Brinckmann, *Baukunst des 17. und 18. Jahrhunderts in den romanischen Ländern* (Berlin 1919), p. 126.

20. Portoghesi, *Guarini* (1956).

21. Even more sophisticated reticence is displayed in the Georgian town houses of London, where components of Orders are implied, rather than applied. 'Where there is no order, a broad band marks the first floor level, and there is often room between the lintels of the top windows and the cornice for the architrave and frieze which are not there. Sometimes an additional (narrow) band runs under the cills of the first-floor windows, in token of an absent pedestal under the order' — Summerson, p. 228.

22. Brinckmann (1931), § 116 B.
23. s.v. 'Guarini', in A. K. Placzek, ed., *Macmillan Encyclopaedia of Architects* (London 1982). Borra also changed Guarini's steps on the north front.
24. More, p. 90.
25. (g), Cat. 43, Mazzo I.
26. Millon, in Placzek, p. 274.
27. For a concise town-planning history of Turin, see the chapter 'Urbanistica' in Marini (1963).
28. I am indebted for the following historical and dynastic details to Ricotti; and L. Tettoni, *Le illustri alleanze della real casa di Savoia* (Turin 1868).
29. Irretrievably, because the Princess failed in an attempt to have the marriage annulled. It was ratified and made public by Luigi Tommaso in 1683.
30. He married Caterina d'Este in 1684, to the fury of Louis XIV, who had wanted to increase French influence in Piedmont by uniting Emanuele Filiberto with a French princess. In due course, however, the young Duke grew up, married and produced his own heir, but, as noted above (n. 1), it was the descendants of Emanuele Filiberto who in the nineteenth century ultimately became the kings of United Italy.
31. Lange, pp. 168 ff.
32. '... l'ingresso nella via di S. Francesco detta degli Ebrei vecchi'. Now Via Barbaroux, Lange, pp. 168 ff.
33. See Abrate, p. 16.
34. 'Alienazioni di Tasso d'appannaggio fatte per convertirne il prezzo nella construzione del Pallazzo nuovo' – Archivio di Stato, Turin (g), Cat. 53.
35. Deed dated 3 August 1622, in the Archivio di Stato, Turin (g), Cat. 53.
36. Passanti (1963), p. 18, gives the size as 81 × 190 metres, covering two city blocks.
37. Undated agreement in the Archivio di Stato, Turin (g), Cat. 53.
38. Abrate, p. 16.
39. Lange, pp. 168 ff.
40. (g), Cat. 51, Mazzo 1, no. 9/9. These drawings were first noted by Giovanni Chevalley in 1920 ('Il Palazzo Carignano a Torino', *Bollettino della SPABA* No. 1–2, 1921). They were first published in part by Brinckmann (1931), Nos. 250–2, while individual sheets have since been featured by D. G. Cravero, 'Il Palazzo Carignano', in *Atti e Rassegna Tecnica della Società degl' Ingegneri e degli Architetti in Torino* V, No. 2 (1951); M. Bernardi, *Tre palazzi a Torino* (Turin 1963), and, in greater detail, by Lange.
41. Cited by Coffin, p. 11, n. 8.
42. See Lange, Scheda 55a.
43. See for instance Lange, Schede 56a, b, and 68 to 75.
44. Bernardi, p. 20.
45. (g), Cat. 51, Mazzo 1, no. 9/7, corresponding to Brinckmann (1931), p. 251A, and Lange, Dis. 57a and Scheda 57a.
46. E. Hempel, *Francesco Borromini* (Vienna 1924).
47. No. 9/6.
48. No. 9/15.
49. No. 9/6 et al. Here shown, for clarity's sake, after measured drawings by S. Molli Boffa.
50. 'giants with their bodies tangled in rope' – Passanti (1963), p. 22. A metaphysical interpretation is suggested by Tafuri, p. 686, n. 1.
51. H. A. Millon, *Baroque and Rococo Architecture* (London 1964), p. 22.
52. Ibid.
53. This explanation is given by Millon (1982); the drawing is reproduced without comment.
54. *AC* II.viii.1.
55. *AC* III.xxv.8.
56. 'Bernini's design of the Louvre I would have given my skin for, but the old reserv'd Italian gave me but a few minutes view ... I had only time to copy it in my fancy and memory' – Christopher Wren, quoted in Summerson, p. 116.
57. G. L. Marini, 'Il mattone nell'architettura civile del Guarini', *Epoche* (Turin) No. 3 (1962), p. 132.
58. In a kiln at the Royal Park near Turin, and brought to the site on mule back. *Registro di mandati al Piovani*, in the Archivio di Stato, Turin (g), Cat. 53, Mazzo 1, no. 3, passim.
59. Lange, pp. 181–7.
60. Benedetti, *GGIB*.I, p. 732.
61. Coffin, p. 10.
62. Battisti, *GGIB*.II, p. 150.
63. *AC* III.xvi.2.
64. Marini (1962), p. 132.
65. Argan (1957), p. 62.
66. Tafuri, p. 686.
67. Argan, *GGIB*.I, p. 36.
68. B. Contardi, *La retorica e l'architettura del barocco* (Rome 1978), p. 119.
69. 'onde fanno una superbissima vista' – *AC* III.xvi.2.
70. Guidoni, *GGIB*.II, p. 231, n. 1.
71. Jean-Louis Vaudoyer, *Italie retrouvée* (Paris 1950).
72. *AC* I.iii.9.
73. The Collegio is not illustrated in *Architettura civile*. The documentary sources are in the Archivio di Stato, Turin (i), Fondo Gesuiti, Collegio dei Nobili, Mazzo 10.
74. Ibid.
75. Portoghesi, *Guarini* (1956), p. [10].
76. Construction started one month after the Collegio began.
77. 'The initial mistake in the formation of character is that the Jesuits have aimed at educating lay boys in the same manner as they consider advisable for their own novices, for whom obedience and direction is the one thing necessary' – R. F. Littledale and E. L. Taunton, s. v. 'Jesuits' in *Encyclopaedia Britannica*, 13th ed.
78. Passanti (1963), p. 50.
79. As displayed, for example, over the side doors on the west front of S. Agnese in Piazza Navona, Rome. See also S. Sitwell, *Southern Baroque Art Revisited* (London 1967), p. 123.
80. '... non potrà dirsi Greca, ma di capriccio, come io la stimo e lodo come bella, ma non come propria' – *AC* III.viii.9. See B. T. La

Greca's interesting observations ad loc. (Poli-filo edition, p. 186, n. 5) on the Mannerist distinction between caprice and propriety.
81. Quoted by Marini (1963), p. 106: He presumably means Gemelli Careri.
82. Chierici, p. 366.

NOTES TO CHAPTER 10

1. Chierici, p. 368.
2. In the Archivio di Stato, Turin, and printed by Sandonnini, p. 496.
3. *Schede Vesme*, Vol. II, p. 551.
4. Ibid., printing a letter dated 24 March 1671, preserved in the Archivio di Stato.
5. Sandonnini, pp. 501–2.
6. Ibid., p. 503.
7. Letter dated 2 July 1672, preserved in the Archivio di Stato, Modena; printed by Sandonnini, p. 502.
8. 'So writes the typical man of the seventeenth century' – Sandonnini, p. 502.
9. Portoghesi, *Guarini* (1956), p. [1]. He omits the word 'dread' (*timore*).
10. Millon (1964), p. 20.
11. Wittkower, *GGIB*.I, p. 26, n. 6 and p. 28.
12. 'Un humore hipocondriaco' – Letter to the Marchese di San Tomaso, 27 April 1677, printed in *Schede Vesme*, Vol. II, p. 553.
13. Report in Archivio Civico, Turin, Ordinati, r. 201, f. 607.
14. Wittkower, *GGIB*.I, p. 28.
15. The correspondence on this matter is distributed between the Archivio di Stato, Turin, and the Cossilla Collection in the Biblioteca Civica. It is excerpted at length in *Schede Vesme*, Vol. II, pp. 552–3.
16. Urgent note dated 22 April 1677 from Gaetano Cizaletto, a Theatine monk, to the Archbishop of Turin – *Schede Vesme*, Vol. II, p. 552.
17. i.e. the Father General of the Theatine Order.
18. 'Questo homo preso per le bone farà quello si desidera, che per altra strada sarà perdere il tempo e l'opera' – letter of 22 April 1677 – *Schede Vesme*, Vol. II, p. 553.
19. Letter dated 12 January 1678, in the Cossilla Collection, Biblioteca Civica, Turin.
20. Letter dated 8 February, in the Cossilla Collection.
21. Dated 19 April 1679 – *Schede Vesme*, Vol. II, p. 554.
22. Archivio Civico, Turin, Ordinati, v. 200, f. 85.
23. Quoted by Sandonnini, p. 504.
24. 'Leaving an unbridgeable gap at Turin' – Tamburini [1968], p. 227.
25. Dated 28 February, in the Archivio di Stato, Modena.
26. In the Archivio di Stato, Modena; summarized by Sandonnini, p. 506.
27. Controllo, r. 175, f. 80.
28. The book appeared later in the year, with a dedication to the Duke of Modena and Prince Emanuele Filiberto di Carignano.
29. Wittkower (1962), p. 27. Cf. L. B. Alberti, *Ten Books on Architecture* VII, c. iv (p. 138 in

30. A situation that continued until the twentieth century, when it was changed by the provisions of the Second Vatican Council (1962–5). Two centralized cathedrals have since been built, at Brasilia and Liverpool, and many parish churches.
31. See J. Quentin Hughes, 'Oval Church Plans' in Hughes and N. Lynton, *Renaissance Architecture* (London [1962] 1965), pp. 181–2.
32. Millon (1964), p. 23.
33. G. Rigotti, 'La chiesa dell'Immacolata Concezione ora Cappella Arcivescovile in Torino', *Bollettino della SPABA* XVI, No. 1/2 (1932), p. 70.
34. Tamburini's essay on the Immacolata Concezione is printed in two slightly differing forms, firstly as chapter xxvii of his book *Le chiese di Torino* (Turin [1968]), and subsequently as a contribution to *GGIB* (La chiesa dell'Immacolata Concezione di Torino, *GGIB*.I, p. 385 ff).
35. O. Derossi, *Nuova guida per la città di Torino* (Turin 1781), p. 18.
36. Tamburini, *GGIB*.I, p. 388.
37. Pommer (1967), p. 81.
38. *AC* III.xiv.1, 4.
39. 'Ettinga' is the Italian adaptation of the Ötting in Altötting, the name of a small town in Bavaria where hundreds of thousands of pilgrims still come each year to venerate a fourteenth-century wooden image of the Virgin. See A. von Reitzenstein and H. Brunner, *Bayern. Baudenkmäler* (Stuttgart 1970), p. 31.
40. H. Schmerber, quoting an eighteenth-century source, in 'Einige Nachrichten über Guarino Guarini', *Monatsbericht für Kunstwissenschaft und Kunsthandel* II (1902), p. 287.
41. Kindly communicated by Dr Vladimír Novotný, of the State Institute for the Care of Historical Monuments.
42. Pommer (1967), p. 80.
43. Giovanni Chevalley, 'Vicende costruttive della chiesa di S. Filippo Neri in Torino', *Bolletino del Centro di studi archeologici ed artistici del Piemonte* Fasc. II (1942).
44. Pommer (1967).
45. Tamburini [1968], chapters xxviii and xxix.
46. Cibrario, Vol. II, p. 601, with details of founders.
47. Decree of 20 June 1675 in the Archivio di Stato, Turin (j) (Sezione III, Art. 687, Patenti, f. 29).
48. Cibrario, Vol. II, p. 606.
49. Ibid.
50. Tamburini [1968], p. 245.
51. Pommer (1967), p. 81.
52. Spatial counterpoint, spatial penetration, spatial expansion.
53. Anderegg-Tille, p. 60.
54. Pommer (1967), p. 81.
55. Portoghesi, *Guarini* (1956), p. [13].
56. Wittkower (1980), p. 386, n. 9.
57. Bernardi Ferrero, *GGIB*.I, p. 417.
58. Sedlmayr (1930), p. 104.

59. Portoghesi, *Guarini* (1956), p. [1].
60. Bernardi Ferrero, *GGIB*.I, p. 418.
61. *AC* II.vii.10.
62. Bernardi Ferrero (1966), p. 75.
63. See Hager's comment, p. 20, above.
64. P. Toesca, *Torino* (Bergamo 1911), p. 87.
65. Wittkower (1980), p. 270.
66. Anderegg-Tille, p. 60.
67. Eyewitness account by F. L. Soleri, 'Giornale dal 1682 al 1721' in the Biblioteca Reale, Turin, Sezione Storia Patria 230, f. 97 v.
68. M. Paroletti, *Turin et ses curiosités* (Turin 1819), p. 151.
69. Chevalley (1942).
70. Pommer (1967), p. 83.
71. Anderegg-Tille, p. 84.
72. Pommer (1967), p. 84.
73. P. Buscalioni, *La Consolata nella storia di Torino, del Piemonte e della Augusta Dinastia Sabauda* (Turin 1938), p. 100.
74. His architectural qualifications, or lack of them, have been subjected to scrutiny by Dr Lange (p. 124, n. 5).
75. See D. de Bernardi Ferrero's essay, 'Il Santuario della Consolata e l'architettura emiliana del Manierismo' in her book *Guarino Guarini e la sua arte* (Turin 1966). The few letters of Don Michelangiolo to Madama Reale which survive (Archivio di Stato, Turin (d), B53 and M49) do not in fact allude to his scheme.
76. Buscalioni, p. 101.
77. 'this banal structure' – Bernardi Ferrero (1966), p. 55.
78. Lange, p. 124.
79. Ibid., Dis. 6.
80. Bernardi Ferrero (1966), p. 58.
81. See Portoghesi (1957), p. 111.
82. In 1667, according to G. A. de Moranti, 'Memorie istoriche della città, e della chiesa di Casale', a manuscript dated 1795 in the Archivio di Stato, Turin (f), H. V. 35, II, p. 216. In 1670, according to H. de Bosio, *De Casalensis ecclesiae origine atque progressu* (Turin 1724), p. 138.
83. C. Ceschi, 'Progetti del Guarini e del Vittone per la chiesa di San Gaetano a Nizza', *Palladio* No. 5 (1941), p. 172.
84. See Lange, p. 115.
85. See the comments of Lange, p. 222.
86. Tantalizingly quoted as direct speech, but without indication of source, by M. Trompetto, *Storia del Santuario di Oropa* (Milan 1967), p. 88.
87. Guidoni, *GGIB*.II, p. 278, fig. 5.
88. Fagiolo, *GGIB*.II, p. 200, fig. 8.
89. H. A. Millon, 'La geometria nel linguaggio architettonico del Guarini', *GGIB*.II, p. 46.
90. cf. H. A. Meek, review of *GGIB* in *Journal of the Royal Institute of British Architects*, No. 12 (1971).
91. Portoghesi (1957), Fasc. 20 and 21, with a 'doverosa postilla' in Fasc. 23.
92. Portoghesi, 'Il tabernacolo' (1956), pp. 16–20.
93. E. Olivero, *La Madonna di Loreto in Montanaro* (Turin 1940).
94. A. Dondana, *Memorie storiche di Montanaro* (Turin 1884), pp. 131, 193.
95. The circumstances are explained in detail, on the basis of archival and other research, by Lange, pp. 222 ff. See also S. Lissone, *Govone. Il commune e il castello* (Turin 1921).

NOTES TO CHAPTER 11

1. Wittkower, *GGIB*.I, pp. 30–1.
2. 'The pupil corrects the Master – it's nothing new' – A. F. Vezzosi, *I scrittori de' Cherici Regolari detti Teatini* (Rome 1780), s.v. 'Guarini'. One can almost see the shrug.
3. 'Sed faciant, per me licet. Talibus infortuniis assuevi.'
4. See Wittkower (1980), p. 275.
5. See the exposition given by M. Chasles, *Aperçu historique sur l'origine et le développement des méthodes en géométrie* (Paris 1875), p. 345. Chasles regards Guarini as an Italian writer on mathematics and astronomy. He appears to be unaware of his architectural work.
6. *Euclides adauctus*, preface.
7. Count Giovanni Andrea Ferrari di Bagnolo, who was so prompt in his payments that (in Guarini's words) 'there is not even one man who could complain of his payment being lost or delayed'. See Lange, pp. 216–18.
8. 'The parabola and hyperbola', he says (p. 165), 'are little if at all known by architects, but could serve marvellously in vaults.'
9. Dr Lange speculates that it may have been the court physician Bartolomeo Torrini, who was also a student of mathematics and astrology – p. 219.
10. See Ch. 7, n. 4. The full title of the book is *Compendio della Sfera Celeste in cui con adattate figure si spiegano tutti i varj giri, che segnano co i suoi movimenti il sole e l'altre stelle*.
11. s.v. 'Fortification and Siegecraft', in *Encyclopaedia Britannica*, 13th ed.
12. The title-page of this quarto volume gives Torino MDCLXXVI, but the imprimatur is only dated 13 April 1677.
13. Lange, p. 210.
14. Ibid., pp. 210–11.
15. See W. Sackur, *Vitruv und die Poliorketiker* (Berlin 1925).
16. Gianni Carlo Sciolla, 'Note sul "Trattato di fortificatione" del Guarini', *GGIB*.I, pp. 513–29.
17. Lodovico was appointed a colonel of dragoons in 1682 at the age of twenty-two, and was killed the next year as a result of falling from his horse in combat with the Turks at the gates of Vienna.
18. Portoghesi, 'L'architetto' (1956), p. 60.
19. *Leges Temporum & Planetarum quibus Civilis & Astronomici Temporis lapsus primi Mobilis, & errantium decursus ordinantur, atque in Tabulas di. geruntur ad Longitudinem Taurinensem GR.30.46' & Latitudinem GR.44.49' juxta observationes tum recentes tum antiquas celebriorum Caeli Inspectorum.*
20. The *OED* defines dialling as the measurement of time by dials (1570). Its use in connection with telephones was not gazetted until Vol. 1 of the Supplement (1972).

21. Fagiolo, 'La "geosofia"', *GGIB*.II, p. 189.
22. Argan, *GGIB*.I, p. 36.
23. He expressed the view that the Holy Office, at the time of Galileo's trial, had considered his views not so much contrary to faith as simply erroneous.
24. See the *Avviso a' lettori* at the beginning of *Architettura civile*.
25. Quoted by Bernardi Ferrero (1966), p. 7, on the basis of a reference by Cicognara.
26. See A. Bertini, 'Il disegno del Guarini e le incisioni del trattato di "Architettura civile"', *GGIB*.I, pp. 597–610.
27. *I 'Dissegni d'architettura civile et ecclesiastica' di Guarino Guarini e l'arte del maestro* (Turin 1966). The title on the spine and dust cover is *Guarino Guarini e la sua arte*, by which shorter name it has been generally referred to in the present work. The facsimile edition is prefaced by some short but valuable essays.
28. H. A. Millon, 'L'altare maggiore della chiesa di San Filippo Neri di Torino', *Bollettino della SPABA* XIV (1960), p. 84.
29. Portoghesi, 'L'architetto' (1956), p. 60.
30. B. A. Vittone, *Istruzioni elementari per indirizzo dei giovani allo studio dell'architettura civile* (Lugano 1760), and *Istruzioni diverse concernenti l'officio dell'architetto civile* (Lugano 1766).
31. Alberti, VI, ii (p. 113 in Leoni's 1755 translation).
32. He believed that inspection and measurement of ancient buildings might supersede the prescriptions of ancient texts.
33. Alberti, VI, xiii.

NOTES TO CHAPTER 12

1. C. Whitaker Wilson, *Sir Christopher Wren, his Life and Times* (London 1932), p. 249.
2. '. . . he was overtaken by death in a foreign land and far from his own people . . . it is certain that he died there miserably, at a still young age' – Sandonnini, pp. 507, 509.
3. Crepaldi, p. 46, quoting contemporary manuscript sources.
4. The one who had written, two years before, 'This chap, if you deal with him gently, will do what you want of him'.
5. This suggested to Wittkower (1980), p. 387, n. 1, that the manuscript was unfinished at Guarini's death. See also above for Amico Ricci's supposed sight of an 'uncut' manuscript.
6. Argan, *GGIB*.I, p. 36.
7. *AC* III.xvi.2. 'It [the gallery at Syon] was finished in a style to afford great variety and amusement' – Robert Adam. The contrast between proud seventeenth-century candour and elegant eighteenth century sophistication is piquant, but the sentiments are identical.
8. *AC* III.xiii.1.
9. See Werner Müller's articles 'The Authenticity of Guarini's Stereotomy in his "Architettura civile",' *Journal of the Society of Architectural Historians* XXVII, part 3 (1968), and 'Guarini e la stereotomia', *GGIB*.I.
10. On Garove (1650–1713), see Chevalley (1942), p. 68, n. 8.
11. Nino Carboneri, 'Guarini ed il Piemonte', *GGIB*.II, p. 355.
12. For an essay of transcendental abstraction on this theme, see 'Oltre Guarini: Juvarra' *GGIB*.II, by Andreina Griseri. Her conclusion is: 'Guarini extracts from architecture a vital fulcrum, an internal centre. Juvarra subjects every point to the law of the ensemble. . .'
13. Cf. the effect on William Kent of his editing *The Works of Inigo Jones* (1727).
14. Carboneri, *GGIB*.II, p. 358.
15. Not to be confused with the one he actually built for the Theatines in this town, in lieu of Guarini's scheme. This church, S. Gaetano, which still stands, has a centralized plan.
16. So described by Wittkower (1980), p. 390, n. 65.
17. 'oscure e difficili e poco ad un semplice misuratore intellegibili'.
18. F. Milizia, *Memorie dei più celebri architetti* (Rome 1768).
19. See Schiedermair, p. 108.
20. See the correspondence published by A. Peroni, 'L'architetto della Theatinerkirche di Monaco, etc.', *Palladio* n.s. VIII (1958), p. 23.
21. H. V. Lanchester, *Fischer von Erlach* (London 1924), p. 11.
22. H. Sedlmayr, *Johann Bernhard Fischer von Erlarch* (Vienna 1956), pp. 18–19. See also W. Hager, 'Zum Verhältnis Fischer–Guarini', *Kunstchronik* X (1957), pp. 206–8.
23. To be found in the Codex Montenuovo, at the Albertina.
24. The fullest treatment of this theme is to be found in H. G. Franz, *Bauten und Baumeister der Barockzeit in Böhmen* (Leipzig 1962). A handy English work is Brian Knox's *The Architecture of Prague and Bohemia* (London 1962), but see my review of it in the *Journal of the Royal Institute of British Architects* No. 12, (1962).
25. Hempel (1965), p. 127.
26. His father was a German captain in the Genoese army.
27. Knox, p. 48.
28. Ibid., p. 49.
29. Compare the arrangements at the Immacolata Concezione.
30. C. Norberg-Schulz, 'Lo spazio nell'architettura post-guariniana', *GGIB*.II, p. 419.
31. On the Guarinian antecedents for Banz, see Frankl, pp. 251–3.
32. An interesting symbolic explanation linking the frescoes with the vaulting system is given by Hempel (1965), p. 150. Millon (1964), p. 46, sees Banz as 'a splendid adaptation of Guarini's Immaculate Conception in Turin'. It is difficult to follow this claim.
33. Curves developed in three dimensions and not capable of being embraced in a flat surface.
34. Millon (1964), p. 47.

BIBLIOGRAPHY

ABBREVIATIONS

AC	see under Guarini, G. *Architettura civile*
Atti del X	*Atti del X Congresso di storia dell'architettura* (Rome 1959)
GGIB	*Guarino Guarini e l'internazionalità del barocco* (Turin 1970). (The papers of the 1968 Guarini Conference in Turin, published by the Accademia delle Scienze in two volumes, here referred to as *GGIB*.I and *GGIB*.II respectively.)
Schede Vesme	see under Baudi di Vesme, A.
SPABA	Società Piemontese di Archeologia e di Belle Arti

ARCHIVAL MATERIAL

Archivio di Stato, Turin
(a) Archivio di Corte. Real Casa. Archivio Savoia Carignano
(b) Archivio di Corte. Real Casa. Lettere principi diversi
(c) Archivio di Corte. Real Casa. Lettere principi forestieri: Modena-Este
(d) Archivio di Corte. Lettere particolari
(e) Archivio di Corte. Materie ecclesiastiche. Regolari di qua dai monti: Teatini
(f) Archivio di Corte. Biblioteca Antica
(g) Ministero delle Finanze, Azienda Savoia Carignano
(h) Archivio della Camera dei Conti di Piemonte
(i) Regio Economato Benefici Vacanti
(j) Controllo Generale delle Finanze

Biblioteca Reale, Turin
Archivi di Corte
Sezione Storia Patria

Biblioteca Civica, Turin
Raccolta Cossilla

Archivio Civico, Turin
Ordinati

Archivio di Stato, Modena
Opera Pia
Giurisdizione Ecclesiastica

Archivio di Stato, Parma
Libro delle croniche della Casa di S. Christina di Parma
Libro dei capitoli della Casa dei PP. Teatini

Archives Nationales, Paris
Registres capitulaires des Théatins
    (taken from A. Lange. 'Disegni e documenti di Guarino Guarini'. *GGIB*.I)

PUBLISHED SOURCES

Abercrombie, P. *Town and Country Planning*. 2nd ed. Oxford 1945.
Abrate, M. 'Elementi per la storia della finanza dello stato sabaudo nella seconda metà del XVI secolo'. *Bollettino Storico-bibliografico Subalpino* LXVII (Fasc. I–II) 1969.
Accascina, M. 'Les soieries siciliennes du "Tiraz" normand'. *Actes du I. Congrès International d'Histoire du Costume*. Venice 1955.
Accascina, M. 'La formazione artistica di Filippo Juvara'. *Bollettino d'Arte* XLI 1956 and XLII 1957.
Alberti, L. B. *Ten Books on Architecture*. trans. J. Leoni (1755), ed. J. Rykwert. London (1955) 1965.
Anderegg-Tille, M. *Die Schule Guarinis*. Winterthur 1962.
Arata, G. V. *L'architettura arabo-normanna e il rinascimento in Sicilia*. Milan 1925.
Argan, G. C. (First) review of Brinckmann (1931) [q.v.]. *Zeitschrift für Kunstgeschichte* I 1932.

Argan, G. C. 'Per una storia dell'architettura piemontese'. *L'Arte* XXXVI 1933.
Argan, G. C. *L'architettura barocca in Italia*. Milan 1957.
Argan, G. C. *Europe of the Capitals*. London 1964.
Argan, G. C. *Storia dell'arte italiana*. Florence 1968.
Argan, G. C. 'La tecnica del Guarini'. *GGIB*.I.
Audiberti, C. M. *Regiae villae poetice descriptae*. Turin 1711.
Baldinucci, F. *Vocabolario toscano delle arti del disegno*. Florence 1681.
Baldoria, N. Review of Sandonnini [q.v.]. *Archivio storico dell'arte*. 1890.
Baracco, C. 'Bernardo Vittone e l'architettura guariniana'. *Torino* February 1938.
Battisti, E. 'Note sul significato della Capella della Santa Sindone nel Duomo di Torino'. *Atti del X*.
Battisti, E. 'Schemata nel Guarini'. *GGIB*.II.
[Baudi di Vesme, A.] 'Guarino Guarini', in *Schede Vesme. L'arte in Piemonte dal xvi al xviii secolo*. SPABA. Vol. I. Turin 1963; Vol. II. Turin 1968.
Beltrami, L. *Vita di Aristotile da Bologna*. Bologna 1912.
Benedetti, S. 'Guarini ed il barocco romano'. *GGIB*.I.
Benevolo, L. 'La chiesa parrochiale di Campertogno'. *Palladio* 1951.
Berger, R. W. "The Church of St. Didier, Asfeld-la-Ville". *Architectura* 1 1973.
Bernardi, M. *Tre palazzi a Torino*. Turin 1963.
Bernardi Ferrero, D. de, I '*Disegni d'architettura civile et ecclesiastica' di Guarino Guarini e l'arte del maestro* [*Guarino Guarini e la sua arte*]. Turin 1966.
Bernardi Ferrero, D. de. 'Chiese longitudinali del Guarini'. *GGIB*.I.
Bertarelli, L. V. *Guida d'Italia del T.C.I.: Piemonte, Lombardia, Ticino*. Milan 1914.
Bertini, A. 'Il disegno del Guarini e le incisioni del trattato di "Architettura civile"'. *GGIB*.I.
Bevan, B. *History of Spanish Architecture*. London 1939.
Blondel, J. F. *Architecture françoise*. Paris 1752.
Blunt, A. *Art and Architecture in France, 1500–1700*. Harmondsworth (1953) 1970.
Blunt, A. 'Guarini and Leonardo'. *Architectural Review* CXLVII 2.1970.
Boase, A. 'Sant'Anna Reale'. *GGIB*.I.
Boggio, C. *Gli architetti C. e A. Castellamonte*. Turin 1896.
Bordoni, S. 'La critica Guariniana'. *GGIB*.II.
Borsi, F. 'Guarino Guarini a Messina'. *GGIB*.I.
Boscarino, S. *Sicilia barocca – architettura e città, 1610–1760*. Rome 1981.
Bosio, H. de, *De Casalensis ecclesiae origine atque progressu*. Turin 1724.
Brayda, C., L. Coli, D. Sesia, 'Specializzazioni e vita professionale nel sei e settecento in Piemonte'. *Atti e Rassegna Tecnica della Società degl'Ingegneri e Architetti in Torino* 3.1963.
Bricarelli, C. 'Guarino Guarini', in U. Thieme and F. Becker, *Allgemeines Lexikon der bildenden Künstler* Leipzig 1922.
Briggs, M. S. *Baroque Architecture*. London 1913.
Brinckmann, A. E. *Baukunst des 17. und 18. Jahrhunderts in den romanischen Ländern*. Berlin 1919.
Brinckmann, A. E. *Theatrum novum Pedemontii; Ideen, Entwürfe und Bauten von Guarini, Juvarra, Vittone* ... Düsseldorf 1931.
Brinckmann, A. E. 'Von Guarino Guarini bis Balthasar Neumann'. *Jahresgabe des deutschen Vereins für Kunstwissenschaft*. Berlin 1932.
Brinckmann, A. E. 'La grandezza di Guarino Guarini e la sua influenza sull'architettura in Germania nel '700'. *Atti della SPABA* XV 1933.
Brinckmann, A. E. 'Tre astri nel cielo del Piemonte: Guarini, Juvarra, Vittone'. *Atti del X*.
Brizio, A. M. 'L'architettura barocca in Piemonte'. *Annuario dell'Università di Torino*. 1952–3.
Brotto, G. and V. Todesco. 'S. Lorenzo a Torino'. *L'architettura: Cronache e Storia* 8.1961.
Burckhardt, J. *Der Cicerone*. Leipzig (1855) 1925.
Buscalioni, P. *La Consolata nella storia di Torino, del Piemonte e della Augusta Dinastia Sabauda*. Turin 1938.
Caramuel de Lobkowitz, J. *Architectura civil recta y obliqua*. Vigevano 1678.
Carboneri, N. Section on architecture in *Catalogo [della] mostra del barocco piemontese*. Turin 1963.
Carboneri, N. 'Vicenda delle capelle per la Santa Sindone'. *Bollettino della SPABA* n.s. xviii 1964.
Carboneri, N. 'Guarini a Modena'. *GGIB*.I.
Carboneri, N. 'Guarini ed il Piemonte'. *GGIB*.II.
Carvalho, A. de. *D. João V e a arte de seu tempo*. Mafra 1962.
Carvalho da Costa, A. *Corografia Portugueza*. Lisbon 1706–12.
Cattaui, G. 'Guarini et la France'. *GGIB*.II.
Cavallari-Murat, A. 'Struttura e forma nel trattato del Guarini'. *GGIB*.I.
Ceschi, C. 'Progetti del Guarini e del Vittone per la chiesa di San Gaetano a Nizza'. *Palladio* 5.1941.
Chasles, M. *Aperçu historique sur l'origine et le développement des méthodes en géométrie*. Paris 1875.
Chevalley, G. 'Il Palazzo Carignano a Torino'. *Bollettino della SPABA* 1/2.1921.
Chevalley, G. 'Vicende costruttive della chiesa di S. Filippo Neri in Torino'. *Bollettino del Centro di studi archeologici ed artistici del Piemonte* (Fasc. II) 1942.
Chevalier, U. *Etude critique sur l'origine du Saint Suaire*. Paris 1900.
Chierici, U. 'Guarini a Torino'. *GGIB*.I.
Chueca Goitia, F. 'Guarini y el influjo del barocco italiano en España y Portugal'. *GGIB*.II.
Cibrario, L. *Storia di Torino*. Turin 1836.
Claretta, G. 'Inclinazioni artistiche di Carlo Emanuele I di Savoia e dei suoi figli'. *Atti della SPABA* V 6.1894.
Coffin, D. R. 'Padre Guarino Guarini in Paris'. *Journal of the Society of Architectural Historians* xv 2.1956.
Collobi, L. 'Carlo di Castellamonte primo ingegnere del duca di Savoia'. *Bollettino Storico-bibliografico Subalpino* XXXIX 1937.

186

Contardi, B. *La retorica e l'architettura del barocco*. Rome 1978.

Cordero di Pamparato, S. 'Il Padre Guarino Guarini teologo del Principe di Carignano'. *Il Duomo di Torino* II 4.1928.

Craveri, G. *Guida de forestieri per la real città di Torino*. Turin 1753.

Cravero, D. G. 'Il Palazzo Carignano'. *Atti e Rassegna Tecnica della Società degl'Ingegneri e degli Architetti in Torino V* 2.1951.

Crepaldi, G. M. *La real chiesa di San Lorenzo in Torino*. Turin 1963.

Currier, C. W. *History of the Religious Orders*. New York 1896.

Darrican, R. 'Les Clercs Réguliers Théatins à Paris'. *Regnum Dei*, Collectanea Theatina. Rome 1954.

Denina L. and A. Proto. 'La real chiesa di San Lorenzo in Torino'. *L'architettura Italiana* XV 1920.

Derossi, O. *Nuova guida per la città di Torino*. Turin 1781.

Dondana, A. *Memorie storiche di Montanaro*. Turin 1884.

Duboin, C. *Editti e manifesti*. Turin 1846.

Dumoulin, M. *Etudes de topographie parisienne*. Paris 1929.

El-Said, I. and A. Parman. *Geometric Concepts in Islamic Art*. London 1976.

Evans, J. *Monastic Architecture in France from the Renaissance to the Revolution*. Cambridge 1964.

Fagiolo, M. 'La "geosofia" del Guarini'. *GGIB*.II.

Fagiolo, M. 'La Sindone e l'enigma dell'eclisse'. *GGIB*.II.

Fasolo, V. 'Sistemi ellittici nell'architettura'. *Architettura e arti decorative*. 1931.

Ferrante, G. B. *Torino 1880*. Turin 1880.

Ferrari, F. *Memorie storiche della regia chiesa parrochiale di S. Vincenzo Martire in Modena*. Modena 1924.

Florensa, A. 'Guarini ed il mondo islamico'. *GGIB*.I.

Frankl, P. Résumé of paper on Guarini's influence on Dientzenhofer. Sitzungen der kunstwissenschaftlichen Gesellschaft in München, 1913–15: Sitzung am 1. März 1915. *Münchener Jahrbuch der bildenden Künste*. 1914–15.

Franz, H. G. *Bauten und Baumeister der Barockzeit in Böhmen*. Leipzig 1962.

Franz, H. G. 'Guarini e l'architettura barocca in Boemia ed in Austria'. *GGIB*.II.

Franz, H. G. 'Guarini und die barocke Baukunst in Böhmen'. *Actes du 22e Congrès International d'Histoire de l'Art*. Budapest 1972.

Fréart, P. de. *Journal du voyage du cavalier Bernin en France*. ed. L. Lalanne. Paris 1885.

Gabrielli, N. *Racconigi*. Turin 1972.

Gallo, G. D. *Gli annali della città di Messina*. Messina 1756.

Giedion, S. *Space, Time and Architecture*. Cambridge, Mass. 1941 et seq.

Golzio, V. *Seicento e Settecento*. 2nd ed. Turin 1960.

Griseri, A. *Le metamorfosi del barocco*. Turin 1967.

Griseri, A. 'Oltre Guarini: Juvarra'. *GGIB*.II.

Guarini, G. *La pietà trionfante*. Messina 1660.

Guarini, G. *Placita philosophica*. Paris 1665.

Guarini, G. *Euclides adauctus & methodicus mathematicaque universalis*. Turin 1671.

Guarini, G. *Il modo di misurare le fabbriche*. Turin 1674.

Guarini, G. *Compendio della Sfera Celeste*. Turin 1675.

Guarini, G. *Trattato di fortificatione che hora si usa in Fiandra, Francia et Italia*. Turin 1676.

Guarini, G. *Leges Temporum et planetarum*. Turin 1678.

Guarini, G. *Coelestis mathematicae Pars I et II*. Milan 1683.

Guarini, G. *Dissegni d'architettura civile et ecclesiastica*. Turin 1686. Facsimile edition, with essays by D. de Bernardi Ferrero (see above under Bernardi Ferrero). Turin 1966.

Guarini, G. *Architettura civile*. Turin 1737. Facsimile edition, Gregg Press, Farnborough 1964.

Guarini, G. *Architettura civile*. Polifilo critical edition, with reset text and reduced plates. Introduction by N. Carboneri, notes and essay by Bianca Tavassi La Greca. Milan 1968.

Guidoni, E. 'Guarino Guarini' in P. Portoghesi, ed. *Dizionario enciclopedico di architettura e urbanistica*. Rome 1969.

Guidoni, E. 'Modelli guariniani'. *GGIB*.II.

Gurlitt, C. *Geschichte des Barockstiles in Italien*. Stuttgart 1887.

Hager, W. Résumé of paper on Guarini given to 5. deutscher Kunsthistorikertag, Hanover. *Kunstchronik* VII 1954.

Hager, W. 'Zum Verhältnis Fischer–Guarini'. *Kunstchronik* X 1957.

Hager, W. 'Guarinis Theatinerfassade in Messina', in *Das Werk des Künstlers. Hubert Schrade zum 60. Geburtstag*. Stuttgart 1960.

Hager, W. 'Guarini. Zur Kennzeichnung seiner Architeketur', in *Zu Ehren von L. Bruhns* (Misc. Bibl. Hertz.). Munich 1961.

Hager, W. 'Guarini e il mondo tedesco'. *GGIB*.II.

Harvey, J. *Gothic England*. London 1947.

Hautecoeur, L. *Le Louvre et les Tuileries de Louis XIV*. Paris 1927.

Hautecoeur, L. *Histoire de l'architecture classique en France*. Vol. II. Paris 1948.

Hempel, E. *Francesco Borromini*. Vienna 1924.

Hempel, E. *Baroque Art and Architecture in Central Europe*. Harmondsworth 1965.

Hibbard, H. 'The Early History of Sant'Andrea della Valle'. *Art Bulletin* XLIII 1961.

Hibbard, H. *Bernini*. Harmondsworth 1965.

Hughes, J. Quentin and N. Lynton. *Renaissance Architecture*. London [1962] 1965.

Jackson, L. C. 'Fortification and Siegecraft', in *Encyclopaedia Britannica*. 13th ed.

Knox, B. *The Architecture of Prague and Bohemia*. London 1962.

Kubler, G. and M. Soria. *Art and Architecture in Spain and Portugal and their American Dominions, 1500–1800*. Harmondsworth 1959.

BIBLIOGRAPHY

La Farina, G. *Messina ed i suoi monumenti*. Messina 1840.
Lanchester, H. V. *Fischer von Erlach*. London 1924.
Lange, A. 'Disegni e documenti di Guarino Guarini'. *GGIB*.I.
Laprade, A. *François d'Orbay*. Paris n.d.
Lavin, I. *Bernini and the Unity of the Visual Arts*. Oxford 1980.
Lees-Milne, J. *Baroque in Italy*. London 1959.
Lefèvre d'Ormesson O. *Journal*. ed. M. Cheruel. Paris 1860.
Le Pautre, A. *Oeuvres*. Paris 1652.
Lissone, S. *Govone. Il comune e il castello*. Turin 1921.
Littledale, R. F. and E. L. Taunton. 'Jesuits', in *Encyclopaedia Britannica*. 13th ed.
Malebranche, N. *Recherche de la vérité*. Paris 1674.
Malle, L. *Le arti figurative in Piemonte*. Turin 1962.
Marconi, P. 'Guarino Guarini e il gotico'. *GGIB*.I.
Marconi, P. '"Virtuti fortuna comes". Guarino Guarini e il caduceo ermetico'. *Ricerche di storia dell'arte* 1976, 1–2; 29–44.
Marini, G. L. 'Il mattone nell'architettura civile del Guarini'. *Epoche* (Turin) 3.1962.
Marini, G. L. *L'architettura barocca in Piemonte. La provincia di Torino*. Turin 1963.
Mauceri, E. 'Colonne tortili così dette del Tempio di Salomone'. *L'Arte* 1898.
Meek, H. A. Review of *GGIB*. *Journal of the Royal Institute of British Architects* 12.1971.
Merlini, C. 'Racconigi e il suo castello'. *Torino* XIX 1941.
Midana, A. *Il Duomo di Torino e la Real Cappella della S.S. Sindone* (= *Italia Sacra*, Vol. I, Fasc. VII–VIII). Pineroli 1929.
Milizia, F. *Memorie dei più celebri architetti*. Rome 1768.
Millon, H. A. 'L'altare maggiore della chiesa di San Filippo Neri di Torino'. *Bollettino della SPABA* n.s. XIV 1960.
Millon, H. A. *Baroque and Rococo Architecture*. London 1964.
Millon, H. A. Review of Crepaldi [q.v.]. *Art Bulletin* XLVII 1965.
Millon, H. A. 'La geometria nel linguaggio architettonico del Guarini'. *GGIB*.II.
Millon, H. A. 'Guarino Guarini', in A. K. Placzek, ed. *Macmillan Encyclopaedia of Architects*. London 1982.
Milner Gulland, R. 'Art and Architecture of Old Russia', in R. Auty and D. Obolensky, eds. *Companion to Russian Studies 3*. Cambridge 1980.
Moissy, P. *Jésuites de l'ancienne Assistance de France*. Rome 1958,
More, J. *The Land of Italy*. London 1949.
Müller, W. 'The Authenticity of Guarini's Stereotomy in his "Architettura civile"'. *Journal of the Society of Architectural Historians* XXVII part 3 1968.
Müller, W. 'Guarini e la stereotomia'. *GGIB*.I.
Mumford, L. *The Culture of Cities*. New York 1938.
Mumford, L. *The City in History*. London 1966.
Murray's Handbook for Northern Italy, 4th ed. London 1852.
Nasti, M. 'Il sistema del mondo di Guarino Guarini'. *GGIB*.II.
Noce, A. del. *Il problema dell'ateismo*. Bologna 1964.
Noehles, K. 'Die Louvre-Projekte von Pietro da Cortona und Carlo Rainaldi'. *Zeitschrift für Kunstgeschichte* XXIV 1960.
Norberg-Schulz, C. *Kilian Ignaz Dientzenhofer e il barocco boemo*. Rome 1968.
Norberg-Schulz, C. 'Lo spazio nell'architettura post-guariniana'. *GGIB*.II.
Oechslin, W. 'Bemerkungen zu Guarino Guarini und Juan Caramuel de Lobkowitz'. *Raggi* IX 3.1969.
Oechslin, W. 'Osservazioni su Guarino Guarini e Juan Caramuel de Lobkowitz'. *GGIB*.I. (Italian version of above.)
Olivero, E. 'La vita e l'arte del P. Guarino Guarini'. *Il Duomo di Torino* 5.1928.
Olivero, E. 'Gli scritti del Padre Guarino Guarini'. *Il Duomo di Torino* 5.1928.
Olivero, E. *La Madonna di Loreto in Montanaro*. Turin 1940.
Paroletti, M. *Turin et ses curiosités*. Turin 1819.
Paroletti, M. *Turin à la portée de l'étranger*. Turin 1834.
Passanti, M. 'Real Cappella della S. Sindone in Torino'. *Torino* XX 1941. (Later incorporated in *Nel mondo magico*.)
Passanti, M. 'Le trasformazioni barocche nel tessuto urbano della Torino medievale'. *Atti del X*.
Passanti, M. 'La cappella della Santa Sindone in Torino'. *L'architettura: cronache e storia* 12.1961.
Passanti, M. *Nel mondo magico di Guarino Guarini*. Turin 1963.
Passanti, M. 'Disegni integrativi di lastre del trattato 'Architettura Civile''. *GGIB*.I.
Passanti, M. 'La poetica di Guarino Guarini'. *GGIB*.II.
Peroni, A. 'L'architetto della Theatinerkirche di Monaco, etc.' *Palladio* n.s. VIII 1958.
Pevsner, N. 'The Three-dimensional Arch from the Sixteenth to the Eighteenth Century'. *Journal of the Society of Architectural Historians* XVII 4.1958.
Pevsner, N. *An outline of European Architecture*. Harmondsworth 1963.
Pollak, O. *Die Kunsttätigkeit unter Urban VIII*. Vienna 1928.
Pommer, R. Review of Passanti (1963) [q.v.]. *Art Bulletin* XLVII 1966.
Pommer, R. *Eighteenth-Century Architecture in Piedmont*. New York and London 1967.
Portoghesi, P. 'L'architetto Guarini'. *Civiltà delle Macchine* January–February 1956.
Portoghesi, P. *Guarino Guarini*. Milan 1956. (20 unnumbered pages, numbered for reference here from first text page, in square brackets.)
Portoghesi, P. 'Il tabernacolo guariniano dell'altare maggiore di S. Nicolò a Verona'. *Quaderni dell'Istituto di Storia dell'Architettura* 14.1956.
Portoghesi, P. 'Guarini a Vicenza'. *Critica d'Arte* n.s. IV (Fasc. 20, 21, 23) 1957.
Portoghesi, P. 'Guarino Guarini', in *Encyclopaedia of World Art*. New York 1963.

188

Portoghesi, P. *Borromini*. London 1968.

Portoghesi, P. 'Il linguaggio di Guarino Guarini'. *GGIB*.II.

Ramírez, J. A. 'Guarino Guarini, Fray Juan Ricci and the "complete Salomonic Order"'. *Art History* IV 2.1981.

Reitzenstein, A. von and H. Brunner. *Bayern. Baudenkmäler* (= Vol. 1 of Reclams Kunstführer Deutschland). Stuttgart 1970.

Ressa, A. 'L'architettura religiosa in Piemonte nei secoli XVII e XVIII'. *Torino* XX 1941.

Reuther, H. *Vierzehnheiligen*. Munich 1968.

Ricci, J. *Tratado de la pintura sabia* and *Brebe tratado de arquitectura acerca del Orden Salomónico entero*. ed. E. Lafuente Ferrari. Madrid 1930.

Ricotti, E. *Storia della monarchia piemontese*. Florence 1861–9.

Rigotti, G. 'La chiesa dell'Immacolate Concezione ora Cappella Arcivescovile in Torino'. *Bollettino della SPABA* XVI 1/2.1932.

Rovere, C. *Descrizione del Reale Palazzo di Torino*. Turin 1858.

Sackur, W. *Vitruv und die Poliorketiker*. Berlin 1925.

Sandonnini, T. 'Il padre Guarino Guarini modenese'. *Atti e memorie delle reali deputazioni di storia patria per le provincie modenesi e parmensi* ser. 3, V 1888.

Scaglione, A. 'Stile e pensiero del barocco fra arte e letteratura'. *GGIB*.II.

Schiedermair, L. 'Die Zeit des Barocks, der allegorischen Dichtung, des Einwirkens deutscher Musik, bis zum Anschluss Bayerns an Frankreich'. *Forschungen zur Geschichte Bayerns*. Vol. X, parts 1 & 2. Berlin 1902.

Schmerber, H. 'Einige Nachrichten über Guarino Guarini'. *Monatsbericht für Kunstwissenschaft und Kunsthandel* 2.1902.

Schubert, O. *Geschichte des Barock in Spanien*. Esslingen 1908.

Sciolla, G. C. 'Note sul "Trattato di fortificatione" del Guarini'. *GGIB*.I.

Sedlmayr, H. *Die Architektur Borrominis*. Berlin 1930.

Sedlmayr, H. *Johann Bernhard Fischer von Erlach*. Vienna 1956.

Sekler, E. *Wren and his Place in European Architecture*. London 1956.

Sicuro, F. *Vedute e prospetti della città di Messina*. Messina 1768.

Sitwell, S. *Southern Baroque Art Revisited*. London 1967.

Smith, P. 'Mansart Studies II: The Val-de-Grâce'. *Burlington Magazine* CVI 1964.

Smith, R. C. Jnr. 'João Frederico Ludovice, an 18th Century Architect in Portugal'. *Art Bulletin* XVIII 1936.

Solero, S. *Il Duomo di Torino e la Reale Cappella della Sindone*. Pinerolo 1956.

Sousa/Viterbo, F. Marques de. 'Guarini', in *Diccionario historico e documental dos architectos, etc.* Lisbon 1899.

Summerson, J. *Architecture in Britain, 1530–1830*. 5th ed. Harmondsworth (1953) 1969.

Tafuri, M. 'Retorica e sperimentalismo: Guarino Guarini e la tradizione manierista'. *GGIB*.I.

Tamburini, L. *Le chiese di Torino dal rinascimento al barocco*. Turin [1968].

Tamburini, L. 'La chiesa dell'Immacolata Concezione di Torino'. *GGIB*.I.

Tavassi La Greca, B. 'La posizione del Guarini in rapporto alla cultura filosofica del tempo'. Printed as an appendix to her edition of *Architettura civile*. Milan 1968.

Terzaghi, A. 'Origini e sviluppo della cupola ad arconi intrecciati nell'architettura barocca del Piemonte'. *Atti del X*.

Tettoni, L. *Le illustri alleanze della real casa di Savoia*. Turin 1868.

Theatrum Statuum Regiae Celsitudinis Sabaudiae Ducis. Amsterdam 1682.

Ticozzi, S. 'Guarini', in *Dizionario degli architetti scultori, pittori etc.* Milan 1830.

Tiraboschi, G. 'Guarini', in *Biblioteca Modenese, o notizie . . . degli scrittori natii degli stati del . . . Duca di Modena*. Modena 1783.

Toesca, P. *Torino*. Bergamo 1911.

Torretta, G. *Un'analisi della cappella di S. L'orenzo di Guarino Guarini*. Turin 1968.

Tricomi, F. G. 'Guarini matematico'. *GGIB*.II.

Trompetto, M. *Storia del Santuario di Oropa*. Milan 1967.

Vagnetti, L. 'La teoria del rilevamento architettonico in Guarino Guarini'. *GGIB*.I.

Vanderperren, J. and J. Kennes. 'De systematische ruimtelijke wereld van Guarino Guarini'. *A+* 31, September 1976.

Vaudoyer, J.-L. *Italie retrouvée*. Paris 1950.

Vautier, A. *Voyage de France. Moeurs et coutumes françaises, 1644–1665*. Paris 1905.

Verzone, P. 'Struttura delle cupole del Guarini'. *GGIB*.I.

Vezzosi, A. F. 'Guarini', in *I scrittori de' Cherici Regolari detti Teatini*. Rome 1780.

Vittone, B. A. *Istruzioni elementari per indirizzo dei giovani allo studio dell'architettura civile*. Lugano 1760.

Vittone, B. A. *Istruzioni diverse concernenti l'officio dell'architetto civile*. Lugano 1766.

Ward Perkins, J. B. 'The Shrine of St Peter and its Twelve Columns'. *Journal of Roman Studies* XLII 1952.

Webb, C.C.J. *History of Philosophy*. London 1916.

Whitaker Wilson, C. *Sir Christopher Wren, his Life and Times*. London 1932.

Wittkower, R. *Architectural Principles in the Age of Humanism*. London 1962.

Wittkower, R. 'Introduzione al Guarini'. *GGIB*.I.

Wittkower, R. *Gothic vs. Classic: Architectural Projects in Seventeenth-Century Italy*. New York 1974.

Wittkower, R. *Art and Architecture in Italy, 1600–1750*. Harmondsworth (1958) 1980.

Wölfflin, H. *Renaissance und Barock*. Munich 1888; English translation by Kathrin Simon. London 1964.

Wren, C. *Parentalia*. London 1750.

Zander, G. B. 'G. B. Montano'. *Quaderni dell'Istituto di Storia dell'Architettura*. XXX 1959; XLIX-L 1962.

INDEX

193

194